FLYING FOR
FREEDOM

FLYING FOR FREEDOM

THE ALLIED AIR FORCES
IN THE RAF 1939–45

ALAN BROWN

First published in 2000
This edition first published in 2011

The History Press
The Mill, Brimscombe Port
Stroud, Gloucestershire, GL5 2QG
www.thehistorypress.co.uk

British Library Cataloguing in Publication Data.
A catalogue record for this book is available from the British Library.

ISBN 978 0 7524 5998 1

Typesetting and origination by The History Press
Printed in the EU for History Press.

Contents

List of Illustrations		vi
Acknowledgements		vii
Abbreviations		ix
1.	The Unexpected Allies	1
2.	Poles and Czechs	25
3.	Czechs and Poles	89
4.	The Free French	148
5.	The Norwegians	180
6.	The Belgians and the Dutch	199
7.	Conclusion	221
	Appendix: Allied Air Strengths, 1940–44	232
	Bibliography	233
	Index	239

List of Illustrations

PLATE SECTION

Between pp. 117 and 118

1. Gen Vuillemin, 1940
2. Gen Charles de Gaulle, 1941
3. Dutch Fokker T.VIII float-planes, 1940
4. Dutch Navy pilots, 1940
5. Polish armourers, 1940
6. George VI inspects Polish airmen, 1940
7. A Czechoslovak airman
8. Czechoslovak air and ground crews, 1943
9. Beer for the troops in Normandy, 1944
10. Flt Off Wustefeld, 1944
11. Rear Adm Riiser-Larsen, 1944
12. Polish air chiefs with pilots, 1944
13. President Edvard Beneš with senior commanders
14. Allied air chiefs, 1944
15. French airmen, 1944
16. Czechoslovak airmen at a briefing

Acknowledgements

This study is an extension of my earlier work, *The Czechoslovak Air Force in Britain, 1940–1945*, which was submitted to the University of Southampton for the degree of Doctor of Philosophy in 1997. Many of the people who assisted me on that project have taken a keen interest in the development of *Airmen in Exile*, and I offer my profound thanks to the staffs of the Public Record Office, Kew; the Royal Air Force Museum, Hendon; the Air Historical Branch, Whitehall; the Hartley Library and New College Library, both of the University of Southampton; the British Newspaper Library, and Eastleigh, Leeds, Portsmouth, Southampton, Winchester and York public libraries, all of whom have played their part in providing expert guidance and flawless service in the procurement of the books, documents and photographs needed for the project.

I have also received very welcome assistance and correspondence from many organisations connected with the experiences of the exiles in Britain. These include: the Air Force History Unit of the Koninklijke Luchtmacht and the Stichting Dienstverlening Veteranen (Holland); the Fédération Nationale des Anciens de la Royal Air Force et de la South African Air Force 1940–45 (Belgium); and the Krigsveteranforeningen 1939–45 (Norway). Special thanks are also due to Lt Gen Av. e.r. Baron Michel Donnet DFC, President of the Belgian Association, and Lt Gen Wilhelm Mohr of the Norwegian Association, both of whom sent me some useful ideas and some excellent material. General Donnet's reminiscences, *Flight to Freedom*, must rank as one of the best aviation memoirs of the war.

There has also been a host of scholars who have shared their knowledge with me and permitted use of their research. These include Christopher Mann (King's College, London), Matthew Buck (Oxford), Paul Latawski (Royal Military Academy,

Sandhurst) and Martin Brown (University College, London). Numerous amateur historians in Europe and America have also contributed information, ideas and encouragement, and I am particularly grateful to Randal Hankla (America), Yves Duwelz and Cynrik de Decker (Belgium), Gert Laursen (Denmark) and Louis Capdeboscq (France). Louis must have a global reputation by now as one of the first dons of the Internet history newsgroups, and it is high time he published some of his work to a wider audience.

Finally, my sincere thanks to my friends and colleagues at Selby College, especially James Broad. Projects of this scale cannot be completed in isolation from ordinary life, and together they gave me a lot of encouragement and plenty of elbow room to see it through to completion. Thanks also to Helen Betteridge, who lent a hand with the research, and to Linda Gray of Chelwood House, Kew, for her excellent hospitality.

Alan Brown
North Yorkshire

Abbreviations

AACU	Army Air Co-Operation Unit
ACAS	Assistant Chief of the Air Staff + (P) Policy; (I) Intelligence; (O) Operations
ACM	Air Chief Marshal
ADC	Aide-de-Camp
ADGB	Air Defence of Great Britain
AFC	Air Force Cross
AFO	Allied Forces Committee
AFOSC	Allied Forces (Official) Sub-Committee
Air Cdre	Air Commodore
AM	Air Marshal
AMP	Air Member for Personnel
AMPC	Auxiliary Military Pioneer Corps
AMSO	Air Member for Supply and Organisation
AMT	Air Member for Training
AOC	Air Officer Commanding
AVM	Air Vice-Marshal
BMR	British Military Representative
C-in-C	Commander-in-Chief
CAS	Chief of the Air Staff
CIGS	Commander of the Imperial General Staff
CNC	Czechoslovak National Committee
CO	Commanding Officer
COS	Chiefs of Staff
COS 120	Common name for paper 120 (1944) by the Chiefs of Staff Committee
D of M	Director of Manning
D of O	Director of Organisation
D of O(I)	Director of Operations (Intelligence)
D of P	Director of Postings
D of Plans	Director of Plans
DAAC	Director(ate) of Allied Air Co-Operation

DAFL	Director(ate) of Allied Air Co-Operation and Foreign Liaison
DCAS	Deputy Chief of the Air Staff
DFC	Distinguished Flying Cross
DGO	Director General of Organisation
DPS	Director of Personal Services
DSO	Distinguished Service Order
ERPC	Expansion and Re-equipment Policy Committee
Flt/Lt	Flight Lieutenant
Flt/Sgt	Flight Sergeant
FO	Foreign Office (British)
GDB	General Duties Branch
GHQ	General Headquarters
GOC	General Officer Commanding
Gp Capt	Group Captain
GR	General Reconnaissance
GRU	General Reconnaissance Unit
HFU	Home Ferry Unit
HO	Home Office (British)
JIC	Joint Intelligence Sub-Committee
LAC	Leading Aircraftman
MAC	Mediterranean Air Command
MAP	Ministry of Aircraft Production
MC	Military Cross
MNO	Ministry of National Defence (Czechoslovak)
MO	Medical Officer
MP	Member of Parliament (British)
MRAF	Marshal of the Royal Air Force
NCO	Non-Commissioned Officer
NEI	Netherland East Indies
OC	Officer Commanding
ORB	Operational Record Book
OTU	Operational Training Unit
PAF	Polish Air Force
PCG	Provisional Czechoslovak Government
Plt/Off	Pilot Officer
PM	Prime Minister
POL	Petrol, Oil and Lubricants
POTU	Polish Operational Training Unit
POW	Prisoner of War

PRC	Polish Resettlement Corps
PRO	Public Record Office (London)
PRU	Photographic Reconnaissance Unit
RAF	Royal Air Force
RAFVR	Royal Air Force Volunteer Reserve
RCAF	Royal Canadian Air Force
RFC	Royal Flying Corps
RNAAS	Royal Norwegian Army Air Service
RNNAS	Royal Norwegian Naval Air Service
RT	Radio Telephonist
SAO	Senior Air Officer
SASO	Senior Air Staff Officer
SEF	Single-Engined Fighter
SHAEF	Supreme Headquarters Allied Expeditionary Force
SHAPE	Supreme Headquarters Allied Powers Europe
Sqdn	Squadron
Sqn Ldr	Squadron Leader
TEB	Twin-Engined Bomber
TEF	Twin-Engined Fighter
USAAF	United States Army Air Force
USAF	United States Air Force
VC	Victoria Cross
VCAS	Vice Chief of the Air Staff
VE	Victory in Europe
VHA	Military Historical Archive (Prague)
VKPR	Military Office of the President (Czechoslovak)
Wg Cdr	Wing Commander
WO	Wireless Operator

CHAPTER ONE

The Unexpected Allies

The summer of 1940 dealt a great many shocks to the government, people and armed forces of Britain. The German attack on France and the Low Countries in May was as sudden as any in the history of large-scale military operations, but although France was politically and militarily unprepared for such a trial, the belief that she could stand firm with British assistance was still the prevailing view among those charged with the central direction of the war. That confidence had been wrecked along with the British Expeditionary Force at Dunkirk. As the allies fell back and were eventually swept from the Continent by an apparently irresistible force, talk of a negotiated peace with the Germans was momentarily heard in the most powerful offices in the land. Such talk came to nothing, but amid the confusion on the beaches of southern England and in the government, new voices were heard from men who had never dreamed that such a calamity could befall the Western democracies. Some had sought refuge with the French when their own capitals had been overrun; others had come directly to Britain in the hope of stimulating resistance at home by their determination to stay free. All of them were simply overwhelmed by the magnitude of the defeat.

These were the governments of Norway, Belgium, Holland, Poland and Czechoslovakia. France, of course, joined the list when she too succumbed. In all cases, the experience of politics in exile brought out the worst in some individuals, who used the instability to further their own political agendas, either to fix the blame for the defeat, secure power for the future, or simply to make trouble in settling old scores. But along with the men of words came men of arms, for in the headlong scramble to escape the Nazi scythe, tens of thousands of troops scrambled onto the boats and joined their political leaders in Britain. Men of foreign navies bravely steered their ships to British ports, and many courageous aviators risked capture at the hands of their own countrymen to fly their machines into British air space and deliver themselves for service once again. Throughout the summer and autumn of 1940, these men re-grouped and re-trained to pledge their committed energies to the common war effort, but in so doing they often became part of the wider political scene as their governments fought internecine battles or struggled to assert themselves with their British hosts.

This book is a study of only one part of that great allied force in exile: the airmen of the six European nations who found refuge in Britain and fought their war from British soil under the ensign of the Royal Air Force.[1] The presence of so many nationalities gathered together in one service arm was an entirely new experience for the British. The possibility that France might be defeated had never seriously been reckoned with, but it had happened all the same. Apart from coping with the shock of sudden solitude, the government and service departments had to devise ways of assimilating the allied personnel into the fighting corps; at the same time, they had to walk the thorny paths of exile politics. This meant that from the very beginning, the history of all the European exiles was inextricably connected to two British departments: the Air Ministry and the Foreign Office. Quite often the former would not act without the advice and agreement of the latter, and when the political activities of the exiled governments interfered with the military establishments nominally under their command – and we shall see how common an occurrence this was – it would be the Foreign Office which had the deciding voice. The two undertakings frequently collided, sometimes with hardly noticeable effects, at other times with explosive results which rocked the very alliances these endeavours were trying to preserve. All parties found the experience to be a steep learning curve indeed, and there is much to be gained from studying these noble but often tempestuous friendships which, though they ended over fifty years ago, still have enough light left in them to illuminate aspects of Britain's interaction with Europe today.

In the following chapters, the essential characteristics, trials and triumphs of each of those alliances will be surveyed, the greatest emphasis being placed upon the British perception of each relationship, but the primary purpose of this introduction is to explore the overall political, social and military environments within which each separate relationship functioned. In the first place, the British government had to create a mechanism which permitted the establishment of foreign armies on British soil, and having created that mechanism, had to ensure its smooth operation in times of crisis. Secondly, the presence of so many different nationalities at once raised numerous problems, all of them important, but none more so than the lack of a common language, and the very real dangers of falling morale and political treachery. Thirdly – and this was to be a consideration later in the war – the question arose of what was to be the policy after victory had been secured? Were the allied governments and their forces to be left to their own policies of reconstruction, or would programmes of closer association finally purge the Continent of the German menace? These were issues of major importance; and as we shall see, the Americans felt that they also deserved a voice in the shaping of postwar Europe. The view from Washington was that Britain was too weak and too closely involved with the European powers to make objective decisions regarding the immediate peace, and through the experiences of the Anglo-European alliances we may glimpse the changing nature of 'the special relationship' and the onset of the Cold War.

However, in 1940, these were issues far removed from the practicalities of the time. The British government was faced with a situation which demanded immediate action, and the most urgent need was to give some legitimacy to the presence of the foreign armies on British soil. The device chosen was the Allied Forces Act, a hastily concocted piece of legislation based upon an earlier model, the Visiting Forces (British Commonwealth) Act of 1933. Under this latter Act, visiting governments would be legally responsible for the conduct of their forces while they were on British territory. This was just what the British government needed: a tool which gave it all the benefits of extra allies and hardly any of the responsibility. With a few modifications, the Allied Forces Act replaced the earlier instrument, and under the terms of Article One each allied government had full military jurisdiction over its service personnel.

But that was not how some sections of the armed forces interpreted it, for although the War Office and the Admiralty were content to allow the incoming forces the right to enforce their own military laws, the Air Ministry fought against national jurisdiction for the whole of the war. As far as the RAF was concerned, a man in their uniform, irrespective of his nationality, was entitled to serve under British military codes rather than his own national variants, which in the main tended to be less lenient and heavier on punishments.[2] This was not because of some noble motive on the part of the RAF, though there *were* occasions when it stepped in to forbid excessive punishment. Much more likely was the need to avoid giving the exiled governments the opportunities to demand independent status for their air forces, and there were two main reasons why they should pursue such a claim. First, after Dunkirk, the primary weapon in defence of Britain was air power. It was visible, active and highly successful, and the various governments sought to exploit the victories of their own pilots by having their national contingents declared independent of the RAF. The right to operate their own military codes in matters of discipline was perceived as a significant step towards that aim. Independence would give them a highly potent propaganda tool to stimulate resistance at home and recruitment abroad; and as a by-product, enhance their own positions as the guardians of national liberty. Second, having an independent air arm would reinforce their status as *allies* rather than 'associated powers', a much vaguer term used by the British when they felt uncomfortable about nominal alliances not formally recognised by treaty.

In the end, it was all about prestige. For wholly understandable reasons, each of the European governments which reconstituted on British soil suffered to a greater or lesser degree from low self-esteem, and one way of increasing it was to have an active service arm under their sole control. To be sure, most had army units recognised as independent forces by the War Office, but with some notable exceptions (especially the Poles and the Czechoslovaks in the Middle East), the army units based in Britain could do little but prepare for action when the day came, and that was not to be until 1944. In short, there were not enough medals being won on land; but in the skies, the exploits of the bomber crews and fighter pilots featured almost nightly on the radio and in the cinema newsreels. Governments hungry for prestige therefore naturally turned to these heroes as symbols of a freedom temporarily crushed, but by no means finished for good. The RAF high command was well aware of these issues, and from the very beginning resisted every attempt made by all but one of the governments to withdraw their forces from the RAF structure and fight as independent allies. Sometimes the high command lost the struggle, as with the Poles and the French; on one occasion they simply granted independence, as with the Norwegians; and sometimes they held firm and got their own way, as with the Czechs, the Belgians, and to a certain extent the Dutch. In each case an entirely different set of circumstances obtained, and at times the mood turned bitter.

It is easier to observe this intransigence than to explain it, for even now, after much study, the motives are not entirely clear.

We can be certain that a deep suspicion was held by many influential and powerful sections of the Air Ministry against virtually all foreigners who came into the country from occupied Europe, and we might argue that to put politically suspect people in charge of a bomber would have been bad policy. But since no conclusive evidence has yet come to light which might confirm that such a fear existed on a widespread basis, we must reject it as mere conjecture. Besides, no allied government even remotely entertained the idea that it might have full operational control over its air force, and each was content to allow its men to serve under the overall direction of the allied high command, which in practice meant the British until the Americans entered the war. It was probably this necessity to fight the air war as one unified arm which motivated the RAF to resist bids for independence until it was forced by political considerations to acknowledge them. Besides, it was quickly apparent to everyone that some of the groups, and in particular the Czechoslovaks, could barely function as national units without substantial help from British ground crew. The Air Ministry took the view that this alone disqualified any pleas for independent status or jurisdiction rights, since it was argued on many occasions that two military codes could not reasonably be applied in mixed squadrons.

To return to the Allied Forces Act, this was one of those occasional pieces of legislation which was denied any realistic chance of debate in Parliament. The National Government had already decided that it should become law long before it reached the floor of the House of Commons, and in the event it passed through all of its stages in a single day, 21 August 1940.[3] Rising at 4.28 p.m., the Joint Under Secretary of State for War, Sir Edward Grigg, urged the House to support the bill, which would 'give legal sanction to the establishment of no less than six foreign armies on British soil, to be trained under their own flags, under their own commanders, and under their own military law.'[4] He then assured the honourable members that civil crimes would still be dealt with by British courts, but in all other respects the responsibilities would devolve upon the allied governments.

In theory, this should have been enough to end the debate and lead to a vote which the government could not lose, but a few hardy souls decided to raise issues for the record which might better have been left unaired. Miss Eleanor Rathbone asked if the allies were to be given powers of conscription over their nationals who had made their homes in Britain, and if any provision had been made for racial and religious differences within the forces concerned. If not, would discrimination be permissible? Grigg fumbled this last point by stating that no specific provisions existed in the military codes concerned, but he saw no reason why it should become an issue. On the question of conscription, he answered with an emphatic 'No.' Miss Rathbone replied that this would mean that each man was technically a volunteer, and Grigg agreed with her.

In both cases, Grigg was unaware of the facts. He was promptly informed that four days earlier the Dutch government had threatened a man with a charge of evading the colours if he did not report for service immediately. Was this not conscription? Grigg did not reply. Others argued that any man who chose to make his home in Britain deserved the protection of British law, and that no allied government had the right or the power to force him into military service if he chose not to volunteer. Behind this concept lay the very real and highly treasured British principle of asylum for political refugees. The British took the view that if anyone chose to leave their home nation on grounds of political, religious or racial incompatibility or persecution, and had been granted the right of residence in Britain, such individuals were entitled to reject the commands of their former country, especially if it meant taking up arms for a cause which they might not support. Conscription was therefore 'off the menu', and although there were numerous cases of allied governments using unpalatable tactics to coerce men into the ranks, the British broadly kept to the policy, particularly if the countries concerned had a history of anti-Semitism or severe political disorder.

This issue of racial discrimination also surfaced in the Commons debate on the Allied Forces Act. Col Josiah Wedgwood declared that the Polish Army in France had been recruited 'more or less under duress', noting that Jews had been given the choice of internment or service. He then made the stinging comment that the Polish and German attitudes towards Jews were comparable, and that many had 'learnt from bitter experience what it is to be under the Polish or Nazi heel'. Supporting Wedgwood, Sydney Silverman added that 'there is something on the Czech side too which needs a certain amount of care and attention'.[5] In an attempt to soothe these concerns, Grigg only fanned the flames by quoting from a specific order issued by the Polish high command forbidding any anti-Jewish behaviour 'humiliating to human dignity . . . upon pain of severe punishment'.[6] An earlier call for an independent Jewish force was rejected by Grigg on the grounds that they had no military system, codes or national government.

There was also the question of jurisdiction. Some members, clearly quite ignorant regarding the military practices of their new allies, very much hoped that flogging would not once more disgrace a British barrack square. Others were concerned about the variations in military codes noted earlier, and the protests were strong enough to force Grigg into assuring the House that he would extract from each government a promise that the death penalty would not be administered if the crime would not attract a similar punishment in the British forces.[7] On the related question of conscription, he also pledged that no government would be given the power to compel its nationals to fight, and he wriggled out of the Dutch example by suggesting that they had acted before any official statement had been made on the subject. The final compromise was an assurance that each and every allied serviceman would be given the opportunity to serve in the British forces if he chose not to don his own national colours, irrespective of the pressures brought to bear on him to do so. This was to be a challenge later taken up by Gen de Gaulle of the Free French, and one which the British lost.

The Allied Forces Act received Royal Assent the day after its passage through parliament. The limits of its scope and authority were to be severely tested and frequently reinterpreted, and it would seem from the evidence that it became progressively less important as the conditions of war changed over the years. It was, after all, an emergency measure. But this cannot be said of the policy to meet the educational and welfare needs of the incoming forces from the Continent. It had been recognised very quickly, and especially by the Air Ministry, that if the allied personnel were to be of any use whatsoever, they would need to learn English at least to a point where they could understand and give commands. As a result, the task of linguistic training was thrown into the lap of the British Council, the initial agreement being that it would provide the teaching and the service departments would pay for it. As this was such a vital aspect of the assimilation of the allied forces, the British Council dedicated much of its own money and intellectual resources to creating effective courses of language instruction, but very soon it became apparent that the service departments regarded the programme with a much lower priority.

The British Council was, and is, one of the cornerstones of Britain's official presence abroad. Formed in 1934, the Council's initial aims were to promote the life, language and culture of Britain.[8] When war came in 1939, the Ministry of Information absorbed much of the Council's promotional work in the affected countries and left it with a greatly reduced range of activities, essentially the education of refugees and the maintenance of Britain's cultural profile. Even these, so the Treasury thought, were 'a luxury in wartime'.[9] The sudden influx of displaced persons from occupied Europe enabled the Council to argue its case with more confidence. By insisting that the cultural welfare of these people fell within the remit of the Council, the Executive Committee successfully lobbied for a range of suitable proposals.[10] Yet this should not obscure the core function of the Council by creating the impression that it was a benevolent, altruistic body posing as the conductor for all things wholesome, decent and British. By its own admission, its primary aim was 'political, or at any rate, imperialistic', and it spent much of its time and its budget encouraging foreign nationals to 'appreciate British friendship', which in practice meant acknowledging that London was the hub of the universe.[11] Content with its mission, the Council pursued these aims and its agenda with considerable success.

Things changed when the military men arrived after the fall of France. Reacting swiftly to the new situation, the Treasury convened a meeting on 28 August 1940 at which it was generally agreed that the Council would assume all responsibility for the cultural and educational needs of the foreigners now in the country. This meant that the direct teaching of English (as opposed to the indirect exposure to it) would now become part of the Council's portfolio of activities. To fund the programme, the Treasury allotted a further grant of £17,000. It was also agreed that the Council would teach the language to the foreign servicemen and internees, 'but only when asked by service departments and the Home Office to do so, when these departments would bear the cost'.[12] This implied that the Council could not act without a direct request from the service departments or without clearing its proposed actions with them beforehand. This was to cause problems, for the chain of supply and demand could be broken or kinked by difficulties in communication or resistance by the Air Ministry or the War Office.[13]

Evidence of this survives in the British Council files. Under the terms of the new financing arrangement, the Council invoiced the Air Ministry for £316 for services provided up to and including 9 September 1940.But decisions on the amount of teaching required by individual units were taken either by the unit commanders or the Education Officer at Fighter Command, Wg Cdr de la Bère. By November 1940, this officer complained to the Council that 'many units in his Command had received no language teaching, nor had they any grammar books', in response to which he was informed that no authority had been forthcoming to appoint additional teachers or purchase new books, hence the Council politely referred him back to the Air Ministry.[14]

By Christmas 1940, the number of teachers employed on behalf of the RAF had increased from 14 to only 16 for a combined contingent of over 10,000 men, and while the Air Ministry paid for the newspapers, fictional and technical works, the basic stuff of teaching – specifically grammars in Polish and Czech – had been translated, produced and supplied at the Council's own expense. By January 1941, the bill had climbed to £2,110, representing services provided between the beginning of September to the end of December 1940. A cheque for the earlier amount of £316 finally arrived in February 1941.[15] In November 1941, an internal note was issued concerning the unpaid invoice for £2,110 'which had been lost by the Air Ministry'.[16]

In April 1941, the Air Ministry sent a summary of the present situation to the British Council. It included a revised list of the technical and general terms which it wanted taught to the allied air crews as part of the general aim 'to teach every allied officer and man to use the English language operationally and technically'.[17] Thus far, the Ministry had employed five methods to further this aim: (1) the widespread use of interpreters, and the dispersal of such men into RAF units 'where possible'; (2) the translated manuals supplied by the Council, and linguaphone records of operational phrases; (3) the use of British personnel commanding either in the air or on the ground; (4) 'use of specially selected allied personnel to lead in theair'; (5) the use of allied personnel in operations rooms for radio communications. Each of these techniques had only limited success, concluded the Ministry, and this still left a force 'that is not fully efficient and has little flexibility', and suffered from a lack of knowledge of operational language, an inability to absorb or read instructions, and the impossibility of employment in composite crews, especially in bomber work. The British Council reacted with astonishment, for it regarded it as audacious that the RAF should complain when it neither paid its bills on time nor seemed keen to develop the language programme at its own expense.[18]

It is tempting to blame the Air Ministry itself for these difficulties, but we must also bear in mind the pressures under which it operated during the second half of 1940. Even so, although we cannot level an accusation of outright negligence in regard to the language training of the allied crews, there is certainly a hint of indifference in its behaviour. Nor was this attitude confined to the Royal Air Force. By November 1940, the Council heard reports that men of the Czechoslovak Army 'had been anxiously awaiting the supply of English teachers since August'.[19] An internal memorandum also referred to a plea from the Czechoslovak Military that 'the lack of mental food for the Czech Army is causing them despair'. There was even talk of writing directly to Churchill.[20] Upon enquiry, the Council was told directly by the War Office that 'any cultural or educational work amongst the allied armies is not required on anything more than a trivial scale'.[21] It was not until April 1941 that a suitable working arrangement had been established, and even then there were delays in its implementation.[22]

It is clear from these scant letters and memoranda that the work of the Council did not feature high in the list of priorities of either the Air Ministry or the War Office, despite the valuable and sometimes valiant efforts of the Council in all other spheres.[23] By January 1942, a survey conducted by the Czechoslovak Air Force Inspectorate indicated that the average level of English held by all ranks was a little under 58 per cent. This figure had been calculated from the end-of-year written and oral tests conducted with the officers and other ranks of 310 and 312 Fighter Squadrons, and it roughly corresponds to the modern-day equivalent of intermediate level: good enough to make oneself understood, but far from any real fluency.[24] Almost certainly, the tendency for the men to associate with their own countrymen, thereby obviating the need to speak English, would have affected their ability or motivation to learn, but it seems that British policy must bear some of the responsibility for these relatively low levels of achievement after one-and-a-half years of exile.

These problems were very real for the men involved, and anyone who has been to a foreign state with little or no knowledge of the language can relate to the sense of isolation this produces. In material terms, however, they lived identically to their British counterparts. They wore the same uniform (in itself a desirable thing to have, especially after the Battle of Britain), they ate the same food, slept in the same bunks, flew the same planes and shot at the same enemy. In most cases they also received the same pay, though this did not always apply if a squadron was regarded as a fully national unit. Nevertheless, pay levels in all the allied squadrons were roughly equal, for too great a disparity would have seriously affected morale.

The service departments also displayed an indifferent attitude when it came to the social welfare of the men. The British Council received several complaints that little or nothing was being done to entertain the allied servicemen, and approaches to the War Office and the Air Ministry for ideas and assistance met with either silence or carefully worded excuses. Consequently, many private individuals took it upon themselves to lend a hand.

Some retired teachers gave English lessons for nothing; others, especially the wealthy, opened their country houses and organised cinema shows, football matches, dances and concerts for allied personnel who happened to be stationed nearby. Somewhat embarrassed by this display of charity, the War Office appointed Sir Thomas Cook MP as a roving welfare officer to tour the air and army camps and report on conditions and general morale. He liaised with the Women's Volunteer Service and the YMCA, which in turn ran clothing drives, book rallies, bring-and-buy sales and other events to raise money to provide home comforts for all of the allied contingents. Cook did an admirable job, and both the British Council and the Foreign Office received many letters of thanks from commanders of allied units. Only once did he cause brows to furrow with one of his lengthy reports. Having visited 310 (Czechoslovak) Fighter Squadron at RAF Duxford, he wrote: 'The men's immediate needs are being well catered for by voluntary women's bodies in Cambridge', in reaction to which a senior Czech officer pencilled in the margin 'Please explain.'

The British Council soon found itself deeply involved with another facet of the welfare provision: the national organisations or 'hearths'. Beginning with the establishment of the *Ognisko Polskie* ('Polish Hearth'), these national centres would act as meeting places for allied personnel where they could enjoy a taste of home. In theory, they were to be the financial responsibilities of the allied governments, but from the start many were heavily supported by the British Council. In the case of the Czechoslovak Institute, the projection for the financial year 1941/2 envisaged a £2,500 subsidy, taking into consideration an expected income of £300 from subscriptions and donations, and a further £100 from overnight room rental. Food and drink would be sold on a limited-profit basis.[25] By 1942, that estimate had increased to £4,820 as the probable subsidy required to keep the Institute viable in 1944. The Belgians, Dutch and Norwegians paid half of the running costs of their own national houses, while the Greeks and the Yugoslavs donated £250 and £300 respectively. The Poles and the Czechoslovaks, however, were noted as offering 'odd amounts only', with the latter being specifically flagged as 'unreliable'.[26]

With such heavy British Council support came a good deal of British Council influence, and very soon the original conception of these national houses as places where civilian and serviceman alike might relax in familiar surroundings soon gave way to the Council's view of what every good foreigner should be exposed to. The houses tended to organise functions which emphasised 'civilised culture' rather than rest and relaxation. Programmes of events which have survived show that the entertainment was very much geared towards the higher thinker. Classical music recitals, literary readings, poetry discussions, historical lectures and similar arrangements formed the staple cultural diet of visitors to the national houses in London.[27] But there were few dances, and though on balance the houses dealt with military and civilian clients in equal numbers, activities and amenities tended to be biased towards the latter.[28]

Furthermore, in 1943 the British Council commissioned work on a short film entitled *Safe Custody*, which was to be based on the activities of the national houses. Part of the resumé concerning the Czechoslovak Institute stated:

> We see a young Czechoslovak student reading a newspaper, then he discards it for a medical book. He has found a haven to pursue his studies in the Czechoslovak Institute, a club with British foundation where Czechoslovakians in Britain can enjoy some of the traditional teachings of their own country. We see the Librarian at work in the Library with its rare copies of immortal Czechoslovakian books. Then we look over the shoulder of a Czechoslovakian officer who is studying a notice-board where we see announcements of concerts, lectures, meetings.[29]

If this oozing sentimentality truly represented the British Council's perception of the Czechoslovak Institute – and it seems plausible to assume that it did – then it is no surprise that most service personnel tended to move through it rather than support it in any meaningful sense. In effect, the national houses were little more than tools of the British Council in its mission to promote British culture, and it had a relatively captive audience and chose to maintain its profile by acting as financier, protecting its investment by packing the controlling directorates with its own people.[30] On the whole, the Council did its best to educate and accommodate all the émigrés – political, civilian or military – from all of the countries which had succumbed to occupation, and it did so with the consent of the government and with funds provided by the Treasury. Yet it is hard to avoid the impression that the average man in an allied unit was largely left to fend for himself in terms of his entertainment. If he came to London looking for gaiety or careless distractions from the pressures of war, he was unlikely to have his needs satisfied at the national house of his countrymen.

In essence, the allocation of comforts and welfare was bound
up with the greater concept of morale. Ever since Roman times,
and probably earlier than that, army commanders have been
keenly aware that high morale in any fighting force is crucial to
its efficiency. No less aware of this was the Air Ministry, but it took
it a couple of years to formulate its perceptions of allied morale,
and how to maintain it, into a policy document of great depth
and considerable length. Unfortunately, space does not permit a
full examination of its many fascinating and varied clauses, but
what follows should convey the overall sense of the document
and, more importantly, the British view of their new allies as it
developed over two years of collaboration and close observation.

The preamble to the document acknowledged that time
had passed since the 'urgent atmosphere' of 1940 and the
subsequent tensions generated by the 1941 air raids, and that
now, after two-and-a-half years, the various allied air forces were
fully engaged in the combined war effort.[31] This was followed
by a broad declaration that 'history revealed no precedent to
guide the Government or the Service in their planning for the
reception, acceptance and operative effect of the allied air forces'.
This could be interpreted as an almost apologetic caveat, but the
object of its inclusion was to introduce the five basic principles
which time and experience had now permitted to emerge as the
guiding philosophy of the Air Ministry in its relations with the
European exiles. These were:

(i) The Principle of Nationality – the preservation of
national, and as far as possible, air force identity; the
retention of national traditions and customs, rituals, religion
and culture.

(ii) The Principle of Legality – the recognition of the right
to be subject to their own national or service laws; the equal
obligation to be subject to British and service laws [*sic*]; the
balance of justice under such dual legislation.

(iii) The Principle of Equality – the recognition of absolute
equality [to include pay and conditions, ranks, trades,
training, vocations and service].

(iv) The Principle of Concentration – as opposed to
indiscriminate dispersal of allied air forces through the
Royal Air Force; the avoidance of disintegration due to over-
dispersal; the advantage of coherent national integral units.

(v) The Principle of Construction – the ultimate creation
of independent self-contained national air forces for future
national use in Europe; the formation of all-allied units

towards that end; the final reconstruction of national air forces on their withdrawal from Britain.[32]

It must be emphasised here that these were the *absolute rules* as far as the Air Ministry and Air Council were concerned when it came to the administration, deployment and use of all the allied air forces then on British soil. Broadly speaking, most of them were adhered to, and we can be certain that from 1942 onwards, all major Air Ministry decisions were made in the light of these principles. The document was circulated to all of the allied air force headquarters in early May 1942, and we can only speculate what the various inspectorates made of the rather syrupy rationale: 'These five tenets shall be the soil upon which allied morale can grow; whether it flourishes or wilts is determined by what it has to weather and the treatment it receives.'

But whatever one makes of the quality of the poetry, the document was certainly considered important by the Air Council because the appended instructions required it to follow the allied squadrons from station to station. Also included was a recapitulation of the existing practices in regard to the command structure within the allied air forces, focusing upon the argument that 'morale at the top is as important as morale "among the troops"'. This, claimed the document, was to be maintained in the following ways:

(a) A full appreciation of the contribution to the war effort by parliament, press, publicity and propaganda.
(b) The conclusion of agreements pledging mutual co-operation towards common aims and ideals.
(c) A sympathetic and co-operative review of all proposals put forward by Allied Air Force Inspectorates or Headquarters.
(d) A ready concession of all just claims affecting the efficient administration of all allied air forces.
(e) The solutions of 'problems' by open conference and discussion in an atmosphere free from bias or prejudice.

We shall see later in this study how (c) and (e) were altered, twisted, or simply ignored in some cases, especially when the question of national independence was at hand; but in the main, these five points said little that was new. Items (a) and (b) were already a reality by early 1942, or committed the Air Ministry to nothing tangible, whereas item (d) was little more than a platitude, in that the next four pages were devoted to describing the

administrative procedures as determined by the Ministry, setting
them in stone for the rest of the war.

With regard to the welfare and morale of the other ranks,
the general policy was 'keep them busy'. The Ministry identified
certain key factors as dangerous to morale. These were: enforced
inaction due to a variety of causes (adverse weather, cancelled
missions, lack of enemy activity, etc.); geographical dispersal
(the separation of squadrons away from concentrated formations
or a particular locality); the stress of redeployment to another
station or group; bad war news, and problems associated with
leave (where to go, what to do, and who to do it with). All of these
elements, claimed the Ministry, had a greater impact on allied
crews than native squadrons.

Inaction was to be mitigated by providing 'entertainment,
shows, dances, games, competitions, lectures and even serious
educational or cultural training for those so disposed'.
Geographical dispersal was not strictly a matter for the allies, for
it was a command decision made at group or command level.
Even so, the Ministry argued that 'the more we are together, the
happier we will be', and permitted small, localised adjustments
to be made in favour of allied squadrons if the principle of
concentration was served. Much the same thinking applied to
redeployment, the theory here being that a squadron move
forced the men to come to terms with a new environment,
possibly even a new dialect of English, and certainly a new station
commander who might or might not be disposed towards working
with allied crews. On the subject of bad war news, again some
form of entertainment was recommended to overcome 'an
unusually heavy mood of depression', but emphasis was to fall
on the engagement of 'prominent allied people' to give lectures
on the war situation or arrange morale-raising tours of arms
factories or shipyards. With leave, the document noted that men
tended to 'stay local' or spend their time in areas where their
home nationals were concentrated. No solution was offered for
the problems arising here, but the Ministry drew attention to the
various hospitality organisations which would advise and assist any
man who approached them. The important factor was to draw the
men away from the station or camp if possible, for it was accepted
that leave – if well spent – was an invaluable boost to morale.[33]

The document closed with a short paragraph on 'Tolerance',
for the Ministry understood that the maintenance of good morale
was ultimately dependent 'upon a tolerant and sympathetic
understanding' of the plight of the allies who were so far from
home. Nevertheless, the Ministry required no outstanding

concessions to be made. In its own words: 'This is no plea for "wet-nursing", it is no plaint for weakness, but rather for increased strength. If anyone who is working with allied personnel feels so die-hard English that he can see nothing good or useful in a "foreigner" then he were better not employed with them.' This was undoubtedly directed at British station commanders or other officers who were likely to come into contact with allied squadrons, and we shall see that this clearly demonstrates that a change of heart had taken place in the two years since the arrival of the men in 1940. Failing that, it was nothing more than a piece of glib propaganda designed to bolster the morale of the allied commanders who read it.

The average British station commander coped in his own way with the new allies on his turf, and he frequently sent back reports on their behaviour, morale and efficiency to command headquarters. In virtually all cases, these tended to be either highly complimentary, or at least benign criticisms, but occasionally we catch glimpses of that raw imperialism which was, or is, so quintessentially British. Many of the early reports focused on the distinctions between the Czechoslovak and Polish pilots. The station commander at Warmwell in October 1940 noted that the Poles were 'keen and enthusiastic about flying for its own sake and would rather fly and fight than do anything else'. Of the Czechoslovaks, he wrote: 'They are as hardworking and conscientious as Polish personnel but not usually so good from the flying point of view and the pilots I have met seem to be less enthusiastic than most fighter pilots.' The station commander at Exeter also had slight reservations about his new comrades: 'The Czechoslovaks without exception appear keen. They have not the terrific hatred for all things German that the Poles have, but they certainly do not compare unfavourably with British pilots in their offensive spirit. Their morale is good, but not so striking as that of the Poles.' Of the Poles themselves, he observed: 'The Polish pilot appears to be almost British. He talks about the same things, enjoys similar jokes, grumbles about the food, and drinks very moderately but makes the most of the party. His manners are better, especially towards women and his superior officers, but he eats less daintily and does not play cricket'.[34]

From 1942 until the Normandy landings in 1944, the Anglo–allied relationships fell into a routine and a pattern rarely broken by any new developments. After that date, most minds turned towards victory in Europe and the liberation of the occupied territories, but with those pleasant thoughts came a plethora of new political and military problems. Two major initiatives

dominated the scene after Normandy. The first was a paper
issued by the Chiefs of Staff known generally as COS 120, and
the second was an umbrella term used to describe a range of
separate yet broadly similar individual agreements: Mutual Aid.
Both instruments were directed towards sustaining and improving
the postwar inter-allied relationships, though it was to be COS 120
which caused the most problems.

On 30 June 1944, a little over three weeks after the invasion
of occupied Europe, Churchill commissioned a policy review
concerning all the allied powers then fighting to liberate their
homelands from the Nazis. It drew its common title – COS 120
– from the simple fact that it was the 120th paper produced
by the Chiefs of Staff Committee that year, but it was correctly
known as *The Equipping of the Forces of Our European Allies.* It
had two objectives: (1) to act as a basis for producing estimates
in preparation for allied rearmament at the war's end; (2) to
ascertain the extent to which demands on British manpower
could be reduced by utilising the forces of the European allies in
the occupation of Germany.[35]

As it reveals much about the predicted conditions in Europe
after the defeat of Germany, including the likely political scenario
as the Red Army advanced, the document is of great value to the
strategic and political historian. For example, the Chiefs of Staff
tentatively forecast that the war against Japan would go on for
another two years beyond the defeat of Germany, and that it was
quite possible that German armament factories would need to be
rapidly restored and pressed into service to meet the munitions
demand. The likely military position of France was also closely
considered, and the COS accepted that the Americans would
require an equal voice in re-equipping and training postwar
French forces. Indeed, the COS believed that such a presence
would be greatly in Britain's strategic interest, and this is worth
recalling when considering the squabbling that began over the
French Air Force in 1945. The arguments for the long-term
provision of British assistance in the liberated territories are also
interesting. It was estimated that the home weapons industry might
enjoy contracts sufficient to supply up to 400,000 men for two
years, these forces being split between those necessary to ensure
each nation's domestic security, and a share of the occupation
liabilities in Germany itself.

Visions of a Soviet hegemony clearly dominated much of
the planning behind COS 120, for the Poles, Czechoslovaks
and Yugoslavs were to have their fighter squadron capability
considerably enlarged as defensive screens against a sudden

Soviet thrust. In the west, France was to receive double the amount of fighters she had been operating from European airfields, as was Belgium. Holland would see an increase to four fighter squadrons instead of the one which formed late in the war, but it was part of the overall strategy that these three nations would participate in the occupation of Germany, therefore an immediate increase of fighter capability was an obvious necessity. Only Norway would see a small addition to her fighter defences: the two fighter squadrons which fought so gallantly during the war would be joined by a third. Squadrons of heavy bombers were also scheduled for delivery to some of the European allies, as were transport and reconnaissance aircraft, with full facilities for training and maintenance provided as part of the package.

This, however, was only the *plan*, and we shall see how wide of the mark some of it was when the halcyon vision was warped by the situation on the ground. In essence, it was the British way of reaping the peace, and although America generally agreed with the principles and estimates laid down in COS 120, she still had plenty to say when these conflicted with her own plans in 1945. Besides, the whole scheme rested squarely upon the ability of the British to supply the aircraft concerned – and, of course, the willingness of the allies to be so equipped when the dust had settled and there were opportunities to think about alternatives. Nevertheless, as we move through the various chapters, references to COS 120 occur from time to time, and it is interesting to watch the cold realities of 1945 unfold in its fading light, first cast while the bridgeheads in Normandy were still being consolidated.

The other programme running alongside COS 120, and to some extent designed to act as the precursor for postwar rearmament, was Mutual Aid. The Mutual Aid protocols signed with the allies in 1944 committed each nation to supplying the British forces with facilities and supplies upon the liberation of her homeland until such time as the Germans were driven out altogether. This was correctly termed 'reciprocal aid' in the jargon of the Foreign Office, as it went some way to repaying the British government for the costs incurred equipping and training some of the allied forces during their exile in Britain. Some of the governments had huge resources from which to draw their expenses – Norway and Holland being two good examples – but others, such as the Czechoslovaks and the Poles, needed extensive financial credits to fund their war effort. Indeed, so meticulous were the men at the Treasury in keeping the books, the Czechs were presented with a bill for £177,236 12*s* 9*d* for

fighter ammunition used in the two years from their arrival in
the summer of 1940 to the end of the tax year in 1942.[36] By the
middle of 1944, the Czechs owed around £5.5 million, but this
pales into insignificance when compared to the Polish debt of
more than £80 million.[37] Mutual Aid was therefore little more
than a gesture of support; and besides, political considerations
in 1945 made much of it irrelevant anyway. Strong-nerved
officials at the Treasury contemplated £100 million write-offs with
scarcely a sign of concern in their frequent notes to the service
departments, but when it became clear that much of the money
would never be refunded, the potential marketing opportunities
implicit in COS 120 became all the more attractive.

Such were the major policies and articles of legislation
which applied to the foreign airmen in Britain, but, before we
move on to examine each nation by turn, a few words must be
recorded concerning the primary focus of the present study.
More than anything, this entire work is an examination of official
Britain's reaction to an unprecedented situation. France had
not been expected to fall, therefore there were no contingency
arrangements to administer the air and land units formed on
British soil by the governments and servicemen of the occupied
nations. They were, indeed, unexpected allies, for if things had
gone according to plan they would have fought their war on the
Continent alongside a resolute France. That turned out not to be
the case, so the British had to cope with things as best they could.
Some might agree that they coped fairly well and assimilated the
allies into the structure of the Royal Air Force with remarkable
efficiency given the difficult circumstances. Others might feel
that the entire relationship was based more on tolerance than a
genuine spirit of alliance and friendship.

But although many of the views expressed by some of the
British make for uncomfortable reading, it is vital to remember
that the officers and men of the allied squadrons were seldom
selected for individual criticism. Many medals were won, many
friends were lost, and the Royal Air Force grew very fond indeed
of these stout warriors who refused to give up the fight for their
homes. Rather, most of the conflict took place at the higher
levels, usually with the allied governments or with the high
commands, for this was the area which generated the greatest
tensions. The men on the ground or in the air simply got on with
the job, and from the dismal days of 1940 right through to the
glorious relief of Victory in Europe, they displayed nothing but
bravery and dedication to the common cause. They lived and
died as airmen of their own countries fighting from the heart of

another, and all the foreign veterans' associations are tenacious in preserving those far-off links with the RAF as defining moments in their respective aviation histories.

Finally, despite all the horrors they had witnessed, the perilous escapes, and the long years in exile during which so many terrible things were heard about conditions at home, we must also note that they displayed a fine sense of humour. Like their British colleagues, they sought laughter wherever they could, for in laughter they might find that extra ounce of comradeship which was so important when the news was bad or the pressures of exile grew hard to bear. Most jokes were usually directed at their political representatives, or at the British for their stuffiness. Language problems gave them no end of fun. One highly popular story, said to have originated with one of the Dutch squadrons, was set in a disciplinary hearing in which a British commander accused an allied pilot of cowardice in the face of the enemy. 'You were told quite clearly that there were bandits at three o'clock,' said the CO, 'and yet you immediately flew back to the station. Why?' Came the nonchalant reply: 'Because it was only half past one.' Another story, this time Polish, poked fun at the British class system. A young lady of high society had volunteered to serve in a tea-wagon, and on the first day she encountered a Polish pilot who had obviously gone to great lengths to master the slang for 'a cup of tea and a sandwich'. After several attempts to understand the chap's requests, she turned to her more roughly hewn workmate and said: 'This fellow keeps asking for "a cuppa cha and a wad". Do you think he knows any English?'

NOTES

1. During the course of the war, Greek and Yugoslav squadrons were formed as the men and materials became available, but these units were based abroad. The focus of this book is the relationship between the British and their allies stationed on British territory.

2. Examples of the Czechoslovak military codes can be found in British archives. A loose minute in the files of the Allied Administration Committee reveals that the penalty of death was applied to cases of mutiny under martial law, desertion to the enemy, cowardice in the face of the enemy, the surrender of a fortified position to the enemy, and the transfer of military materials to the enemy.

By contrast, the Polish list was more severe. The death sentence could be awarded for murder, crimes against the state, treason, espionage, crimes against the national economy, sabotage, shamming, self-wounding, desertion in the face of the enemy, refusal to obey an order in the face of the enemy, the failure of a commander to hold on to an objective, or capitulating without good cause, and the surrender of military materials (FO 371/24373: Loose minute, June 1940).

3. The National Government was the longest-serving coalition government in modern British history. It had originally been created in 1931 as a temporary administration to deal with the impact of the Depression, but it gained such enormous public support that it survived through the recovery period and into the deepening crisis presented by the European dictatorships. For most of its life it was dominated by Conservatives, and it had four prime ministers: Ramsay MacDonald (Labour), Stanley Baldwin, Neville Chamberlain and Winston Churchill (all Conservative). It was finally put out of office in July 1945 by Clement Attlee's Labour Party.

4. *Parliamentary Debates, 5th Series*, vol. 364, cols 1,350–1,414. All subsequent references to the debate are drawn from this source unless otherwise indicated.

5. The available evidence promotes conflicting assessments of Czech and Slovak anti-Semitism. In a despatch from Prague in 1939, George F. Kennan noted that 'the mass of the [Czech] people appear to have little or no interest in anti-Semitism', whereas the Jews 'are the object of widespread resentment on the part of the Slovak population' (Kennan, G.F., *From Prague After Munich: Diplomatic Papers 1938–1940* (Princeton UP 1968): 'Despatch of February 1, 1939 to the Department of State on the Jewish problem in the new Czechoslovakia', *passim*).

On the other hand, an article dealing exclusively with Jews in the Czechoslovak armed forces examines a range of testimonies which indicate that anti-Semitic behaviour on behalf of the officer corps was rife, pointing the finger especially at Gen Sergěj Ingr, Chief of Staff of the Czechoslovak Army in Britain and later Minister of National Defence in the Government-in-Exile. (Dagan, A. et al., *The Jews of Czechoslovakia* (The Jewish Publication Society of America 1984); Kulka Erich: 'Jews in the Czechoslovak Armed Forces During World War II', pp. 371–6).

6. Anti-Semitism in the Polish forces is admirably reviewed by David Engel, who also examines the impact of *Jestem*

Polakiem, a rightist periodical published by a faction within the Polish government which had strong anti-Semitic undertones and attracted criticism from the British popular press and various religious newspapers. During the Commons debate, Sydney Silverman observed that credits granted by the British presumably paid for the publication. Engel draws the valid conclusion that this and other evidence of anti-Semitic attitudes made the Polish government 'concerned about their negative public image in England and its possible political repercussions ever since the first month of the war'. The British government held similar views. (Engel, D., *In the Shadow of Auschwitz: The Polish Government-in-Exile and the Jews, 1939–1942* (University of North Carolina 1987) pp. 70–7).

7. A major example here would be cowardice. This was abolished as a capital offence under British military law in 1930.

8. Donaldson, F. *The British Council: The First Fifty Years* (Jonathan Cape 1984), pp. 29–30. In his inaugural speech, the Prince of Wales described the Council as 'a proper organisation to spread knowledge and appreciation of its language, literature, art, science and education'.

9. Eastment, D.J., *The Policies and Position of the British Council From the Outbreak of War to 1950* (PhD, University of Leeds 1982), p. 27.

10. BW/68/3: 39th Meeting of the Executive Committee, 21.9.39. The scope of activities was to be selective, concentrating on only the most educated persons, and only those who were stranded or alone in the country. The main elements of the new scheme were the reunion of foreign nationals; further integration between refugees and British citizens; the procurement of free tickets for the theatre, cinema and concerts, and the organisation of 'receptions', lectures, recitals and cultural events particular to the foreign nationals, such as traditional dancing and art exhibitions (Donaldson, pp. 112–13). It can be seen from this programme that the Council was by no means geared to catering for the recreational needs of the average soldier or airman who arrived bedraggled and tired during the summer of 1940.

11. BW/2/47: First meeting of the Advisory Committee on the Teaching of English to Foreigners, 21.6.40. A further note complained that too many foreigners tended to learn English 'for their own private purposes' and that 'comparatively few care for culture and even fewer want to be anglicised'.

12. Donaldson, p. 114.

13. It is worth noting in passing that the Admiralty had very little interest in language training for foreign sailors because most allied ships were self-contained units.

14. BW/2/231: Correspondence, 9.9.40 to 5.11.40. De la Bère also expressed his sincere thanks for the work already done by the Council, 'but his anxiety to have more language teaching is caused by the fact that a Czech squadron holds the record of 105 brought down last month, and he feels there must be many other Czech and Polish pilots who would be equally useful, but who must know some English before they can be let loose in the skies'.

15. BW/2/231: Invoice to Air Ministry, 9.1.41. The Council was deluged with pleas from Allied stations for books, films, magazines – anything which could either improve the men's command of the language or at least entertain them in some measure. In many cases, the Council met the costs from its own funds. It should also be noted that there are many letters of thanks from RAF stations all over Britain for the efforts made by the Council to meet all their educational needs.

16. BW/2/231: Internal memorandum, 10.11.41.

17. This list of 'operational and technical language' included such terms as 'PBI' (Poor Bloody Infantry), 'FA' (Football Association), 'in the drink' (to ditch an aircraft in water) and 'NBG' (No Bloody Good). During the following month, the Council suggested to the Ministry that such colloquialisms as 'it lies plumb on your route' might confuse the learners, but the Ministry replied – reasonably enough – that this was the type of language the foreign crews would hear all the time, so they had to get used to it (BW/2/231: 2.5.41).

18. BW/2/231: Memorandum from the Air Ministry to the British Council, 23.4.41.

19. BW/2/51: British Council Advisory Committee on Foreigners in Great Britain; Minutes of 7th meeting, 7.11.40.

20. BW/2/229: Memorandum to the Secretary-General, A.J.S. White, 12.11.40.

21. BW/2/229: Correspondence of 28.1.41. White further admitted that this attitude was causing no little resentment among the allied governments.

22. Donaldson, pp. 116–17.

23. Donaldson, pp. 112–23. See also BW/2/51 (Advisory Council on Foreigners in Great Britain), and BW/2/45 (Resident Foreigners Hospitality Committee). Both of these files contain exhaustive information on the cultural activities of the Council from the outbreak of war to December 1942.

24. ČsL VB 131/CI-3/1/76: Examination Results, January 1942. The results ranged from 5 per cent to 95 per cent.

25. BW 27/3: Undated fiscal projection issued before April 1941.

26. BW 108/1: Estimate of expenditure, 17.11.42. This file contains the general records of the National Houses in London.

27. HO 294/72: Copies of the monthly programmes are held in this file.

28. BW 27/3: Letter of 8.10.41 from the British Council to the Food Office at Caxton Hall.

29. BW 108/1: Unsigned and undated resumé, but probably issued in early 1943, judging from its position in the file. The proposed narrative for the other main National Hearths was couched in similar terms with similar images.

30. All of the source files used in this section contain numerous references to the Council officials who directed the affairs of the national houses in London.

31. ČsL VB 121/CI-2d/1/175: 'The Maintenance of Good Relations and Allied Air Force Morale', p. 1. Oddly, no copy of this document surfaced in British archives during the research for this study, either in the files of the DAAC/DAFL or the Air Council.

32. Ibid., pp. 1–2. Some lesser elements have been omitted from this list to conserve space.

33. Ibid. pp. 7–10.

34. ČsL VB 119/Cl-2d/1/75 (VHA Archives, Prague). Reports, September– December 1940.

35. Various copies of COS (44) 120 exist in British files, but the main version, complete with appropriate commentary, may be found in CAB 80/44.

36. The VHA archives in Prague are full of such data. Within three weeks of the first two Czechoslovak Hurricanes being lost in the Battle of Britain, an invoice for £13,140 to cover aircraft costs and training fees was sent to the Czechoslovak authorities. To be fair to the British, however, the allies themselves insisted on such accurate accountancy to balance their own budgets.

37. FO 371/42299: Treasury figures, 11.6.44.

CHAPTER TWO

Poles and Czechs

THE FIRST PHASE: SEPTEMBER 1939 TO JULY 1940

'Machines will beat machines,' said Winston Churchill to the French Prime Minister, Paul Reynaud, as all serious resistance to Germany was coming to an end in June 1940. It is difficult to determine whether the British statesman was speaking from the heart at that moment or merely groping for any suitable words which might inject at least some more self-belief into the tottering French government. In all probability it was the latter, for in the same discussion on 11 June, the French had asked for yet more British fighter squadrons to be sent to their aid, and again Churchill had refused. Furthermore, the British had lost a good deal of their *own* machines at Dunkirk, and the prospect of fighting any kind of war on the Continent – let alone a mechanised one – was rapidly diminishing.

Churchill's comment was almost certainly inspired by the grim fascination with which he and others had watched the German advance. Machines on the ground and in the air had dealt Europe a blow of savage intensity not seen since the days of Napoleon. Indeed, the entire doctrine of *Blitzkrieg* depended on machines. If one recalls the dominant images of the First World War, most likely they will involve men in trenches being pounded by artillery, and both resources were considered to be available in almost inexhaustible quantities. By the time of the Second World War, the lesson had been learned – though more quickly by the Germans than anyone else – that mechanised warfare was the future. The man on the ground would necessarily become subordinate to the aeroplane and the tank; and if one wishes to pursue that progression to its logical conclusion, the soldier of today is even more of an irrelevance. In 1940, however, the

French and British military still relied most of all on the trooper to win the field; and he, no matter how valiant, was no match for the piston and the propeller.

The air war in 1940 was essentially a question of pilots and planes. The French had at their disposal not only their own national force, but a good number of Poles and Czechoslovaks, many of them trained fighter pilots, who had reorganised on French soil when their own nations had been overrun. But the French problem was not one of pilot availability, for these they had in relative abundance. Neither the Poles nor the Czechoslovaks were employed by the French in any great measure, and those who did see combat (and several were decorated for bravery) did so in largely obsolete aircraft ranged against state-of-the-art fighting machines. As a result, when the air war over France drew to its close in mid-June 1940 and the RAF withdrew its remaining reserves, many of the pilots of the other allied nations sought evacuation to Britain, some hoping to continue their war against Germany, many others hoping to play a part in it at last.

Both the Poles and the Czechoslovaks would bring various grievances with them to British shores. Neither contingent was particularly impressed with the French war effort, and each group had political scores to settle, though in this respect the Czechoslovaks had the longest agenda. Both groups felt bitter and under-employed. Air Ministry staff who were detailed to interview the men on arrival in Britain grew accustomed to vehement complaints hurled at the French for having treated them as second-class fliers with no useful purpose to serve – until the going got rough, when they were thrown into the fight with scarcely any training on unfamiliar aircraft. The sharpest condemnation of all was reserved for the attitudes of the French personnel who had actively tried to prevent them escaping after the Armistice. These and other criticisms rang in the ears of RAF personnel officers until serious work had begun on the reconstruction of the allied units. Had both groups known the whole story, however, their anger would have been magnified tenfold.

To begin with the Poles, it is well known that the British and French guarantees to Poland formed the basis of the Western allies' entry into the war in September 1939. It is less well known that the British guarantee issued by Chamberlain in March 1939 had included the French without their formal agreement. Chamberlain was gambling on the fact that France, still smarting with guilt after the Munich betrayal, would not treat Poland in a similar fashion, but the French not only doubted whether

Poland was on Hitler's list, they also had grave concerns over the fighting capabilities of the Polish forces, meaning that if a German attack *did* occur, the odds were heavy indeed that France would be plunged into another war. Thus, from the start, French commitment to the Polish cause was always going to be lukewarm, and Britain's scarcely warmer, since neither party had any real admiration for the Polish state or its right-wing government.[1] In essence, the whole business was about containing German expansion, not defending Poland. However, once given, the assurance had to be honoured for neither France nor Britain could withstand the international condemnation which would follow a 'Polish Munich'.

Shortly before the German attack on Poland, the British had signed a pact of mutual assistance with the Polish authorities. This arrangement, though largely political in nature, rather compelled the British toengage in staff talks with the Poles. The procedure was ponderous and meticulous; sub-committees were formed, satellite discussions took place, and all the details were carefully fed back to the Foreign Office in London. The first conference took place in the afternoon of 25 October 1939, and over several hours the delegates reviewed the options available. In essence, there were only three. The first was to retain all Polish air personnel in France. This idea was supported by Gen Zajac because this meant a better chance of active service upon the opening of a hot war in the west. But if this were to be the case, the French argued, then all the Poles would be sent forward to the front line in units or sections and then attached to existing French squadrons. The Poles would have none of this, insisting that their air force retained its independence as a national fighting arm. Zajac made it quite clear that sufficient men were available to form, operate and maintain eight complete squadrons of any combination if either ally undertook to supply the equipment and the locations.

The second option was to send all the men to Britain. This was also supported by Zajac, for three reasons: first, it would strengthen the bonds which united Poland to Britain; second, the imperial connection might make recruitment in the Dominions that much easier (and here he had Canada in mind); and third, the Polish maintenance personnel were more familiar with British aero-engines. Both the British and the French rejected this option, the British claiming that they had neither the space nor the equipment to assimilate the 5,000 or so men involved, and the French because they feared that a lengthy training period would surely be necessary, and in effect this would render the contingent useless for too long. It will be seen that this was so much hot air on behalf of the French, but the French DCAS, Gen Romatet, sweetened the pill by suggesting that the entire contingent be split equally down the middle, one portion to serve on the continent in independent squadrons, the other to embark for Britain for refitting with the RAF.

This was the third option, and Romatet went on to elaborate his vision for the Polish Air Force reborn. He explained to Zajac that 'within a few months' France would create a Polish fighter division consisting of two squadrons, or thirty-eight planes in all, and one bomber division, again of two squadrons, with a total of twenty-six aircraft. AVM Douglas Evill then chipped in on behalf of the RAF. He flattered Polish aspirations by stating that His Majesty's Government would be 'very proud' to have Polish units fighting side-by-side with the RAF, and his trump card was to hand a note to all the delegates committing the British to forming two first-line light-bomber squadrons with two more in reserve, the latter acting as operational training units. Thus, the target of the eight squadrons which Zajac had asked for would be met by the policy of division, and neither he nor the new Polish Prime Minister, Gen Wladyslaw Sikorski, had much option but to accept it, primarily because it was the only offer on the table, but also because it represented a realistic chance of getting Polish airmen into action again with reasonable resources at their disposal. Zajac later wrote to the former British air attaché to Warsaw, Gp Capt Alexander Davidson, and stressed that any units formed 'would constitute a part of the Polish Air Forces'. This meant independent status, and with that, so Zajac argued, came the rights of inspection and creation of a separate high command. He also demanded a firm promise from both the allies that the squadrons would fight on the western front when it became active, and that all units would be returned to Poland in their entirety at the end of the war. Davidson's reply is not known, and in any case such matters were far too lofty for a group captain to pronounce upon, but what is significant is that these issues in one form or another were to dog the Anglo–Polish relationship in the air until victory had been won, and even after.

The conference closed with each of the three parties declaring the scheme to be workable, and Evill returned to Britain in the evening and informed the Air Ministry and the Foreign Office accordingly. To the latter, Evill summarised the situation, concluding that the terms of service should be 'embodied in a charter' that would formalise the arrangement above and beyond the official treaty of alliance. He also sounded the first warning

about 'the administrative, disciplinary and psychological problems'
which would certainly arise from the formation of Polish units
in England. Finally, in a sentence which was to cause problems
in the near future, he added that the Poles had been told that
any further arrivals of personnel would be concentrated at Lyons
'and similarly dealt with'. He also knew, but did not mention, that
another 6,000 Poles then resident in France had been targeted by
the Polish High Command as potential recruits, but when this had
been brought to the attention of the allied conference, both the
French and the British threw up their hands and declared that any
use of these personnel would constitute an entirely new proposal
above and beyond the present arrangement which involved only
those men in uniform at that time.[2]

The transfer of the airmen did not begin until after the Anglo-
Polish Naval Agreement was signed on 18 November 1939. Within
the scope of that Agreement, which was designed to incorporate
Polish naval operations within the structure of the Royal Navy,
provisions were made for the movement of the men to Britain
at the rate of 200 or so at a time. This was to make the task of
accommodating them easier, or so the story went. A few weeks
after this, the first cohort arrived at Eastchurch. Much to the
annoyance of the Polish authorities, each man was to be enrolled
or commissioned into the Royal Air Force Volunteer Reserve
(RAFVR). Formed in 1936, the primary function of the RAFVR
was exactly what the name implies: to provide a pool of volunteer
personnel from which reinforcements and replacements for the
regular Air Force could be drawn. This was intensely irritating
to the Poles, for they insisted in France – and would insist many
times more in the future – that their position as a formal ally
entitled them to fully independent status. In return, the British
used an argument upon which they would fall back many times.
RAFVR enrolment, they declared, was a much simpler method
by which the new influx could be swiftly assimilated; and besides,
it was impracticable to have an independent Polish Air Force
in existence when half its strength would be in another country
altogether. The Poles had no choice but to accept, though they
were to discover that the British had secured for themselves by far
the best part of the deal.

Thus, as far as the British were concerned, they had fulfilled
their agreement to the letter. Groups of Polish airmen continued
to arrive at Eastchurch until February 1940, but on their arrival
they quickly discovered that there was nothing to do but sit in
classrooms and learn English, be constantly drilled on the parade
ground, and be force-fed RAF regulations. The attitude of the

British officers did not help either. As Adam Zamoyski wrote, the RAF commanders thought the Poles to be 'a rung or two lower on the ladder of civilisation'.[3] There were numerous disciplinary infringements and the language barrier seemed almost impenetrable. In short, service life with the RAF seemed as inert as the situation they had left behind in France.

On 17 February 1940 the French Air Minister, Guy le Chambre, signed the Franco-Polish Air Agreement with Sikorski, now C-in-C of the Polish Forces as well as Prime Minister. The arrangement provided for the reconstitution of the Polish Air Force on French territory. Naturally enough, Sikorski expected the French to supply all possible assistance to achieve that aim, but Air Ministry records hint at a different agenda. As early as 9 January 1940, the French had been pestering the British to speed up the transfer of the Polish cohort, claiming that the delay was holding up the training of the men who were to remain in France. The British Foreign Office concurred with this view, arguing that 'the Air Ministry's handling of this from the very beginning has not been convincing'. As far as the Foreign Office was concerned, the whole deal had been concluded without much forethought, and in a desire not to sour relations with the French, the decision was taken to put more pressure on the Air Ministry to honour its commitments. Any action, however, should be undertaken with caution. As Roger Makins phrased it: 'We must be careful how we set about stirring them up.'[4]

Makins wrote to Archibald Boyle, the Director of Intelligence within the Air Ministry, a man with considerable power in the field of allied air relations. Boyle had won the Military Cross in the First World War and had a range of contacts spread across Europe, which might have accounted for him being the RAF's representative on the Joint Intelligence Committee. According to AM Sir Victor Goddard, who knew him well, his primary duty was 'assessing the attitudes of people, including the shady ones and the twisters, British and foreign, who had associations with air power'.[5] When he received Makins' gentle urgings to move things along at Eastchurch, he threw part of the blame back onto the Poles themselves, insisting that they were contributing to the delay by dithering with the selection of suitable officers and men. The other part of the problem involved preparing the station itself for the incoming crews. At the time, only about 350 men had arrived, though he believed that a figure of 200 a week could be reached given favourable conditions.[6]

The Foreign Office was not convinced, believing that the French would not be pacified with such an excuse. Then the

British Air Attaché in France, Gp Capt Alfred Collier, weighed
in with his own views. Writing to the British Ambassador in Paris,
he began by agreeing with Boyle that the Poles were showing
'considerable muddle-headedness', but he argued that the French
were making matters worse by continually moving the men from
camp to camp, and had made little or no effort to co-operate with
their British allies in the transfer programme. He added:

> They have received the Poles . . . without any proper
> arrangements for them, with the result that they have
> suffered seriously in morale and in health from the
> appalling conditions in which they have been kept. If we
> have not wished to take the Poles more rapidly, it has been
> because we were determined not to accept them until
> they could be properly housed and warmed. The French
> have done nothing with regard to the training of the Poles
> allotted to them.

He closed by drawing the Ambassador's attention to the fact that
three months earlier, the French 'were clamouring and insisting
that they must have all the Polish aviators. What, one wonders,
would they have done with them if we had agreed to their
suggestion?' When a copy of the letter reached the Foreign Office,
Makins pencilled a caustic note in the margin: 'What would the Air
Ministry have done if they'd had them all in the UK?'[7]

Thus, the Poles were in an invidious position. The French were
keeping them in conditions so bad as to endanger health, while
at the same time trying to push them out of the country into
the arms of the British. For their part, the British Air Ministry
was trying to blame the French *and* the Poles for the lack of
progress. Small wonder, therefore, that discontent was spreading
throughout the entire contingent. As one pilot so graphically put
it: 'They treated us like white niggers.' Under heavy pressure and
'with a great deal of fuss', the Air Ministry finally relented and
agreed to take 250 men a week, though the Foreign Office was
by now well aware that future dealings with the RAF ought to be
approached with much caution.[8]

That should have been the end of the affair. Throughout
February and March 1940, the 2,200 officers and men were
shipped over to Britain and installed at Eastchurch. Though
conditions were cramped and there was much grumbling, the
Air Ministry was still satisfied that it had kept its side of the
bargain. Then, in late March, a new row erupted when the French
approached the air attaché in Paris and informed him that

a further 4,000 men were due to arrive from Romania, having escaped from occupied territory, and under the terms of the October Agreement the British had agreed to take half. Would they now do so?

An absurd argument then developed, rooted in pedantry and semantics. The British argued that, yes, they *had* agreed to take 50 per cent, but that figure was based on a total of 5,000 men, an estimate supplied by the Poles themselves. Nothing had been said about any further batches of escapees. The French retorted by pointing to the spirit of the agreement, insisting that no figures had ever been agreed upon in writing by either side. The Air Ministry then threw itself upon the mercy of the Foreign Office, and the latter promptly took the side of the French, checking the text of the October Agreement and curtly informing the Air Ministry that no precise expression of total numbers existed within it. The French, however, were on solid ground. It will be recalled that Evill, in summarising the October conference to the Foreign Office, mentioned that he had told the Poles that any further arrivals would be 'similarly dealt with': The French were well aware that any decent diplomat would interpret this as a firm promise because they immediately threw Evill's words straight back at the Foreign Office, which in turn volleyed them on to the Air Ministry.[9]

The Air Ministry had been cornered; it had no option but to comply absolutely with the Agreement signed on its behalf by Evill in October, and this meant an obligation to take a further 2,000 men. This is not to say that compliance needed to be swift. In the wake of the Foreign Office's decision on the matter, the Air Ministry copied letters to all relevant departments, arguing that it was the Polish High Command who were the real villains of the piece. One of the British staff in Paris interviewed a senior French Air Force officer and drew the conclusion that the Poles' own estimates had 'fallen far short of the true number', and instead of informing the French and British governments of the position, they had 'merely kept quiet and let things drift'.[10] The French sympathised with this view, and also with the pleas of the Air Ministry that any further transfers would place an intolerable strain on RAF resources. Yet it made no difference – the October Agreement was sound, and promises had been made. The French repeated their demand to know when the transfers would be taking place.

The Air Ministry then changed tactics and retreated to a policy which, using the terminology of today, might be called 'massive retaliation'. More to the point, once it discovered that it worked – for no further transfers of Poles took place before the attack on France – it became an essential part of the Ministry's armoury. As we shall see later, it was a weapon used whenever the Ministry felt itself to be outflanked by the Foreign Office on the question of allied air personnel. Having tried hard to convince anyone who would listen that they had fulfilled their obligations to both allies, and that they were struggling already with problems of training, accommodation and equipment, they circulated memoranda and reports which – to put it mildly – cast the Poles in an unflattering light. The most crucial of these was a paper by an officer attached to the RAF reception squadron named as Flt Lt Landau. Boyle read the report and discussed its findings with Landau in late March, shortly before the Foreign Office verdict on the question of further transfers. He then sent a copy to the Foreign Office in early April.

Landau argued that Polish discipline and organisation left much to be desired, and that officers and NCOs had little control over the other ranks. To explain this, he identified a range of causes, beginning with the defeat of Poland itself. This, he said, had caused the men to lose confidence in their commanders, and the long periods spent in Romanian and French camps had had 'a demoralising effect on the discipline of the Polish airmen'.[11] He then attacked the Polish military tradition itself, suggesting that their concept of discipline 'has never been up to the standard required in the RAF'. This he blamed on 'the inherent individualism and egotism of the Poles', and the observation that the officers seemed to treat the other ranks with 'a lack of consideration unknown in our service'. Then, somewhat mystified, he observed that officers would also 'fraternise with airmen, walk about with them and play cards with them', and we may only conclude that Landau felt this had a confusing effect on the men, to the overall detriment of good military practice.

But all of this was only the preamble. Warming to his theme, Landau informed Boyle that promotion within the Polish Air Force was due largely to favouritism, and that this, too, gravely undermined discipline and efficiency. Then, in a swipe at the fighting spirit of the Poles, he added:

> It had been hoped that the initial enthusiasm which inspired our Polish guests would enable them to overcome the difficulties arising out of the new surroundings and the new methods. Unfortunately, once they were put into British uniforms, given British ranks and British pay (far above their pay at home) and felt safe ground under their feet, this

enthusiasm has worn off and matters of rank, prestige and, above all, 'having a good time' have become predominant.

This lacklustre attitude, he believed, might possibly be dispelled by pushing forward the programme of flying training, but more importantly, by encouraging the Poles to mix with their British colleagues so that they might 'learn by example'.

If these were the problems, what were the solutions? First, Landau argued, 'if the Polish air units in this country are ever to become efficient, their command must never be taken out of British hands'. He went further than the practice of duplicating senior posts, advocating that the Poles needed a British counterpart right down to flight sergeant because they were incapable of running things for themselves. To accomplish this duplication without giving too much offence, he suggested a programme of education through which the Polish authorities might come to know the complexity of the RAF organisation, appreciate the language difficulties, and fully comprehend 'the extremely high standards' expected from all who wore RAF blue. The British must supply as many liaison officers as it took to achieve these aims, and the Air Ministry should be prepared for the programme to last between six and nine months. Finally, to cure the problem of favouritism, he recommended that all such decisions of promotion and rank should finally rest in British hands, 'even though outwardly the impression might be maintained that the Poles themselves had the final word'.

Some might see this as nothing but rampant bigotry; others might choose to argue that war is war and tough decisions have to be made, unpopular or not. But we can be sure that Boyle concurred with much of this, and the essence of the report – though presumably in greatly sanitised form – would be conveyed to Sikorski through the Chief of the Air Staff, Sir Cyril Newall. Sikorski himself wrote directly to Neville Chamberlain on 4 April asking him to intervene personally and have the quota limitations cancelled, and urging him to accept all Poles from the Continent. Chamberlain replied with platitudes, promising that the matter would 'be examined with the least possible delay'.[12] Sikorski again then directly requested a seat on the Supreme War Council, but the refusal from both the French and the British was as swift as it was blunt. The British Ambassador in Paris wrote to Makins at the Foreign Office agreeing with the view that a Polish military representative should be present at War Council meetings only for matters of Polish concern. 'To give the Poles anything else,' he added, 'would be dangerous. They are much too emotional and indiscreet to be entrusted with secret plans relating to the conduct of the war.'[13]

Meanwhile, Boyle had hatched a new scheme, one which involved pacifying the French while avoiding the transfer of any more Polish airmen to Britain. The new total estimate of Polish personnel was placed at 10,000, and Britain was still bound by the October Agreement to accommodate and train half of them, or another 2,500 men in addition to the group at Eastchurch. It was argued that the Air Ministry's main justifications for refusal should be lack of accommodation itself (though Boyle well knew, thanks to Landau's report, that some of the earlier Polish contingent had been posted to stations across the whole of Britain, meaning that absorption would have been possible had the will been there), and the language difficulties presented by such a high number of non-English-speaking personnel. Also questioned was the likely impact on the war effort as a whole if resources were diverted to these men; this perhaps demonstrated that he too was in agreement with Landau's view that the Poles might lack the morale to fight.

Boyle's solution, therefore, was to inform the French that any surplus numbers should be either sent to the Polish Army in France or demobilised and employed in the French war industry. That way, the numbers would be dispersed without any serious impact on resources. It would also mean the virtual destruction of the Polish Air Force as a viable entity, though of course this was not mentioned in the plan. It was suggested that the French be told, politely but firmly, that there was simply no hope of forming more than two operational squadrons in Britain, with two more in reserve, and though Britain might be able to absorb 'a few hundred mechanics at most', this would almost certainly irritate the Poles into refusing such a limited transfer. Either way, Britain secured a few hundred trained specialists for nothing, or no more Poles at all. He obviously liked this idea, for he concluded his letter with: 'We should therefore prefer no mention to be made of it, except under great diplomatic pressure, and then as the absolute limit of possible concession.'[14] Thus, the Air Ministry dug in its heels: there would be no more Poles except under irresistible circumstances, and even then this would be the pick of the crop and only a fraction of the allotted number.

'The reason why nothing was happening [at Eastchurch] was British confusion and dithering'; so wrote Adam Zamoyski in _The Forgotten Few_.[15] But it seems clear from the full report as examined above, that it was not 'confusion and dithering' which the British were displaying, but an active distrust, and even dislike, of their new allies. Zamoyski also entirely ignores the debate over the excess numbers and the British commitment to absorb them, but it is apparent from the evidence that neither the French nor the British really wanted anything to do with the Poles, and that the whole thing from first to last had been an exercise in allied 'solidarity' which had gone hideously wrong for all parties concerned.

Zamoyski's interpretation of Landau's report can also leave the reader with the impression that the British to some extent *caused* the reduction in discipline and other factors by this 'confusion and dithering', when it would seem from the timing of the memoranda that the report was precisely gauged to add a powerful contribution to the continuing debate over whether or not the British should take more Poles. This is not to say that Landau's report was accurate or even fair, but it is indicative of the lengths to which the RAF would go in order to avoid having its organisation interfered with by mere diplomats. Neither was this a solitary incident, as we shall see.

Of greater importance, perhaps, is not *what* the Air Ministry did, but *why* it did it. The answer lies deep within the pre-war relations with Poland as a state, the British military tradition in general, and the Anglo-French interpretation of East European politics. In the first place, the Chamberlain guarantee to Poland in March 1939 had little or nothing to do with protecting the Poles; rather, its primary function was to signal to Hitler that the Western democracies would tolerate no further expansion. An added bonus might be the weakening of Hitler's position within Germany if his general staff could be persuaded to take seriously the threat of an all-out war with much the same coalition which defeated them in 1918. Secondly, Chamberlain – and to some extent the French also – was obliged for reasons of credibility to save face after the Munich betrayal. This was particularly important because, at the time, both Britain and France were entertaining hopes of Soviet resistance to Hitler – hopes dashed by the Nazi-Soviet Pact of August 1939. By taking a tough line on Poland, Chamberlain might convince Stalin that the West was prepared to fight this time, and it was simply impossible to reverse the guarantee once the Russians had signed their devil's covenant with Berlin. Chamberlain, by nonchalantly offering to protect Polish honour, effectively committed Britain and France to war in defence of a country which had itself behaved disreputably during the Munich crisis and was governed by an unwholesome bunch of militarists and right-wingers.

This last point was also a factor in the guarantee. The West was fully aware that Poland could fall into the German orbit given

sufficient territorial compensation and an agreeable policy over
Danzig, hence the desire to strengthen Polish nerves with the
offer of assistance. But Poland had delusions of Great Power
status, and under Foreign Minister Josef Beck, had followed a
policy of arrogant resistance far beyond her capabilities to
support by force if necessary, so the West was bolstering a power
which was fatally under strength at its core. The French, on
their part, had signed a formal alliance with Poland as early as
1921, but even this was in connection with the French policy of
preventing a resurgence of German aggression, and only loosely
directed towards mutual interests. Poland therefore had no
'friends' in the West as such, only many fine words and promises
of support from two nations which were in fact serving their own
interests and completely failing to grasp the implications of the
promises they had made.

For these reasons, when the Polish collapse in 1939 was so swift
and resolute, France reacted not with outrage but with horror,
for now all the diplomatic chickens would come home to roost.
The alliance of 1921 had provided for military staff talks and a
mutual exchange of German-related intelligence, but in reality
there had been few moments of substantive communication
between the two. The French had been similarly aloof with the
Czechoslovaks, with whom they signed alliances in 1924 and 1925,
and by 1939, largely through ignorance and lack of commitment,
the French had formed opinions of the Polish and Czechoslovak
military which were wholly negative, which accounts for the bleak
treatment the air crews received when they decamped to French
soil. The French held the Polish military entirely responsible not
only for their own defeat, but also for the necessity of France
declaring war on Germany at all. Worse still, it now appeared that
Germany was free of all Eastern entanglements and at liberty to
hurl her entire weight against the West. Thus the Poles became
the scapegoats for French resentment and – we might say – fear of
what was going to happen next.

The British position was more remote. To some extent, the
Poles were an inherited ally: they came attached to the French
like a bolt-on accessory to a domestic appliance. The British were
only committed to liaise with the Poles after they had signed the
agreement on mutual assistance shortly before the outbreak of
war, and most of the knowledge the British possessed regarding
the capacity and capabilities of the Polish forces was acquired
second-hand from French sources. The Polish Military Mission
arrived in Britain in August 1939 complete with four ships loaded
with supplies. As 'allies' they expected much, but they obtained

very little. They demanded promises of immediate intervention in the event of a German attack, but they were not to know that as early as May 1939, both the French and the British had resolved not to attempt direct military assistance.[16] Neither of the general staffs expected the Poles to be able to resist a German attack for very long (and at the time this did not include the possibility of a parallel Soviet invasion from the east), and to send forces in support of such a doomed cause would amount to a suicidal strategy and might even provoke a German attack in the west. Therefore, when the defeat of Poland occurred with such resounding finality, this merely confirmed the prejudices of the British and French service chiefs that the Polish forces were simply not viable allies in combat. In the eyes of the British, the Poles were a French problem first and foremost, and that is why the Air Ministry took such a firm stance against the further transfers in early 1940.

One other factor needs to be considered: the way Britain viewed military alliances in general. As Lord Salisbury said, 'Britain does not solicit alliances, she grants them,' and this was very much the prevailing view in 1939, echoes of which may be detected in the way Chamberlain committed the French to the Polish guarantee without their prior approval. In one of A.J.P. Taylor's musings on the nature of British foreign policy, he wrote: 'Most countries have their foreign policy dictated to them by their situation and by the behaviour of their neighbours.' To this he added Palmerston's view that an alliance between equals is impossible, and that 'one Power has to be dependent on the other and need protection'.[17] Britain had *chosen* to go to war in September 1939, whereas Poland had no option but to respond to the German thrust. Moreover, Polish pre-war foreign policy was in large part a reaction to the policies of Germany and Russia, her two most powerful and dangerous neighbours. This choice on the part of Britain created in her a sense of moral superiority, for yet again Britain saw herself as acting in Europe's best interests by attempting to maintain the balance of power. With moral superiority comes the righteous belief that one should hold the levers of power, and although this was difficult to achieve in regard to the French, it was easy when it came to the Poles. From the very beginning, therefore, both the British and the French regarded the Poles as 'the dependent power', to be seen and not heard while the bigger boys got on with the business of war.

All of this explains why the Poles were held in such contempt by the French, and why Polish frustrations at Eastchurch were interpreted by the British as evidence of slovenly tradition, unwarranted arrogance, overblown prestige and a hint of defeatism. It also explains why the Poles were so emphatically denied a permanent seat on the Supreme War Council. Only twice before the fall of France were Polish political and military representatives allowed to witness the Council's deliberations, on 23 and 27 April 1940, and on both occasions the main topic of Polish interest was not allied action against their conquerors, but Polish contributions towards the Norwegian campaign. They were literally sent from the room when the Council turned to matters of strategic policy. In fact, almost the only words the Poles heard were 'sentimental and bland expressions of sympathy and appreciation for Polish heroism'.[18]

Then, on 1 May 1940, at the first meeting of the Allied War Committee, similar tributes and promises of complete liaison were bestowed upon Col Leon Mitkiewicz-Zoltek, the Polish representative. Here was a man who had not enjoyed a smooth passage to this gathering. He had initially been proposed by the Poles as their representative on the Supreme War Council, and in itself this had been prompted by questions in the House of Commons in February regarding the likelihood of a Polish candidate for a seat at the top table. Encouraged by the publicity, the Poles nominated Mitkiewicz-Zoltek as their man at the centre, so in mid-March he went about his formal rounds to introduce himself to his new colleagues. But when he arrived at the War Office, he was all but ejected from the premises by officials who claimed to know nothing about him. Beside themselves with fury, the Polish authorities bombarded the Foreign Office with demands for answers and apologies, and the Foreign Office in turn (rather shocked, to judge by the tone of the correspondence) demanded answers from the War Office. It was eventually told by Gen Marshall-Cornwall that the Pole could not be received because the War Cabinet office had not been officially informed of his appointment. Worse still, the French claimed no knowledge of the man at all. The General suggested that the Poles should apply to the French for approval, then the French would inform the British. A minute to file in the Foreign Office conveys the exasperation: 'This all seems to be unsatisfactory and to a certain extent ridiculous.' This would seem to be a reasonable assessment, for the next two weeks were spent laboriously circumventing protocol to receive a man who for many years had been on first-name terms with the air attachés of Europe, and it was only after the War Office, under intense pressure from the diplomats, informed the French without debate that Mitkiewicz-Zoltek had been appointed that order was eventually restored.

Even so, the whole affair merely illustrates still further how easy it was for the major powers to alienate and aggravate their ally – not by deliberate action, but by the perhaps more wounding and humiliating method of simply disregarding it in small but highly significant matters of prestige.[19] It also reinforces the view that, as far as the British were concerned, the French still bore the greater part of the responsibility for Polish affairs.

We may therefore only imagine Mitkiewicz-Zoltek's frustration at that meeting on 1 May as he was showered with lusty welcomes and bonhomie. He thanked the Committee, and then admitted rather apologetically that Polish input to the war effort thus far had been 'rather limited'.[20] Given that his country then had at least 8,000 airmen in France and ten times as many soldiers, few of whom even had a regular pay packet to look forward to, we must record this as a monumental piece of restraint on his part. What is more, that situation changed very little when the Germans launched their assault in the west ten days later. The feeling among Polish air crews was that the French could not possibly ignore their determination to continue the fight now that the war had been brought so close to home. Of the 8,000 air force personnel, approximately 1,000 were pilots, many of whom had seen action in the battle for Poland, and it seemed inconceivable that such a wealth of training and combat experience could be disregarded. Yet it was, and to a considerable extent. It has been estimated that only 150 or so men actually flew in combat, and though at the height of the battle the Polish Air Force in France consisted of seven squadrons (four fighter, two reconnaissance and one bomber), the action was limited in the extreme, the bomber squadron being entirely unused.[21]

Hence the French were still locked into their grand hallucination. Testimonies by both the Polish and Czechoslovak air contingents clearly indicate that neither was assigned to any meaningful combat duties, save a few individuals who found themselves flying within French squadrons. Defeatism was rampant, made worse by the scale and speed of the assault. When the shockwaves hit Britain, it might have been expected that attitudes towards the Poles would have been inverted overnight, but this was not the case. Two weeks into the new war, the Deputy Chief of the Air Staff convened a meeting to discuss 'the desirability' of forming allied flights within existing RAF Hurricane and Fairey Battle squadrons, working on the principle that 'around 70' pilots with operational and/or combat experience were then in the RAFVR. The meeting instructed Boyle to prepare papers accordingly.[22]

The Air Ministry's figures of 'around 70' were based not on actual data of men who had seen action in the various theatres of war, but on the numbers who, at the time, were involved in operational training of one form or another – in other words, men who were being trained to RAF standards as opposed to the skills acquired from service with their own national forces. For example, by late March, the Poles had 63 officers and 163 other ranks engaged in training at the new Polish Operational Training Unit (OTU) then forming at RAF Hucknall. By late April, only a very small percentage of these men had been trained to the levels required by the RAF, and when added to the other individuals from other nations who had been inducted into the RAFVR, they formed this nucleus of allied pilots which, as the situation in France swiftly worsened, the Air Ministry now deemed it necessary to employ. By late May, the estimated number of suitable allied personnel ready for service was placed at fifty bomber pilots with combat experience and a possible ninety with other operational experience. Even so, Davidson fought shy of using Polish aviators in bombers, arguing that Poles were 'individualists' and that their temperament was not suited to service in aircraft with a large complement.[23]

The Poles themselves had already seen the need for a rapid increase in trained men ready to fly at a moment's notice. To that end, they had made a direct offer to the Air Ministry, giving their permission for individuals to be seconded to British fighter squadrons. Sholto Douglas, writing in early June to the Air Member for Personnel, Sir Richard Peirse, gave his blessing to the idea.[24] Boyle himself had only recently accepted the concept of utilising the Polish experience. From early June, therefore, it seemed that the Polish crews which had been so neglected at Eastchurch might at last find themselves back in the war.

However, while it would be pleasant to record that sheer necessity had forced the hand of the British – even if this implies that progress on the Polish issue would have remained sluggish if that necessity had not arisen – there was an added impetus behind the drive to get some of the Poles into action. On 24 May, in a long memorandum directed towards the decision-makers in the Air Ministry, Wg Cdr Cyril Porri argued that 'an explosive representation' might be made by the Poles unless something positive was done soon.[25] He added that the vast majority of the men encamped at Eastchurch had done little in the way of active war work since their arrival, and he noted that those men who had opted for service with the French were now in action, 'and the French express the greatest admiration for their efficiency, usefulness and enthusiasm'. As we know now, the sincerity of this last statement is open to question, but Porri's central message was clear: unless a number of Poles saw action soon, morale and efficiency would take a serious downturn, and the blame would rest squarely with the Air Ministry.

This note was read the day before the conference, which immediately gave the signal to explore the possibility of using Polish personnel, hence we may draw our own conclusions about its effectiveness. Porri emphasised his argument by pointing out that several Dutch pilots had only recently arrived in the country, yet they were already in RAF uniform and being readied for action while the Poles still languished in Kent. Porri was too canny to target any individuals as being responsible for the dilatory attitude regarding the Poles, but he skilfully laid the blame at some appropriate doors by highlighting four factors, pointing first to the 'multiplicity of Air Ministry branches dealing with organisation and procedure'. This threw into stark relief the bald fact that the Air Ministry had no preconceived strategy for dealing with allied pilots, and proves conclusively that the 'British half' of the Polish contingent was taken without any basic planning being involved, making it no more than an empty gesture to the French. This was underlined by his second and third points: that the aerodrome (Eastchurch) was 'insufficient' in terms of suitable accommodation, and that the availability of training aircraft and RAF instructors was also poor. Finally, he pointed to a total inability 'to obtain authoritative decisions which might accelerate action', a charge which would have stung Sholto Douglas and Peirse as they were ultimately responsible for the allied crews.

Porri's brief examination of the intrinsic problems within the Air Ministry would later give rise to a new RAF directorate dedicated to the administration of the allied air forces, but in the short term his observations undoubtedly inspired action, albeit limited. Approximately twenty trained Polish pilots were transferred to British squadrons in early June, but the remainder were left to continue their long vigil. Why, exactly, is a matter for our interpretation of the events and motives. Zamoyski's view leaves the reader with the impression that British distrust and disorganisation were the principal reasons for the shambles at Eastchurch, and this assessment is not without merits, as we have seen. But we must also add the element of disinterest, for as discussed earlier, in many respects the British and the French did not even see Poland as being a viable belligerent in 1940. She had been knocked down and counted out, and the thousands who gathered in the west were, if anything, just the remnants of a shattered force to be pushed into a corner and left out of any meaningful equations.

This explains why neither the French nor the British had any assimilation programmes in place, and why they made no serious attempts to design any such programmes until they were forced to do so by political pressure, impending disaster or the threat of insurrection. To be sure, distrust played a part for military, political and even racist reasons; and sheer bloody-minded snobbery was not far beneath the surface either. In the final analysis, however, the Poles were unwelcome allies on *both* sides of the Channel, not because they were unfit for service or were of questionable commitment, but quite simply because they were in the way.

Confirmation that this was the dominant attitude can be found in the British and French treatment of another group of Slav exiles, the Czechoslovaks. Their experience was almost identical to that of the Poles; in fact, if anything, their position was worse. Many Czechoslovaks had been in France longer than the Poles because Hitler's *coup de grace* on the torso of Czechoslovakia had occurred in March 1939, and from that date a steady stream of men managed to escape the country by a variety of routes and offer their services wherever they would be wanted. Unlike the Poles, however, the occupation of Czechoslovakia had taken place without a fight, so the contingent had to rely entirely on promises of valour, rather than proof of it.

Most of the early escapees headed for Poland, but relations between Poland and Czechoslovakia were ice-cold after the Polish seizure of the Těšín territory at the time of the Munich vandalism. As a result, many men sought the embrace of Soviet Russia, only to be met with instant internment.[26] However, those who succeeded in crossing Poland's border discovered that the first obstacle to be overcome was their new national status. For Germany had not merely occupied the Czech lands of Bohemia and Moravia in March 1939, she had declared the territory to be a Protectorate of the Reich. This meant that all citizens of the two provinces – mainly Czechs – were henceforth citizens of the Third Reich, and Berlin was well within its rights under international law to demand the repatriation of all such persons who might arrive on foreign soil. Similarly, all Slovaks were under intense diplomatic pressure too. At the time of the occupation of the Czech lands, Slovakia had declared herself to be an independent state, but she automatically fell within the orbit of German influence. Political pressure from the new government in Bratislava might have forced neutral or threatened countries to repatriate all Slovaks too, therefore the target nations for the exiles – principally Poland,

Romania and Hungary – all had to take into account the political consequences if they aided Czech and Slovak escapees. To the credit of the Polish authorities, however, they rejected the option of sending the men back, but equally they had no intention of provoking Germany by openly integrating them into their forces. A few Czechoslovaks did see action with the Polish Air Force after the German invasion, but these were mainly men who had Polish connections and had chosen to stay behind after the bulk of the contingent left for France at the beginning of August 1939.

France was the natural destination for the Czechoslovak group because she was legally an ally by treaty. French desires to bolster her potential resistance to the Germans had led her during the interwar years to seek alliances in Eastern Europe, mainly with the small states created at the end of the First World War which were vulnerable to renewed German aggression. It seems to have escaped the wit of French diplomats that by following such a policy they were recreating the same pattern of allied encirclement which so haunted Germany before 1914. Nevertheless, French insecurity drove the policy forwards, so by 1921 she had signed an alliance with Poland, followed by the Treaty of Alliance and Friendship with Czechoslovakia in January 1924. This treaty had outlined the military dimensions only, and merely committed the powers to confer on matters of foreign policy. But after the Locarno Pact of 1925, when it became apparent that Germany's eastern borders were still negotiable, minds in Paris and Prague were suddenly concentrated on the awful prospect of a resurgent Germany, and hence the full alliance – the Treaty of Mutual Assistance – was signed in October 1925. France also strengthened her relations with Yugoslavia and Romania.

It has been argued in the past that British reluctance to commit herself to French security forced the latter to seek her protection elsewhere.[27] Equally, one could level the charge at France that by unilaterally developing her own security system, she was by implication demonstrating little faith in the capacity of the League of Nations to function as an arbiter of international disputes, and this was hardly encouraging behaviour from so prominent a member. Either way, the alliances were made, and in 1939 both the Poles and the Czechoslovaks threw themselves upon the welcome of their 'ally'.

The attitude of the French towards the Czechoslovaks was little different to the position they adopted towards the Poles. As the men arrived in France they were told quite bluntly that they would be temporarily enlisted in the Foreign Legion, and that this was not an option – refusal to comply would mean expulsion back to the occupied territory.[28] Some men were also told that they faced deportation to the Reich itself. Furthermore, as with the Poles, the French held the military capabilities of the Czechoslovaks in little regard. A series of derogatory articles had been published in the middle 1930s through the military journal *Bulletin des armées étrangères* until Gen Faucher, a high-placed sympathiser, had them stopped.[29] When the men arrived in the summer of 1939, a confidential report produced for the Czechoslovak Ministry of National Defence (MNO) suggested that the primary holding camp at Agde was little more than an internment area. Although they had enough food, they suffered from lack of accurate war information and the disdain of French officers to all things Czechoslovak.[30] Ignorance rather than blatant contempt may have been the cause here, however. The Alliance of 1924 had allowed for staff talks between the French and the Czechoslovaks, but there had been little consultation at a practical level. The French, it would seem, placed greater faith in Czechoslovakia's defensive capabilities than her offensive strength.[31]

By most accounts, Legion life was a grim experience. Units were sent to North Africa for training, much of it characteristically brutal, and some of it, perhaps by dint of malicious irony, under German NCOs.[32] After the fall of Poland, limited active service was offered to both army and air personnel, but as with the Poles, the air contingent was used sparingly, joining combat as part of French Air Force detachments rather than as independent units. One reason was that Czechoslovak airmen, having completed basic Legion training, were posted to French colonial bases well away from the forthcoming front line on the Continent.

It was not until the outbreak of war with Germany that France drew on this manpower, but by then it was far too late to successfully integrate air crews who had been lightly trained on outdated equipment.[33] Of approximately 1,000 airmen in France, one estimate places only eighty-five in combat roles, with the others 'kept well behind the lines'.[34] This conflicts with the official Czechoslovak tally of 123, but this figure also includes men who flew either individually or in small groups with French squadrons.[35] Whichever figure is correct, it is clear that action was seen by very few. In itself, this would have been a grave disappointment to the Czechoslovaks. In a report drafted early in 1940, optimism for a fully independent force with at least one fighter squadron and two bomber squadrons ran high. Prestige was a major motivating factor, for the Czechoslovaks felt able to compete with the best the French Air Force could muster, but they were not to have that chance. Although a Franco-Czechoslovak military agreement was signed in early May 1940, it was little more than window-dressing, and actual usage remained at the levels outlined above.

The undignified scramble which attended the defeat of France in June 1940 ultimately brought these men, and the remainder of the Polish group, to England. One might suppose, not unreasonably, that the British would have undergone a rapid change of tune towards both contingents now that their Continental ally was busily engaged in making a separate peace and an invasion of the British Isles seemed more than a distinct possibility, but it should come as no surprise to discover that very little changed at all. The sudden prospect of many thousands of Slavs fetching up on British shores greatly alarmed those men of influence who had pushed back the earlier commitments to the Poles, and they continued to resist even though there was, quite literally, nowhere else for them to go. Indeed, it is tempting to speculate what would have happened if the energies of one man had not been applied to a programme of assimilation. For it was Churchill who insisted that all of the displaced allies be made welcome – a brave policy for a man whose position as Prime Minister was by no means secure. Many of the people he pointedly directed to facilitate the evacuation and absorption of the allied groups had an intense distrust and dislike of their new 'allies', and it will be seen that resistance continued for some time.

The headlong retreat from the Continent after the fall of France was caught by a combined naval operation sometimes referred to as OPERATION AERIAL, though in practice this is an umbrella term for many small, independently arranged sailings ranging from Cherbourg in the north of France down to the Bay of Biscay. While neither as large nor as famous as the Dunkirk evacuations a month earlier, AERIAL rescued what remained of the British forces in France and the many tens of thousands of foreign personnel who, actively or otherwise, had been in the service of the French. The figures are impressive: a total of 163,225 men and women during mid-summer 1940, rescued by a flotilla of ships flying the whole range of allied flags, plus some Egyptian and Swedish vessels which were in French ports at the time.[36] In addition to the naval operations, the call went out to innumerable pilots and air crews to fly their machines – or any aircraft available – to Britain. Many of them made the crossing successfully, though there were reports of some French officials disabling planes or refusing to allow allied pilots access to them. The terms of the Armistice dictated by the Germans led to many such ugly scenes as former allies turned against one another, and men of all nationalities have recalled personal moments of anxiety as they desperately tried to get away, only to be hampered by over-zealous Frenchmen, glad that their war was finally over.

In Britain, the War Cabinet watched developments with increasing alarm. On 18 June, Eden drew to the attention of his colleagues that 12,000 Czechoslovak troops were in or near Marseilles, information supplied to him by the Czechoslovak National Committee in London. The following day, Sikorski told Churchill that many thousands of Polish personnel were also in dire need of assistance if they were to reach safety. Eden declared that he had spoken to the Admiralty on both counts, and embarkation plans now existed for Bordeaux and Marseilles. Even so, although he said that he was prepared 'to take off any Czechoslovak troops who wished to leave', he added that he 'would much prefer to embark Polish troops'. This indicates that rescue from French beaches was not entirely conducted under a blanket policy, and that if the situation became desperate, Polish forces would have been given preferential treatment. It has also been claimed that the British were going to give priority to Polish airmen.[37]

The most interesting part of Eden's speech is the comment about those Czechoslovak troops 'who wished to leave'. This begs the question, why should they not? In fact, a sizeable proportion did stay behind. Accurate figures for Czechoslovak casualties during the German offensive are difficult to establish due to the immense confusion, but one report estimated that the tally in May and June stood at 20 killed, of which 8 died in combat, the others having perished in flying accidents or from unknown causes, and a further 12 unaccounted for.[38] One writer has estimated that fully two-thirds of the Czechoslovak forces stayed in France after the Armistice, many of them choosing voluntary demobilisation, most of them other ranks.[39]

This estimate is firmed up by a Chiefs of Staff report which was submitted to the War Cabinet on 26 July, placing the number of Czechoslovak servicemen then in Britain at a little under 4,000.[40] Of these, the bulk were army personnel, but of the 1,000 airmen who had been encamped at Merignac, about three-quarters made their escape. Most of these men were officers or senior flying NCOs, a factor which was to plague the Czechoslovak Air Force throughout its time in Britain as it struggled endlessly against a shortage of ground crew. Furthermore, a good number of Poles chose not to leave France either. The Polish military had a total cohort of some 83,000 men in France at the time of the German attack. It has been calculated that over 27,000 reached England in the main wave; 16,000 were captured, and a further 54,000 remained in France, sought alternative escape routes through Spain, or were stranded in Switzerland with a French corps, this latter figure being placed at 11,000. This left 29,000 men still in France or trying to reach England, and by no means that amount reached Britain later in the summer.[41]

It can be seen from these data that a higher proportion of the Czechoslovak group remained in France, roughly 66 per cent. Even if we allow for *all* of the 29,000 Poles to have stayed behind, this only accounts for 35 per cent of the total. The issue is clouded further by contemporary figures, for the Chiefs of Staff report placed the number of Poles then in Britain at 14,000 (not 27,000) and the Swiss contingent at 25,000 (not 11,000). Curiously, these figures almost balance each other out, and it is unlikely that we shall ever know the true statistics. What we can be certain of, however, is that the signals received by the British regarding the Czechoslovak numbers were not encouraging. If two-thirds chose to stay and seek reasonable treatment at the hands of the occupying powers, what did this say about the commitment of the Czechoslovaks to continue the fight? This explains Eden's remark, and his thoughts may well have been informed by earlier prejudices.

For example, in late May 1940, the Czechoslovak Air Attaché in London wrote to the Air Ministry with a feasible scheme to utilise Czechoslovak bomber crews, at that moment entirely redundant in France even though the battle was in full flood. The Attaché, Lt Col Josef Kalla, argued quite strongly for the formation of at least one bomber unit on British soil which could then be sent on specialised missions to attack enemy locations in the Protectorate. Kalla insisted that the men could be hand-picked for their geographical knowledge, and in forwarding the proposal to Boyle on 28 May, Wg Cdr Porri agreed that it would be wrong to 'leave such potentially useful war personnel idle at this moment'.[42] Fleshing out the idea, he suggested that seventy or eighty pilots could be absorbed into long-distance squadrons as second pilots or observers, but the reply from Boyle was unequivocal:

> I very much doubt if this is worth pursuing. We don't know (1) if there are any pilots worthy of the name and if they are available; (2) their integrity (I am doubtful of many Czechs); (3) whether their terms of agreement with the French makes them available.[43]

Here again we see a senior British officer casting considerable doubt upon the efficiency and trustworthiness of men engaged in the common fight, with scarcely a shred of evidence upon which to base his judgement. Note also that he found it convenient to throw the responsibility back onto the French once more. Even so, he advised Porri to canvass Kalla on the availability of the men, and to explore the possibilities of incorporating those trained on fighters into home squadrons; and it is clear from later correspondence that he intended to pass the whole matter on to a higher power.

Boyle was clearly uneasy about dealing with the Poles and the Czechoslovaks, but Porri acted swiftly and interviewed Kalla, who assured him that the men were fully trained and experienced personnel with total commitment to the war effort. On 10 June Porri replied to Boyle and suggested that perhaps only thirty of the best pilots and an equivalent number of wireless operators and observers should be selected for service 'after their integrity has been certified by the Czech Legation.'[44] To support his case, he enlisted the help of the former British Air Attaché to Prague, Gp Capt Frank Beaumont. This officer drafted a truly glowing tribute to the legend of Czechoslovak gallantry, to their 'fibre, efficiency and indomitable spirit', but we cannot know if these sentiments had any effect on the opinions held at the Directorate of Intelligence because by this time the French surrender was imminent. A quick response from Boyle merely stated that the matter had been forwarded to Sholto Douglas for a policy decision; and a further note on 17 June effectively shelved the issue altogether, drawing attention to the impending collapse of French resistance and suggesting instead that thoughts should now turn to evacuating *all* the Czechoslovak personnel from French territory.

Clearly, the French defeat had saved some high-ranking members of the RAF from a potentially embarrassing decision, but events had overtaken them. Edvard Beneš had already written to the new Secretary of State for Air, Sir Archibald Sinclair, requesting help with the evacuations, adding that the first group of thirty pilots had landed at Hendon on the night of the 17th. So, whether the Air Ministry wanted the Czechoslovak pilots or not, they were already at the door.[45]

Nor were the Czechoslovaks the only contingent to be so coarsely assessed, for the Poles were also to suffer the lash of British xenophobia. Air Cdre Charles Medhurst became rather alarmed at the prospect of so many Poles arriving on British shores. Medhurst would soon be installed as the first director of a new Air Ministry department custom-built for dealing with the European air contingents, the Directorate of Allied Air Co-operation (DAAC). Early in 1941 this department was given a major overhaul and became the Directorate of Allied Air Co-operation and Foreign Liaison (DAFL), though by that time Medhurst had moved on to other duties. When it became clear at the end of June that very large numbers of Czechoslovak and Polish servicemen would shortly be arriving in the country – not by choice or invitation but by force of circumstances – the suspicious attitudes hardened. Medhurst, writing to Sholto Douglas on 3 July, warned that nearly 10,000 Polish airmen would soon be arriving, and forecast intense political pressure upon the RAF to form an independent Polish Air Force 'entirely under Polish control'. The Army, he said, had already agreed to a form of independence for the Polish land forces, so such pressure applied to the RAF would be hard to resist. He strongly advocated that the RAF must insist on any new units being incorporated into the home force and falling directly under British command. Neither did he express his opinion of the newcomers in ambivalent terms:

An additional reason for attempting to secure this principle is that the senior Polish Air Force officers, I have been reliably informed, are completely useless and are only out to line their pockets in filling cushy jobs.[46]

With views such as these, it is quite possible that he had been influenced by Landau's negative report in March – not that such opinions were by any means unusual in the Air Ministry, as we have seen. He went on to suggest that a definite number of Polish squadrons should be decided upon at that moment, thus limiting places and excluding 'the unskilled and inferior material' who might be re-trained for service with Army Air Co-operation Units or ferrying duties. He estimated that no more than 40 per cent of the influx would be 'really good material', and surplus stock should be handed over to the Polish Army for absorption. Although Medhurst's comments on the Czechoslovak contingent are not noted, it might reasonably be assumed that he held them in no higher regard.

On the same day that Medhurst was penning his vision of the future, Sholto Douglas received an assessment of the Czechoslovak air strength. In all, 327 flying personnel had arrived from France, of which approximately 50 per cent were officers. A further 177 ground crew had escaped, though their numbers would soon be swollen by another 300 mechanics believed to be in transit. This gave a rough officers-to-men ratio of one to five, and even the Czechoslovaks admitted that this was far too high for comfort. The reason for the imbalance was that the majority of the men

who escaped occupied Czechoslovakia were career fliers, and
these in the main tended to be officers or flying NCOs. When the
agreements with the French allowed for the reconstitution of the
Czechoslovak forces on French territory, Czechs and Slovaks who
had otherwise settled in France during the 1930s were mobilised.
Of these, Slovaks made up by far the greatest proportion of the
ground crew in France, and after the French defeat these were
the men who stayed behind together with their comrades in the
Czechoslovak Army, returning to their families after the Armistice.
It has been calculated that only about 14 per cent of the entire
Czechoslovak Air Force which fought from Britain during the
war were Slovaks, and the majority of these saw service with 311
(Bomber) Squadron, mainly as gunners, radio operators and
ground crew.[47] Therefore, although most of the original 'French'
contingent of 1,000 men chose evacuation, most were Czechs and
about 20 per cent were officers, and this gave rise to some serious
problems which will be examined in Chapter Three.

This flurry of correspondence on 3 July was due to a minor
conference taking place on the same day, the principal item on
the agenda being the absorption of the Czechoslovak airmen
into the RAF structure. Porri, Kalla, Gen Karel Janoušek and Lt
Col Alois Kubita all agreed that each man should, if possible, be
employed within ten days, if only to maintain what was described
as 'excellent morale'. It was also agreed that there existed
sufficient trained personnel to form one fighter squadron and
one light-bomber squadron immediately, but in the first instance
the whole cohort would be sent to a flying station, RAF Cosford,
for initial assessment. Frank Beaumont, presumably because of
his earlier enthusiasm for the Czechoslovaks, was nominated as
commanding officer. Four training aircraft would be supplied at
once and, in a revival of the earlier scheme, surplus fliers would
be transferred to an Operational Training Unit to be readied
for long-range bombing raids on enemy locations within the
Protectorate. Men still without work after these selections would
be trained for ferrying duties, and once fully operational the
new bomber unit would be sent to a south-eastern station for
raids against targets in France, preferably with its own fighter
support to minimise the language difficulties. This last point was
rejected by Sholto Douglas when the report reached him. Striking
out the proposal, he commented: 'We cannot have the Czechs
conducting separate little operations of their own.'[48]

A charitable interpretation of this remark might be that
Sholto Douglas preferred to hold the new units rigidly under
British command. Much more likely, however, is that it

represented the prevailing spirit of distrust, for on 5 July he implicitly confirmed Medhurst's anxieties concerning the new Polish influx. The latter's suggestion for a limited formation of units found expression in the decision of the DCAS to create two fighter and two bomber squadrons from the Polish group, though this would clearly leave a vast amount of men awaiting employment from a contingent of 10,000. Untrained or partly trained men should be kept within arm's reach for replacement purposes, though the emphasis fell upon maintaining the availability of skilled mechanics whose talents could be utilised inany squadron once they had become familiar with British machines. Medhurst's comments on the quality of the men were neither refuted norrebuked.[49]

Two Polish units were then in the process of formation: 300 Squadron, technically created on 1 July, and 301 Squadron, which existed on paper but would not be formally established until 26 July. Both units were to be equipped with Fairey Battle light-bombers, but neither could function without British personnel for maintenance and administrative purposes. The proposal was to follow Medhurst's idea of creating two new units from the 'French' contingent of Poles and simultaneously replace the British personnel in 300 and 301 Squadrons with Polish mechanics. This carried a disadvantage, in that two otherwise front-line units wouldbe lost while being made operationally fit, but with the two new squadrons at least all four Polish units would be in the same group. Proposing this scheme to Sholto Douglas, the Directorate of Organisation added a sarcastic quip: 'This would also satisfy Polish aspirations since it would go a little way towards their wish to have the squadrons grouped in what they are pleased to call "a unique command".'[50] To some extent this was an unfair comment, not least because those aspirations had been partially encouraged by the British themselves. The war had been scarcely three weeks' old when the Chief of the Air Staff, Sir Cyril Newall, had written to the Polish Military Mission, newly arrived in London, and expressed the earnest wish that he would soon 'see members of the Polish Air Force beside us in the Royal Air Force' – a phrase which deeply implied independent status and one which set a clear precedent from the viewpoint of the Poles.[51] He also added, 'Need I say that I shall count it as an honour to have them thus with us', and this must have rung hollow indeed with the Polish High Command after the squabbles over the transfer of men to Britain before the battle for France.

Much of the responsibility for assimilating the Poles and Czechoslovaks was now devolving upon Medhurst, yet he was still to be convinced that the RAF's new allies were worth having. His principal concern was 'the anxiety and trouble' it would cause station commanders who would have to administer the Slavs in the early days. It was deemed impossible to allocate dedicated stations at that point in time, so his remedy was to supply liaison officers, one to each unit, and four or five interpreters, if that many could be found. On 7 July, he called for a full list of personnel from both groups. Armed with this information, he said: 'we shall be able to pick out the best of the available material and grade the rest for future use if and when we want them.' On 16 July, he wrote to all the relevant departments within the Air Ministry and further expanded his fears:

> The political importance of preserving the *appearance* of a fully independent Polish Air Force will be strongly pressed [but it would be] detrimental to efficiency, and to national security, to permit Polish units to serve in the complex RAF organisation unless the RAF has full operational and disciplinary control . . . It is undesirable from every point of view to sacrifice operational efficiency to a point of prestige; the latter may be satisfied in many ways, the former must run no risk.[52]

Thus Medhurst set out his stall. He had been compelled by adverse military circumstances and political decisions made at the highest level to do something with the thousands of Slav exiles streaming in from the Continent, but he did so with great reluctance and considerable apprehension.

As we have seen, there were deep political reasons behind some of this negativity, and those which surrounded the Czechoslovaks are even more complex due to the Munich affair and its aftermath. We shall examine these points at a later stage, but we may close this section by demonstrating just how flexible Medhurst could be in his official dealings with the Poles. On the same day that he warned the Air Ministry of creeping Polish expansion, he wrote to the Polish Military and Air Attaché and assured him that 'we are, as you know, very eager to give all possible recognition to the Polish Air Force as having the status of an independent allied air force', and he offered to release from the RAFVR all the previously enlisted and commissioned personnel 'if the Polish Government feels it to be desirable', which it most certainly did.[53] And yet even here, despite the apparent hypocrisy of his position, he was offering something which had already been decided, for the Polish High Command under Gen Zajac had taken a firm stand against any further enlistment of men into the RAFVR, insisting that all future registration should be handled by the independent Polish forces, and that *all* personnel formerly shovelled into the RAFVR be released forthwith.

Two days later, on 18 July, Medhurst was still clinging to the view that this policy was fraught with peril, minuting all departments that by serving within the RAFVR all men would be subject to RAF procedures and not Polish Air Force law, but under an entirely separate Polish command all control would be lost. He reinforced his opinion by adding: 'The establishment of this precedent will undoubtedly cause trouble with the other foreign contingents, and possibly also the dominions.'[54] The only crumb of comfort was that the Poles had acceded to the British demand that the latter retain operational control.

A great deal, therefore, had occurred in thirty-eight days. The period began with some senior members of the Air Ministry holding a strong aversion to the creation of even a token Czechoslovak bomber squadron in Britain, and it ended with the establishment of 310 (Czechoslovak) Fighter Squadron at Duxford in Cambridgeshire on 10 July 1940. This was closely followed by the formation of 311 Bomber Squadron at Honington on 29 July, both units using the best-trained personnel from the Czechoslovak group which had arrived from France. Similarly, 'completely useless' Polish officers had, in the space of a week, been placed in positions of responsibility with dual command over hastily selected personnel. From the comments and decisions examined in this section, it is clear that there had been no sea-change of opinion within the Air Ministry during this time; and, bluntly put, the Royal Air Force had been presented with reinforcements that it did not want and did not trust. No one in July 1940 had any clear idea of what was to be done with these men, and the criticisms did not stop there, as we shall see.

THE SECOND PHASE: AUGUST 1940 TO DECEMBER 1943

Whatever negative feelings Medhurst, Boyle, Sholto Douglas and the others may have harboured towards the Polish Air Force in the desperate summer of 1940 were substantially mollified by events come the winter. All of the Polish crews proved themselves worthy of allied status ten times over during the Battle of Britain, and though little criticisms remained – such as their tendency to monopolise the radios during combat flying – by 1941 all of the serious doubts had been swept away. Indeed, even in the summer, attitudes had been changing noticeably. At first Medhurst had insisted that the 'French' and 'British' Poles were not to be mixed in squadrons if at all possible, mainly to protect the latter from defeatist influences, but Gp Capt Leslie Hollinghurst, the Deputy Director of Organisation, recorded that: 'as a result of closer acquaintance with the "new" Poles, they [Air Intelligence] have decided that they are not such bad fellows after all and have withdrawn their objection'.[55] This view was reinforced during the autumn of 1940 when most of the senior RAF commanders and politicians from both countries conducted high-profile visits to the Polish stations, presenting medals, giving speeches, and generally talking up a relationship which was settling into a satisfactory condition.

Although the alliance was stabilising in military terms, the Poles still had two political issues which were not fully resolved from their point of view. The first was British assistance in establishing recruitment schemes abroad so that their very healthy core stock of air personnel would not be diminished by combat losses and unavoidable demobilisation due to age or disability. The second was the perpetual quest for independent status. The question of recruitment will be dealt with in Chapter Three, primarily because the Polish experience was broadly in line with that of the Czechoslovaks in that both groups suffered when they tried to export their enthusiasm to a largely disinterested North America. But, disappointing though these efforts ultimately were, the all-important need for prestige drove both of them into head-on confrontations with the British over the question of independence. It was a battle which the Poles eventually won, and one which the Czechs lost with great indignity.

Even by late 1940, the British were still reluctant to discontinue the practice of duplicating middle- and high-ranking posts within all the allied air forces (a not unreasonable decision considering the language difficulties and lack of a thorough knowledge of RAF practice on behalf of the allies), but this did not slow the political momentum behind Polish desires to achieve fully independent status. Success in this quest would be measured in various ways: (1) an agreement between the two nations that would formally enshrine the bilateral aspects of the alliance; (2) the creation of a separate Polish Air Force Inspectorate that would have full powers in the field of promotion, selection, training and administration; (3) equal, or at least substantial, representation at strategic level. This last point should not be confused with the creation of an independent stratum of command regarding missions and routine flying, for the Poles, as junior allies, were always prepared to follow the British lead when it came to active operations. Rather, as with their earlier requests for a seat on the Supreme War Council, the Poles felt entitled to a say in what course the war took, especially regarding operations or plans which affected the home territory. It was to be an unfulfilled objective, partly for political reasons on behalf of the British, many of which surfaced in the last years of the conflict, and partly because with the entry of the USA into the war after Pearl Harbor, that power automatically put many of the lesser groups into the shade, assuming an ever-greater dominance in strategic affairs which even Churchill had difficulty in resisting at times.

In 1940, however, no such obstacles existed, and it fell to the Polish High Command and political representatives to make the best possible case for the creation of independent armed forces. Indeed, *all* of the European allied powers felt entitled to independence in one form or another, and more often than not the air contingents were the focal point of their efforts. For its part, the War Office had no great objections to forming Army units which reflected the national character of each ally, but we should bear in mind that in 1940 there was no land war and it was relatively easy to create free-standing organisations which could, if need be, be smoothly integrated with the home Army. That was not the case in the air. Given the crises of that summer, and the obvious implications that air power would henceforth be a major strategic tool, the RAF felt wholly justified in its insistence that it retained as much control as possible over the allied groups. Equally, each allied government felt to a greater or lesser degree that the air units stood as elite representatives of their own national freedom and their determination to resist the invader, therefore the potential for conflict was vast.

As we have seen, the agreement to split the Polish air personnel between Britain and France was a separate issue dealt with in October 1939. However, the Polish terms of service were another matter, and the British side-stepped any unnecessary complications by simply rewording the Anglo-Polish naval agreement which legally formalised the collaboration at sea. This was not enough for the Poles, for in essence it meant that they were seen and described as an associated power simply assisting the British government with its war against Germany, when what they wanted, quite reasonably, was a level of international standing much higher than that. Even before the attack on France, Sikorski had been campaigning for greater recognition for the Polish presence to be embodied in the military agreements. He tried first with Chamberlain – meeting with little success – and then Churchill, who demonstrated that although the spirit was willing, the influence was weak. As far as Sikorski was concerned, Polish sovereignty rested largely upon the process of officer promotion and selection – a power which the British intended to reserve for themselves. As things stood in May 1940, the RAF had first and last say over who would receive commissions in the Polish section of the RAFVR – something which Sikorski strongly rejected. The British argument rested upon the constitutional point that only the King, 'as advised by the Air Council, can promote officers belonging to that force'. Furious with this ill-judged and almost feudal declaration, Sikorski complained directly to Churchill, who put pressure on the Foreign Office to intervene. Within days the Air Ministry had relented, but not entirely, for the subsequent re-draft of the agreement merely permitted promotion to be considered by a joint board of Polish and British representatives, with the Poles having the final approval.[56]

The air war over Britain that summer slightly delayed the negotiations leading towards the finished document, but by August all the outstanding issues had been resolved, or at least were in a state of compromise. The Poles had initially pushed for Polish military law to be applied in all cases, but this was refused by the Air Ministry with the not unsound argument that it would be unworkable where both nationalities were serving in the same squadron or on the same station. The compromise here was to insist that RAF law would apply at all times when a Polish individual was serving with the RAF in any capacity, and although in theory he would be subject to Polish military law, when the terms of Polish military law and Royal Air Force law differed, the latter would prevail. Furthermore, all disciplinary courts would consist of an equal number of British and Polish officers as judges, but with a British officer serving as president of the court and holding the casting vote. On the question of promotion, it was decided that all recommendations were to be generated by unit commanders then forwarded to the Polish High Command by the RAF for the former's approval, but only if the RAF agreed with the recommendation in the first place. As a nod to Polish sovereignty, however, all men were permitted to take an oath of allegiance to the Polish Republic, and the agreement provided for the creation of an independent Polish Inspectorate theoretically responsible for all matters relating to the force, though in practice it represented the interface between the two air ministries, the primary channel of communication through which the RAF could monitor the condition of the Polish Air Force and, perhaps more importantly, the means by which the RAF could make its wishes known. But the Poles, and to some extent the British too, had taken for granted the creation of a formal Inspectorate as early as March 1940. In any case, it served both parties to have such a body in place: from the Polish side, it enabled them to monitor and maintain the development of the air force in exile, and from the British viewpoint, it relieved them of the burdensome task of day-to-day administration, allowing them to concentrate on the major issues of policy and deployment.

The first incumbent was Gen W.J. Kalkus, the existing head of the Inspectorate since September 1939, but when the transfers to Eastchurch were well under way, Polish requests to have him sent to Britain were at first rebuffed. The Directorate of Organisation was clearly displeased with the prospect of a senior commander viewing the shambles at Eastchurch, minuting Porri in March 1940, '[His visit] would not serve any useful purpose because any shortcomings that he might discover would certainly be well known to us' – the implication being that the RAF could not stand before him covered in shame when as far as they were concerned they were only doing what was expected of them.

The attitudes changed when Davidson, the station commander at Eastchurch, supported the proposal and enlisted the help of the British Attaché in Paris. The latter described Kalkus as a man 'with very pleasant manners', the only serious drawback being that he spoke no English or French. Davidson concurred with this view, though he warned that the proposed Inspectorate might prove to be larger than imagined because the Poles had a few surplus officers which they wished to employ. However, the argument was clinched when the attaché added: 'I should say that he is not a very strong man, and this impression is borne out by his nickname among his own people which is "the sheep in lion's clothing".'

This was more than enough to sway even the devout sceptics like Boyle who minuted all departments that Kalkus was clearly the man for the job, and that the creation of an Inspectorate within the RAFVR would 'enhance the levels of control' over the units in Britain. At a meeting in May, it was decided that Kalkus would be given the immediate rank of Air Commodore and have a staff of twelve, though there was still some foot-dragging over the powers he would be endowed with, and whether this would lead to a form of *de facto* independence by the back door. Davidson argued that the Inspectorate must be formed with all possible speed because the workload placed upon him was at times intolerable, and that the senior Polish officer, Capt Stachon, was forced to refer to his superiors in Paris before even the smallest decision could be taken. Then, in late May, AVM Paul Maltby, the AOC No. 24 (Training) Group, which shouldered most of the responsibility for the training programme at Eastchurch, wrote directly to the Air Council and complained about the expectations placed upon Davidson at Eastchurch:

> [He] is becoming far too involved with all matters concerning the various Polish contingents in this country, no matter where they are stationed [and] he is being consulted not only by various branches of the Air Ministry and the Polish authorities, but even by politicians. I submit that it is quite beyond his capacity to command his station . . . if he is expected to act as an advisor on widespread policy matters at the same time.'

He closed by urging the creation of 'some central authority' at once, and henceforth all doubts were cast aside and Kalkus was formally installed at the beginning of June. If anything, this little episode demonstrates yet again that the British were totally unprepared for dealing with the Poles in any capacity, but also that any proposals for improving the situation had first to run the gauntlet of suspicion that by passing greater autonomy to the Polish High Command, the British would lose more of what little control they had to begin with.[57]

The first Anglo-Polish Military Agreement was signed on 5 August 1940, with appropriate appendices covering the respective air, sea and land forces. Apart from defining the powers of the Polish Inspectorate, it also officially removed the entire contingent from the RAFVR and placed them under their own national banner. It went some way towards fulfilling Polish aspirations, but it had one crucial omission: it did not include any promise by the British to restore the territory of Poland once victory had been assured – something which did not pass unnoticed by the Poles. The preamble only committed the two governments 'to prosecute the war to a successful conclusion', a vague and slippery objective which meant that the British could avoid indelicate matters of territory and frontiers at the war's end.

Furthermore, the Poles were not the only group whose postwar ambitions were kept at a distance by the British: the Czechoslovaks too were to discover that their new friends were inclined to shuffle and mumble when the question of 'afterwards' was raised, and it was even more galling to both these nations when the agreements with the other allied countries of Western Europe proudly proclaimed restoration and deliverance. This is one reason why the British preferred all of the national agreements to be kept secret between the contracting parties, and why they were never elevated to state treaties, for this would have meant parliamentary ratification, and therefore publicity. In short, although the various allied military agreements were, in the main, little more than carbon copies of each other, the essential differences lay in the amount of power each group had over its own forces, and what policies the British government intended to follow once the war had been won. Nevertheless, and perhaps wisely, the Poles did not seek further conflict over this matter, for had they done so they would have faced a wall of opposition from the Foreign Office and the Cabinet. But in 1940, looking around at the grim state of the war, this was a minor point of contention compared to the very real business of getting on with the fighting.

In the years that followed, the Polish Air Force superbly demonstrated that getting on with the fighting was something it could do without prompting from the French, the British, or anyone else. By mid-1941, most of the doubts and suspicions of darker days had been dispelled by the sheer tenacity and determination of these men in exile, to the point where the RAF started to throw open hitherto shuttered doors to selected members of the Polish High Command. This still did not extend to what might be termed 'secret information' or strategic briefings, but when Sikorski requested that certain of his officers might serve for a time in Command or Group Headquarters so they might learn more about the central organisation of the RAF, both the DAFL and Portal (then the CAS) signalled their wholehearted concurrence. Polish officers were gradually seconded to British squadrons, and like senior officers in other allied forces, eventually placed in command of some of them.

The social dimension was also a positive one for the Poles. Zamoyski spends considerable time describing how attractive the Poles were to British women in the first half of the war, and there can be little doubt that the Polish airman or officer was very much an exotic creature until the arrival of the Americans in large numbers. But what he lacked in spending power, the Pole amply made up for in charm, 'traditional' values and sheer symbolism, for he represented merely by his existence in British uniform all that was mythically wonderful about Britain's crusade against tyranny. The Czechoslovaks also enjoyed this backwash of sympathy, though perhaps their social acceptance was promoted by a pinch of guilt over the Munich affair. Men from both groups made friends easily in Britain; several hundred married British women. For a while, too, the Pole was a social accessory in the upper reaches of the British class system. The huge amount of radio and newspaper publicity generated by their successes in the air made a token Polish officer *de rigueur* at any cocktail party worth the name, and although things were to turn very sour indeed for the Poles by the war's end, the eighteen months between the Battle of Britain and Pearl Harbor proved to be a happy hunting season for all the Slavs.

If the medals, the public acclaim and the sexual conquests were indicative of the bright side of the Polish exile, there were darker aspects which exercised the diplomatic skills of the politicians. The application of Polish military discipline raised some eyebrows in the service departments and Whitehall, for although the British were the final arbiters in matters of gross infringement, minor issues were dealt with at a local level and occasionally drew unfavourable comments regarding harsh treatment meted out to men who had for whatever reason managed to transgress the Polish codes of honour and service.

Part of the cause was the defeat of Poland itself, which led to an urgent need to rebuild and restore national pride through the service arms in exile. This led some Polish officers to interpret indolence, dissent or simply fatigue as evidence of cowardice or disloyalty, and there were examples of men being humiliated or punished for offences which would have attracted lesser reprimands in the British forces. The Air Ministry decided that this was a hangover from the pre-war days, declaring some of the older Polish officers to be 'too rigid and inflexible in outlook'. In the early part of the war, the RAF applied pressure to the Polish High Command to transfer or reassign officers whose very presence gave rise to disciplinary problems in Polish squadrons, and they also adduced this conflict between ideals and codes of practice to explain much of the tension which had plagued the exiles in the Eastchurch era. Even as late as Christmas 1940, the British were still having difficulties integrating RAF officers into some Polish squadrons within the system of dual command, and it was not until the summer of 1941 that most of the problems had been resolved. By that time, the RAF had successfully collaborated with the Polish High Command to reduce or remove the small cohort of career officers whose enthusiasm for order had threatened the stability of some Polish squadrons.[58]

A case can be made for the Polish attitude, however. Having twice been on the losing side in a vicious war, the like of which had never been seen before, it is perhaps easy to understand why any behaviour which appeared to be defeatist or contrary to the cause should be swiftly and sometimes severely suppressed. Morale was a tender plant indeed in 1940, and the hideous reports of what was happening at home did nothing to raise it. As we shall see in Chapter Three, the Czechoslovaks also fell foul of the British in matters of discipline, but then it is true of all the exiled nations that they each had more at stake and more to prove, and they therefore had more to lose if they should falter again.

It is difficult to make a case for that other Polish vice, anti-Semitism. This was a Foreign Office issue, and reports of incidences of anti-Semitic behaviour within the Polish forces are evenly spread throughout the war years. We saw in Chapter One how the issue was first aired in the House of Commons during the debate on the Allied Forces Bill in 1940, but it is important that Polish anti-Semitism should not be overblown; rather, it is better to conceive of it as something which was consistently present throughout the Polish forces but rarely manifested itself in serious form. We should also be aware that anti-Semitism was present to a greater or lesser degree in every European nation. What made the difference as far as the Poles were concerned was that they had made no secret of it in the interwar years, that it was a faint but visible part of their public presence in Britain during the time in exile, and that in itself represented a facet of Nazism which everyone was aware of and which stood, albeit marginally, as an evil against which Britain was supposedly fighting. Even as late as 1944, the Foreign Office was still receiving letters of complaint concerning anti-Semitism in the Polish Air Force, and although this was a matter which the Air Ministry liked to brush aside – perhaps because it posed no serious threat to efficiency or discipline – the diplomats were still saddled with the problem at the war's end. Indeed, there was a lengthy parliamentary debate on the subject in April 1944, leading again to the issuing of orders from the Polish High Command forbidding maltreatment of Jews. Eventually, this proved to be a trait which ultimately sullied the Polish experience in exile, and it contributed to the public backlash against them in 1945.[59]

THE THIRD PHASE: JANUARY 1944 TO OCTOBER 1946

The Polish air crews were unique among the European allies in exile because they alone were denied a triumphant return home at the end of the war. After nearly six years of bitter and intense fighting, their reward was to fall into the political abyss created by the sudden upsurge in tension between East and West, and as the major powers positioned themselves ready for a new confrontation, so the Poles were swept along virtually powerless to direct events.

They themselves were aware of what was happening – or likely to happen – as the war in Europe ended. A Polish forces magazine, *Robotnik*, published several letters from men who complained of anti-repatriation propaganda being spread by some officers. These scare tactics, generally consisting of blood-curdling warnings of deportation or internment by the communists, were interpreted by the Foreign Office as useful indications of the growing political divisions within the Polish forces, attitudes which had been slowly developing since January 1944, when in a meeting of the Post-War Reconstruction Committee, at which a Polish representative was present, it became apparent that Poland would inevitably be occupied by Soviet forces after the defeat of Germany. 'This had, not unnaturally, created a considerable commotion in Polish circles,' ran a Foreign Office minute. 'We had better deal with this dangerous rumour immediately. Our explanation would be that the Moscow Conference had a document before them – not subsequently agreed to – concerning the general administration of the liberated territories.'[60]

The conference to which this rather unsettled note referred was the meeting of foreign ministers in the Soviet capital between 18 October and 30 October 1943. Their brief was to set the agenda for the first meeting of Churchill, Roosevelt and Stalin in Tehran at the end of November, and again the Polish government-in-exile tried in vain to have a voice. Polish–Soviet relations at this time were sour indeed. Stalin had used Polish outrage at the discovery of the massacre at Katyn to break off all diplomatic relations with the London group in April 1943, and by the end of that year the arrival of the Red Army in Polish territory was imminent. The Poles attempted to persuade Churchill to take up their case with Stalin, but the former was outflanked and isolated at Tehran by the other two leaders, and the latter had nothing to lose by ignoring the desires of the Polish government in London. In the event, the Tehran Conference decided that Poland would be shifted westwards on the map, with Stalin gaining enormous territories in the east, and the Poles being compensated by German land in the west. At Tehran, the carve-up of Poland had begun in earnest; in fact, the eventual dismemberment of all of Eastern Europe was set in motion there. When the news reached

London, the Polish government redoubled its efforts to have the Western allies stand firm, but it was always going to be a fruitless exercise. The overwhelming need to have Stalin continue the war in the east and not make a separate peace with Hitler was enough incentive for Britain and America to petition him with little more than vague hopes for a sunny Polish future; anything concrete would have been waved aside. Furthermore, Churchill's scheme for a second front rooted in a Balkan invasion was also scuppered at Tehran. Such an expedition might have brought some relief to Poland, or at least the troops of Western allies on her soil, but it was never to be. On the night of 3 January 1944, Russian troops crossed the Polish frontier, and there they were to remain for a long time.

Rumours of the talks in Moscow and Tehran gradually filtered down to the Polish forces in exile, and the *de facto* occupation of Poland by the Red Army made the rumours metamorphose into grim expectancy. However, this did not lead – as one might have expected – to a sudden downturn in morale. On the contrary, the commitment to the defeat of Germany and an honourable peace remained as high as ever in the Polish forces. But, like the Czechoslovaks, the pervasive effect of the Soviet advance made itself felt in political terms. The Polish government's efforts to play down the dark reality of events at home by continually pointing to the fact that nothing had been firmly settled and that a satisfactory deal with Stalin was still possible led men to believe that victory might still mean freedom. That attitude was not to last long, however, because the true horror for the Polish people erupted on 1 August with the Warsaw uprising. Throughout the two months of struggle, the powerlessness of the Western allies to be of any assistance was forlornly monitored by the Polish forces in Britain and Europe, and although it is doubtful that the West could have provided any substantial military aid, Stalin's refusal to allow Western planes to use Soviet airfields for supply drops merely confirmed in the minds of many thousands of Poles that they had been sold out in the West, leaving their beleaguered homeland to be inexorably drawn into the Soviet orbit.

The Warsaw uprising and its subsequent failure dealt a shattering blow to Polish morale. Worse still, other exiles alongside whom they had fought for five years were gleefully anticipating their own return home. August 1944 had seen Gen de Gaulle, dodging Vichy snipers, marching in triumph through Paris; the battle for Belgium, though still with all too much life left in it, was going to be won sooner or later; and also in August, the Free Dutch Army's Princess Irene Brigade began the liberation of the Netherlands, and it was only the allied failure at Arnhem which greatly stifled the process. Nevertheless, the war was clearly being won; Germans were on the run all over Europe, and yet, as one Polish pilot said: 'As we sat around the radio, we died a little during each of those 63 days of the rising.'[61] The slaughter and hideous reprisals meted out by the Germans left Warsaw as little more than an open wound, and it was all the more unbearable with so much joy all around.

It was this pain and uncertainty about what the future held which triggered the factious elements within the Polish forces. As the last full year of the war came to a close, the Chiefs of Staff report for the final quarter of 1944 merely recorded the continuation of 'restlessness' in the Polish Air Force, but added: 'It has not weakened either spirit or discipline in the squadrons.' This was true enough, but there were deeper elements at work in the minds of men who had given so much for what appeared to be so little. For it seemed to many that the cause had been lost, and that their allies had given their consent to Poland being swallowed by a hostile power. Then the final blow to Polish hearts was cruelly delivered – not by Britain, America or even Stalin – but by those very ordinary people who had once been their unreserved champions: the British public.

It was a combination of two factors, tenuously connected by the same theme: communism. As the war neared its end, and the workload fell away from the millions under arms throughout Europe, a morbid apathy descended on many Poles. The prospect of going home to what was almost certainly going to be life under a regime hardly distinguishable from the one they had fought so hard against led many men to drop their guard. Many turned to drink in an attempt to assuage the sadness which victory had brought them. Also, communist ideas were now at large in Britain in the form of pamphlets, meetings and public debates on how far the British people should move to the Left if a better world was going to emerge from the years of suffering. In short, Stalin was no longer seen as the monster he had been painted as during the interwar years, and much of the responsibility for this new political openness must lie with the British government, for it had designed and conducted the marvellous propaganda campaign in the summer of 1941 to transform Stalin's image abroad. Communist and socialist ideas had become, if not fashionable, then at least acceptable in Britain by the end of the war, and this would reach its zenith when Attlee's Labour Party defeated Churchill in the election of 1945.

The Poles were to reap a bitter harvest from this shift in British attitudes. The press turned against them, holding them responsible for the continuing tension in the east; graffiti appeared, taunting them with the old anti-Semitism and their pre-war sympathies with the Right; and complaints from the public and its representatives flooded the authorities. A clipping from a local paper in Peebles, Scotland, carried various complaints from town councillors who resented the continuing presence of the Poles in Scotland: 'They have overstayed their welcome,' claimed a spokesman, 'and it is high time they were sent back to their own country.' Individuals also made their views unequivocally known. Kathleen Chapman from Sheffield wrote:

> It is time they were back in Poland, great lusty fellows simply idleing [*sic*] about, with nothing to do but frat[ernise] with our girls while Poland needs them *now*. They are all without exception anti-Russian and have no good word for our own fine brave allies.

And a Mr A. Aspinall penned the following from his home in Harrow, Middlesex:

> As a ratepayer, I should be much obliged if you would inform me why a large Polish Army (RAF) is kept standing in England? It is well known that, in the districts where Polish forces are stationed, a great deal of immorality takes place and, more particularly, to the ruin of British girls. In writing this letter I am expressing the views of very, very many British people whose families are being pestered by the Poles. How much longer is this pest to continue?[62]

There is much to mock here from a safe distance of over fifty years, and much to deride as British xenophobia of the worst kind. One wonders also if Kathleen Chapman, when speaking of 'our own fine brave allies', would have had second thoughts had she known of the excesses of which the Red Army was capable. The Poles certainly did. Then again, maybe Kathleen Chapman did too, and didn't care.

It was crystal clear to the British government that something would have to be done, but to begin with it was at a complete loss for answers. The two service groups from the east, the Czechoslovaks and the Poles, were faced with a serious problem of which each had been aware for some time: the occupation of the home territory at the war's end by Soviet forces. Yet this was the only mutual element, for the Czechs had a slight advantage in that their troops from Britain had accompanied Patton's Third

Army into Czechoslovakia when it was partially liberated from the north-west. Patton, however, had been forbidden to go further, with the result that Soviet troops had downed tools in the majority of Czechoslovak territory. Even so, the Czechoslovak government-in-exile under Edvard Beneš had gained a small but significant military foothold when it tried to re-establish its position. But the Polish forces of the west could only watch as Soviet troops swept across their home territory with considerable assistance from the Polish Army of the east.

As Jozef Garlinski has shown, the Polish units formed by the communists were always in a much better position in terms of manpower than their countrymen in the west, benefiting from conscriptive powers and the steady flow of recruits from the Polish Home Army, most of whom were compelled to join the ranks under direct threat of deportation into the depths of Russia.[63] Much of the home territory was thus controlled by a mixture of Polish and Russian forces, making Stalin's ambition of absorbing Poland into his empire all the easier since he faced virtually no resistance. From London, the view was bleak indeed. Everything hinged entirely on Stalin's undertaking, made at Yalta in February 1945, that he would permit free Polish elections. In the mean time, a Council of National Unity would be established, consisting of representatives of all parties, followed by a Polish Provisional Government of National Unity as soon as negotiations had been completed. That was all Churchill could wring from Stalin at Yalta, and everybody knew that the arrangement could only be to the benefit of one party. Since there was no other option on the table, though, the Polish forces in the west could only sit and wait upon events.

The Polish forces knew all about the decisions taken at Yalta, and that Stalin had insisted upon the eastern Polish territories as war booty for himself. This had the most impact upon the men of the Polish Second Corps, then in Italy, a great many of whom were natives of those lands. Morale slumped disastrously, and their ebullient commander Gen Wladyslaw Anders threatened to pull them out of the fight until he was persuaded otherwise by the British and the Americans. Nevertheless, in this one action he made a name for himself as a potential threat to stability – something which none of the major Western powers needed at such a sensitive time. A wave of communist arrests of prominent Polish political leaders in March also confirmed in the hearts and minds of tens of thousands of exiles that any return home would at best be a deliverance into the hands of the man who had colluded with Hitler in the destruction of their country six years earlier. It was a ghastly prospect, and nothing short of a major diplomatic crisis for the British.

In July 1945, the Air Ministry signalled all commands that the deteriorating situation in Poland might cause difficulties within the units awaiting repatriation. Black propaganda circulated at all levels, and the bitter political in-fighting between pro-communist elements and those who wished to continue the fight against the Russians threatened a possible collapse of discipline. 'Any violent dissent or victimisation must be dealt with,' ran the Air Ministry's order, adding: 'You are authorised to take any steps you consider necessary.'[64] With over 112,000 men in the Polish Second Corps alone, and a further 14,000 in the Polish Air Force, the British realised that a complete breakdown could lead to a disaster of considerable magnitude. Two days later, the Chiefs of Staff Committee met to discuss the position of the Polish forces in exile. Churchill had given them the lead by suggesting that a policy of segregation might be implemented. By forcibly separating those who wished to return and those who did not, Churchill hoped to smother the powderkeg before it really ignited, though he accepted with resignation that the whole issue rested on three points: (1) the wishes of the new Polish government in regard to the Polish forces abroad; (2) the readiness of those forces to obey the Polish government; (3) the British government's intentions towards those who did not obey.

The Polish Provisional Government of National Unity had been formally created in Moscow on 21 June 1945, with seventeen communists providing the government, and only four of the London group symbolising the unity. Stalin had won total victory in Poland, and those members of the Resistance or the Home Army whom he had not imprisoned in Moscow were utterly isolated and in fear for their liberty. The Western allies could do nothing but protest. Red Army control of the eastern regions was complete; and besides, neither the British nor American public would have tolerated a renewal of the war against the Soviet Union. The last-gasp effort by free Poles to eject the communists came through the final manifesto issued by the Council of National Unity even as the government created in Moscow was preparing for business. Its *Testament of Fighting Poland* was a hybrid of a bill of rights and a demand for self-determination. Its publication was unanimously approved, and at that point the last vestige of democratic Poland voted itself into oblivion. Five days later, the Americans and the British formally recognised the communist-dominated government in Warsaw and withdrew their wartime recognition of the London government-in-exile.

Thus, by the first week of July 1945, the Poland for which nearly a quarter of a million men had fought had ceased to exist as a free state. A few were prepared to chance their luck and go home; others actually welcomed the change, believing the old regime to have been corrupt, militaristic, and considerably worse than the one which had replaced it. But the vast majority were dejected and confused. When the Chiefs of Staff met in July 1945, they learned that the remnants of the London government intended to hand over all their property in Britain to the British, declaring themselves to be the only true government with popular support. Churchill argued that if this were permitted to happen, 'total breakdown of discipline might occur'. Furthermore, he reminded the service departments that Britain had footed the bill for the Polish war effort, to the tune of £5 million per year for civil costs, and a thumping £20 million per year for the military. Of this total, approximately half had been acknowledged by the Polish government in London as being a genuine debt for later repayment, the rest being written off under the Mutual Aid scheme. It was anyone's guess whether the new government in Warsaw would honour this debt. Added to this was the burden of feeding, clothing and housing the armed forces and approximately 50,000 refugees and dependants, and it was Churchill's view that the only option was to open negotiations with Warsaw about repatriation and keep a tally of the expenses ready for presentation when the right moment came.[65]

The Foreign Office was also deeply involved with this new dilemma. Sir Alexander Cadogan wrote to the CIGS, Alan Brooke, and warned him that 'this Polish question is full of dynamite', and although he felt that a sizeable number of men would eventually return if the propaganda was sound enough, 'out of our obligations of honour' they could not force the Poles to go back against their wishes. As far as the Air Ministry was concerned, a secret ballot of Polish Air Force personnel might reveal a substantial number of volunteers for repatriation, and they added that no serious impairment to RAF operational efficiency would follow if the Polish Air Force fragmented.[66] By the end of the month, the Foreign Office had issued a formal note to the Polish government outlining British policy. His Majesty's Government would: 'ensure so far as possible that these officers and men should have proper opportunity of making an unbiased and unhurried decision, with a full understanding of the facts, free from fear or compulsion . . . [and] none should be compelled to go [back] against their will'.[67]

The British requested the views of the Polish government regarding this policy, but again this brief quotation serves to underline the newness of the situation with which the West was faced, and the stark lack of understanding on behalf of the British of the nature and strategy of the new regime in Warsaw. For the Polish government had no intention whatsoever of forcing the men to return; it suited them admirably to have such huge numbers of restless troops dependent on their ideological opponents in the West. Besides, the return of more than 200,000 men who had been contaminated by capitalism would have been immensely destabilising. The 'facts' would never be presented to the exiles, but they were to have plenty of time for their 'unhurried' decisions.

On 1 August, the Polish government responded with a proclamation that equal rights would be extended to all Polish service personnel abroad who wished to return to their homes. Not good enough, said the Foreign Office. Large numbers of the Home Army which had survived the uprising of 1944 were now held in Soviet internment camps, and the British government wanted an absolute guarantee that freedom, not imprisonment, would greet the exiles if they went back. Meanwhile, the pressures on the British were mounting. The complaining letters from the public had start to flow in greater numbers, pro- and anti-communist propaganda was circulating freely within the Polish forces, and the service departments were warning the politicians of dire consequences if the situation was not resolved soon. In late August, the Air Ministry told the Foreign Office that it had initiated a freeze within the Polish Air Force, halting promotions, recruitment and non-essential training. The levels of guard capacity at Polish air stations had also been drastically reduced and the side-arms decommissioned.

Essentially, the Western allies were powerless in this whole tragedy, and the communists knew it. The Warsaw government issued a further statement which promised a safe return to all Polish forces in the west only if they travelled in their existing military units. Again, this was rejected by the British and the Americans. It was believed by both that the communists were fully aware of the political divisions which were widespread throughout the Polish forces; a unit-level repatriation would almost certainly provoke the consenting and dissenting elements within each group to turn upon each other. The British suggested a piecemeal return based on a slow demobilisation; the Americans argued for the return of the entire force *en masse.* Both proposals were rejected by Warsaw as impractical. By September 1945, therefore, the stalemate was complete.[68]

The communists continued to play their games. The British representative in Warsaw, Victor Cavendish-Bentinck, summarised his reading of the situation in a long memorandum to the Foreign Office in early September. He had spoken with Wladyslaw Gomulka, the Polish deputy premier, who would later be imprisoned by his own creed for advocating an independent path to socialism. Gomulka claimed that he wanted to repatriate only those men who would support the new order, but he would be happy enough to see the return of complete military units whatever their political composition might be. Cavendish-Bentinck thought this to be a lie. Gomulka had informed him that a military mission to London would soon be proposed, and all problems would be resolved through that, but the Foreign Office was promptly warned that such a mission would almost certainly exacerbate the tense situation in Britain and would lead to the break-up of the Polish forces. Such an event would play directly into the communists' hands, for in all probability most Polish officers would urge their men to resist. This could lead to a complete loss of control, and any action they might take would be portrayed as 'Fascist repression'. Cavendish-Bentinck closed by urging London to do everything in its power to get the Polish forces to return as complete units, whether they liked it or not, because failure to do something could lead to a civil war on foreign soil.[69]

A day later, he wrote again. This time, he urged what was tantamount to the forcible repatriation of all the Polish forces in the west, preferably as complete units after segregating the 'irreconcilables'. He argued that the potential for serious disorder was too great, and that it suited the communists to have the men sent back in twos and threes. It suited Gen Anders too, for he had been loudly advocating the return of those pro-communist elements in his forces whom he perceived as 'troublemakers'. Both sides knew that the men who volunteered for repatriation would almost certainly support the new government and help to thwart the return of the dissenters.

These notes disturbed the Foreign Office, for on 8 September it strongly advised the immediate segregation of all those who did not want to go home, and the repatriation of those who did, without delay.[70] The service departments needed no persuading. A meeting at the War Office on 1 September had already recorded 'two mutinies simmering in Scotland', and a letter from Lord Murray, who had enjoyed close contact with the Polish forces in Britain throughout the war, spoke of mounting disorder in all three services. He argued that three broad political groups existed: men, mainly from western Poland (many of whom were farmers and skilled artisans) who wished to return at once to reclaim their land and their jobs; men who had lived in eastern Poland and had suffered at the hands of the Soviets in 1939, who did not want to return at all, and younger men who hoped, rather than expected, to find work and a normal life in the country of their birth. He also referred to an extant plan to gather up all the volunteers in southern England, claiming this to be a mistake:

> I don't think official quarters . . . realise the amount of persecution which [they] have suffered during the last few weeks. The officers can avoid it as they remain in their lodgings, but the men are pestered wherever they go.

He concluded by suggesting that the government should issue an official request for people 'to stop abusing these unfortunates', thus striking a blow against the Chapmans and the Aspinalls of middle England.

None of the Polish squadrons were even close to going home by September 1945 – which must have been particularly galling because the Czechoslovaks, after much dithering on the part of the British, had revelled in their own return the previous month and flown in triumph over Prague. To the dismay of the Poles, the only air display to take place over Warsaw was composed entirely of Russian aircraft which had fought over the eastern front. The British Air Attaché in Warsaw, Gp Capt Burt-Andrews, described the whole performance to the Foreign Office in a long memo, commenting: 'There is good reason to believe that many of the pilots were Russians, and all of the ground staff visible were certainly so.' In the speeches that followed, no mention whatsoever was made of the British contingent, though the attaché's attention was inexorably drawn to the Russian orchestra, 'which played with more volume than melodiousness [and] greeted the entry of His Majesty's ambassador and his staff with a vigorous Russian version of "Roll Out The Barrel".'[71]

Whether or not the British party enjoyed the experience of being welcomed by a crude drinking song is not recorded in the files, but the men in Whitehall were growing hardened to the apparent hopelessness of the situation as the Soviets and their puppets began to consolidate their position. What little chance remained of a reasonable settlement lay with the Polish Military Mission, led by Gen Modelski, scheduled to arrive in Britain in mid-October. But in the event it came, it went, nothing of any

substance was discussed, and despite official urgings to clarify
matters, Modelski merely repeated his orders to refer all matters
of policy and practice to his superiors in Warsaw. Cavendish-
Bentinck had offered a ray of hope when he reported a
conversation with Marshal Rola-Zymierski, the Polish Minister
of Defence, who solemnly promised that no officer returning to
Poland would be deprived of his rank or suffer molestation by
the security police, and if he was so molested, he was 'entitled
to withdraw his revolver and fire'. This was brushed aside by the
Foreign Office. For one thing, it spoke only of officers and not
other ranks; and besides, they took all such oaths with a pinch of
salt. One clear detail emerged from the conversation, however:
there could be no place in the new Poland for Generals Anders
and Sosnkowski, both of whom could be relied upon to cause
trouble if given the opportunity.[72]

By the autumn of 1945, all the service departments were deep
into the process of calculating who would go back and who
would not. The War Office and the Admiralty reported that of
a combined total of 207,000 men and their dependants, only
37,000 (or roughly 18 per cent) were prepared to return to their
homeland. The Air Ministry produced even more disturbing
figures. From a total of 14,700 men, only 7 officers and 50 other
ranks had volunteered for repatriation. Sholto Douglas, then in
command of the occupation air forces in Germany, sought out
Rola-Zymierski in Warsaw. The latter expressed his government's
wish to have a couple of middle-ranking officers fly to Warsaw and
begin negotiations; senior officers, said the Marshal, were likely to
be 'contaminated with political ideas'. He then astonished Sholto
Douglas by expressing his surprise that the entire air force had
not already been sent home, and according to Sholto Douglas he
implied that the British were keeping them back for some obscure
purpose of their own. Sholto Douglas partially agreed, but added
that his government felt obliged to retain them in Britain because
they could not be repatriated 'without any guarantee of their
subsequent treatment'. Rola-Zymierski thought these sentiments
to be noble indeed, and although he was happy to welcome back
the entire air contingent *en bloc*, many senior officers who were
politically compromised would not be welcome.[73]

This cut no ice with the Foreign Office. As far as they were
concerned, the official position remained the same: Warsaw
would accept only unit-level returns. But at least the Poles had
one true friend left. A headteacher named Alice Chatterson
wrote from Braintree in Essex and implored the government
not to forcibly send the Poles home 'to a land whose politics

are distasteful to them'. She added that the British 'must never forget that in 1940, the Polish were almost our only friends . . . many of them laying down their lives to save us in the battle of Britain'.[74] She was promised in reply that no man or woman would be sent back against their will, and although it is unlikely that Ms Chatterson changed British policy with her letter, she wrote at a time when everyone officially connected with the Polish forces was undergoing a change of attitude. British foreign policy is renowned for its cautious and ponderous nature, but by November 1945 it was becoming pretty clear to most that diplomacy was failing and that Warsaw held all the aces. Furthermore, the strain on the exchequer of supporting 200,000 men and dependants with little or no hope of reimbursement was becoming so great that politicians began to steel themselves to accept defeat. A new idea was needed.

Sholto Douglas had one last crack at Rola-Zymierski. He suggested that two Polish group captains should visit Warsaw and smoothe the way. Since this was the Marshal's own preferred plan, Sholto Douglas was on to a sure winner, but again it was vetoed by the Foreign Office. They were not convinced that Rola-Zymierski spoke with sufficient authority; and besides, they had recently been informed by Warsaw that the army would be dealt with separately from the navy and the air force. Whitehall was convinced that this was yet more obfuscation designed to split the Polish forces into manageable units and destroy whatever solidarity remained. Sholto Douglas was disappointed, for he believed that he had it within his grasp to secure the promise of return for the whole Polish Air Force, yet it seems to have escaped his notice that virtually none of them wanted to go at all.[75]

Just before Christmas 1945, an inter-departmental committee met at the Foreign Office and declared that the climax of the crisis was fast approaching. Warsaw had cabled to tell London that all Polish personnel would be unconditionally received back into their homeland, and they refused to elaborate or continue with seemingly pointless negotiations. The British decided that every man would be informed, and would have six weeks to make up his mind. The meeting prepared itself for large numbers who would choose not to return, and they presumed that the Polish government would immediately denationalise them, effectively making them stateless refugees. If that should come to pass – and it was likely – then the entire burden of maintaining them would fall upon the British.

In early January 1946, the Inspector of the Polish Air Forces, Gen Mateusz Izycki, wrote to Lord Tedder and informed him that more than 99 per cent of the men under his command would refuse to return. This marked the turning point in the RAF's attitude towards the Polish Air Force. It was at once apparent to all that the loyalty which the Poles had shown throughout the war, despite all the troubles in the past, was of such magnitude that no matter what the politicians did or said, the RAF would ensure that their debts to their allies would be repaid. There would be no pressure placed by the RAF on the Poles to go home.[76]

Evidence that the sea change of attitude had taken place exists in the British reaction to a new scheme hatched by Rola-Zymierski. In mid-January he wrote and offered to send another mission to Britain, this time with full powers to negotiate on behalf of his government, but it was swept aside by the Foreign Office. The Marshal was curtly informed that the British were reviewing their position, and that his offer, though carefully noted, was being placed in suspension until that review had taken place. This moment also marks the division between the attitude of the service departments and the politicians. The new British Foreign Secretary, Ernest Bevin, was about to inform the Cabinet that 'information of a discouraging nature about the prospects for those who did not return' was going to be circulated among the Polish forces. In other words, he would use black propaganda designed to frighten or coerce the men into going home.

Bevin's statement to the Cabinet was discussed at the Air Ministry in mid-January 1946. No one doubted the reasons for using such methods to encourage repatriation – and it was noted that the trades unions were uneasy about such huge numbers being thrown onto the British labour market – but it was decided that when the 'hard core' of the Polish Air Force was exposed to such pressure, the RAF would 'reserve [its] right to dispose of it under such conditions as will in every way fulfil our obligations.' In a lengthy paper prepared for the Cabinet, the Air Ministry insisted that certain factors made the Polish Air Force a special case. The main points were:

1   under the existing agreement, all men of the Polish Air Force were eligible for service with the RAF;
2   the two forces had lived and fought side by side for more than six years;
3   they came to the aid of the allies in their time of need, and greatly expanded their force under allied direction;
4   they knew more about Britain and the RAF than a great many of the Polish Army, '100,000 of whom have never lived in Britain';

5 Polish officers and airmen were, for all practical purposes, already in the RAF, and because the two forces were so closely integrated, the Air Ministry felt that it had 'a nearer and more intimate responsibility' for the Polish Air Force than had the War Office for the Polish Army.

Thus the Air Ministry set out its stall, and in so doing positioned itself for potential conflict with Attlee's government. Of course, purists might argue that time had confused the Ministry's memory a tad, but the basic message was clear enough. It was felt that men who had served for more than three years should be considered for British citizenship, and if they rejoined the RAF after the Polish Air Force had been dismantled, naturalisation should be automatic. The Air Ministry was also the first to suggest that advice on employment and the rigours of civilian life should be offered to each man through a dedicated agency. In an eloquent passage, the RAF sealed its honour thus:

Whilst fully understanding the cold and dispassionate attitude which must at this stage be adopted by His Majesty's Government in handling a situation of tremendous difficulty, we cannot escape the fact that the Royal Air Force have both a great regard for and obligation to the Polish Air Force, and we feel that neither they nor the British public would condone unfair treatment of [the] strongest, the most loyal and faithful, and the most persistent European ally of all those who fought with us in the air in the west. The debt owed [can] only be satisfactorily repaid by giving them special and generous consideration at a time when their Air Force, of which they were intensely proud, and which they had built up with such hopes for the future, crashes to the ground.[77]

These fine words and noble sentiments demonstrate that the wheel had indeed turned full circle, that Medhurst's 'completely useless officers' of 1940 had been transformed by courage and loyalty into allies of the first order. More to the point, the Poles were allies by whose side the RAF was going to stand firm.

Bevin was also in the mood to stand firm. He said in Cabinet on 22 January that while he understood the position of the service departments, his policy of leaning on them to go home would remain unchanged. The presence and maintenance of the Polish forces, he argued, 'was a source of increasing political embarrassment in our relations with the Soviet Union and Poland', and he placed the financial costs to the Treasury at

£2.5 million per month. The only crumb of comfort seemed to be in his reluctant acceptance that some might eventually join the British forces.

But Bevin's intentions depended entirely on a factor beyond his control – the Warsaw government. It had recently informed London that any Polish air units returning intact would remain as viable squadrons, but the Foreign Office doubted this, not least because the Polish civil air service, LOT, was under the extensive influence of Moscow, therefore it seemed unlikely that military formations would receive special consideration once they were on home soil. The Air Ministry concurred with this view, and its own policy was to give no hint to the Polish air personnel that they might be permitted to join the RAF if they stayed behind. It was a shrewd decision, for at once they could not be accused by Warsaw of placing temptation before the men to refuse repatriation, and they could also avoid the Cabinet's wrath by not deliberately cutting across ministerial policy. It was the Air Ministry's belief that a substantial hard core of men would not return at any price, but a few of the lower ranks might go back, if for no other reason than that they perceived their chances of advancement in Britain to be limited.[78]

In a letter to Viscount Stansgate, Bevin said that he understood the RAF's plea for special consideration for the Poles, but nevertheless he could not grant it: 'Great though our obligations are, are they necessarily any greater than to those Poles who fought at Tobruk, Monte Cassino and Arnhem?' In the margin to this letter, copied to the Foreign Office files, an unknown hand pencilled 'Yes.' Whether this is true or not is largely a matter for each individual to decide, but there can be no question that support for the Polish Air Force was gathering weight and momentum. If his own ministers and mandarins were starting to fall in behind the Air Ministry (an unusual event in itself), then Bevin was in for a hard fight indeed.[79]

Bevin prepared his message to the Polish forces slowly. Versions of it appear in numerous files, and various changes to the text are apparent. By mid-February 1946, however, it was in print waiting for distribution. In essence, he was going to scare them into going home by bluntly stating that the British government could promise no more than assistance to start a new life outside Poland, but this did not extend to preserving the structure of the Polish forces, which would be disbanded in a short while; and neither would he guarantee that any man would be offered British nationality or rights of settlement in British territory. It was calculated that this threat of being stateless and homeless would be sufficient motivation to drive the men back in their thousands.

However, three problems loomed suddenly before the Foreign Secretary. The first was the declaration by Warsaw that the Polish Army in Italy constituted a threat to the Yugoslav–Italian frontier. It meant nothing in real terms, and both sides knew it, but it sent a signal to Bevin that the communists were getting ready to play rough. The second was a cable from the British representative in Italy which warned of the potential for serious disorder if Gen Anders was not permitted to return to England to open negotiations concerning repatriation. Here, the Foreign Office and the Air Ministry parted company in their assessments of Anders: the former saw him as a reactionary who would stir up trouble against repatriation, and the latter held him to be the key to the whole problem, knowing him to be an officer who commanded enormous respect within the Polish Air Force. Finally, Warsaw threw everything into confusion. A telegram from the British Embassy to the Foreign Office on 19 February indicated that the Polish government was preparing to break relations with the USA and Britain. To force the hand of the West, it declared that no mass repatriation would be acceptable any more, leaving each man to apply individually through the Polish consulate if he wanted to return home. Cavendish-Bentinck interpreted these moves as a deliberate attempt to wreck the British proposals to return as many home as possible, and it laid in ruins all of Bevin's hopes at one stroke. It was estimated that it would take five weeks to have his open letter to the Polish forces printed in sufficient numbers and distributed to a quarter of a million men at the same time on the same day, but it would be a bankrupt policy long before then if Warsaw could not be persuaded to retract from its new position.[80]

The Polish note also stated that all men of Polish nationality were to be placed under the command of officers appointed by Warsaw, and would henceforth have to obey any orders generated by them or the Polish government. The Foreign Office saw this as a deliberate attempt to provoke rebellion within the Polish ranks – disturbances which the British would be forced to suppress. Nevertheless, it was decided to push ahead with Bevin's plan. The Air Ministry cabled all commands on 12 March and warned them (rather hopefully) to expect a wave of potential volunteers for repatriation, the calculation being that if men came forward in large enough numbers, the Warsaw government might scrap the plan for personal applications, or at least waive it pending further developments. Warsaw had promised that 'no punitive measures or reprisals would be carried out against returning officers or men' (save those who had aided or served with the Germans), and the British hoped this might be enough to inject confidence into the great mass of undecided men. The date for the publication of Bevin's statement was set as 18 March, following which a period of six weeks would be allowed for consideration.[81]

On 15 March, Gen Anders arrived in Britain from Italy. As Poland's most senior soldier abroad, no one doubted his influence with the men, or his capability to make or break policies in an instant. At once he was taken to meet Attlee and Bevin, who impressed upon him the need for orderly thought and the maintenance of military discipline. The publication of Bevin's statement had been put back two days at Ander's request to allow him time to speak with other senior commanders, but he saw an advance copy and promised his full support for the policy. As all three men agreed, demobilisation was inevitable sooner or later, so if Warsaw was holding out even the thinnest of olive branches, perhaps now was the time to grasp it. On 16 March, the Air Ministry cabled all commands and instructed all RAF personnel to support the policy of His Majesty's Government no matter what their personal views might be. The telegram also reinforced the RAF's own policy that not one word should be spoken about the possibility of future RAF membership for men who refused to go. This was the Air Ministry's own trump card, and it was keeping it well hidden.

A thoroughly tragic letter from Gen Izycki landed on Lord Tedder's desk towards the end of March 1946. The Inspector-General promised that he would not fight political battles and would uphold the British policy, as was his duty. And yet, he argued, it would not be Bevin's 'enticements or persuasions' which would help the men to make up their minds, but 'the true picture of the situation in our unhappy country'. Many thousands were only too aware that their long-cherished dreams of freedom had vanished. He reminded Tedder that the Polish Air Force had suffered much, yet not once had it turned from its duty. It had been abused, ignored, ridiculed and condemned, but had fought from the first day of the war to the last, longer than any other nation save Germany itself, and now here it stood on the eve of its destruction. Izycki closed by justifying his thoughts and the letter itself, 'as history will one day hold me responsible for the destruction of the Polish Air Force'.[82]

The day before, on 21 March, Bevin's statement had been distributed to a quarter of a million Poles 'without incident and in an atmosphere of calm efficiency'. Anders had given orders that no man, of whatever rank, was to engage in political conflict with any other; and no one, under pain of severe punishment, was to attempt to persuade any man to reach a judgement against his will. It was widely expected that no one would make his decision until Anders had spoken his own thoughts, but no one in the Foreign Office by now doubted that the respect Anders commanded was enormous. It was also felt that if this campaign did not produce the desired results, then Warsaw would immediately launch a violent propaganda campaign and do everything in its power to provoke what would be a communist uprising in exile.

On 27 March the Assistant Chief of the Air Staff (Policy), AVM William Dickson, prepared a series of briefing notes for a private meeting between Tedder and Izycki, called at the latter's request in his earlier communication. Dickson felt that the Polish general was seeking 'just one word of encouragement' from the British to do his utmost to preserve the core of the Polish Air Force intact. He had already blessed the formation of a Polish Air Force Association (Great Britain) and had asked for RAF recognition. This had been denied pending 'very high level consultation', but had been viewed sympathetically for all that. He had also let it be known that he might approach the RAF to become procurator of all Polish Air Force records, histories, funds and so on, but all of this was technically the property of the Polish government in Warsaw. As Dickson wrote, 'whether we like them or not, we could lay ourselves open to receiving stolen property'.

The end of March 1946 saw a complete change of policy by the British. One can view it as a pragmatic approach to an insoluble situation, or simply a total capitulation in the face of an invincible opponent. Either way, the decision to give up trying to get the Poles back home, and to find an alternative means of dispersing them must be interpreted as a defeat for the British in the opening skirmishes of the Cold War. On 4 April, the first meeting of a new Polish Forces Committee with a very high-level membership convened to discuss the structure of what would eventually become the Polish Resettlement Corps (PRC). During that meeting, the RAF won its case and secured a promise that the majority of men in the Polish Air Force could join the RAF, and with that came an undertaking to lower the waiting time for nationalisation from five years to two. Men who refused to re-enlist in any service would be offered other means of supporting themselves, either through the labour market in civilian life or by emigration to sympathetic countries. No man would be compelled to follow any of these routes, but his only option would then be to risk the uncertainty of a displaced persons' camp. In all, nearly 14,000 men and women of the Polish Air Force would be offered the chance to continue their careers in peacetime or, depending on the point of view, accept a life in permanent exile.[83] The concept of the PRC was given almost unanimous support, the only serious dissent issuing from the War Office, which thought the project unworkable.

In all, less than 10 per cent of the Polish air personnel had responded favourably to Bevin's repatriation campaign. Many men and their families were expected to go to America, which had signalled its approval of the policy of encouraging emigration there, but had stipulated that only men with recognised trades would be accepted. In a moment of fine historical irony, it was Sir Douglas Evill who suggested that the RAF could absorb 4,000–5,000 men at once, and the rest in phased intakes. The smaller numbers involved with the Polish Air Force were less of a concern to the RAF than the huge task which faced the War Office, but the Air Ministry immediately offered to share the burden by making temporary jobs for 7,000 Poles to work with prisoner-of-war gangs clearing sites and dismantling stores. Towards the end of April, the Air Ministry announced that it would turn the former Polish depot into a resettlement centre and use the existing Polish Air Force headquarters as the primary channel for communications. Evidence that such creative thinking and commitment was urgently needed came when the six weeks deadline expired for Poles to register their desire to go home. Out of a quarter of a million men, only 2,600 opted for repatriation.[84]

On 19 May, the Foreign Office despatched a wonderfully defiant telegram bluntly informing the Warsaw administration that His Majesty's Government had now established a Resettlement Corps, and that no man would be confronted regarding his repatriation options, and neither would he be expected to decide by any firm date. It was emphasised that the entire scheme was non-compulsory, but the British position now was to give every assistance to those who chose to remain in the West. There were private concerns that the Polish government would retaliate with a black propaganda campaign against the PRC, but a delighted Izycki met Slessor at the Air Ministry on 21 May and brushed aside any such complications. Hopes for a separate air wing within the PRC were mentioned by the Poles, but it was clear that the RAF had pledged its full support for the scheme and the absorption of as many Poles into its organisation as possible This did not stop the Poles protesting the need for the PRC's very existence, however. Their primary concern was that the Warsaw government would now completely abandon any plans to hold free elections or maintain democratic principles, but their greatest fear was that the PRC should not be seen as 'the closing chapter' to the story of Poland's war. In Italy, Anders issued a statement informing all Polish personnel that the national war aims had not been achieved, but although it was full of bluster and rhetoric, it contained no criticisms of the PRC or British policy in general.[85]

The royal warrant which legally established the Polish Resettlement Corps was signed in August 1946, followed shortly by two more which created a women's section and, much to Izycki's satisfaction, a special RAF division. But his request for the Polish units to remain intact within the RAF was rejected by the Foreign Office. To have an exiled force permanently established on Western soil while the politicians grappled with the complexities of the developing Cold War would have been too strong a provocation to the East. It was part of British policy from the start to ensure that the Polish armed forces were disbanded and demobilised. Anders complained, but Bevin would have none of it. Izycki also lobbied for a skeleton Polish Air Force to remain intact, but this too was refused. In truth, neither of the two commanders relished the prospect of telling their men that the Polish forces had ceased to exist after all they had been through, but there was no other option.

The PRC was split into two broad divisions: the army and navy in one part, and the air force contingent in another, for with only 4,000 personnel in the navy, it seemed an unnecessary extension of the scheme to provide a separate administration. The Air Ministry undertook the responsibility of controlling its own section, while the War Office took charge of the rest. The whole scheme came under the auspices of the National Assistance Board. The RAF made six airfields available for billeting and initial registration, and by June 1946 most of the personnel had been assembled. The ground crew presented no problems, for most of them had been trained and trade-tested up to RAF standards, but many pilots found themselves on ferrying and transport duties, or assigned for further training as Britain moved towards a peacetime footing. As for the Polish Air Force, its symbolic demise came on 18 September with a farewell parade at Coltishall attended by every brass hat who could be mustered. Glorious speeches were made and returned, ensigns were exchanged, hopes for the future solemnly expressed, but no one could hide the fact that it was all over.[86]

All that remained was to complete the process of assimilation and dispersal as smoothly as possible and with minimum impact upon the tired and unhappy Poles. A Cabinet report in early October 1946 reveals that 75 per cent of the men had opted to enlist with the PRC, some 17 per cent were considering repatriation (in large part motivated by Warsaw's threat to denationalise them if they remained in voluntary exile), and 8 per cent flatly refused to do either. This last group was to be told firmly that they had one month to make up their minds or face transfer to a displaced persons' camp in Germany to join 280,000 of their countrymen left stranded by the war. This figure dropped sharply after this knowledge became common, and the eventual number transported to the Continent in early 1947 was about 200, some of whom had served time in British jails.

As for the Air Ministry, it maintained its support by producing a bilingual pamphlet outlining all the options available to the air personnel, and only fifty-seven of the total number of 14,000 chose to go home. In mid-November, Izycki issued a proclamation urging the men of the Polish Air Force to accept this new challenge to them and their homeland, for theirs was to be a permanent exile. They had fought hard with dignity and courage, but the long battle for liberation had been lost. Paying tribute to the Royal Air Force and its loyalty to their Polish comrades, he reminded his men that Polish freedom would live on in the hearts of all who kept the memory alive, and those who had fallen had not died in vain if their sacrifice would never be forgotten.[87] It was to be many years before their Poland was truly free again, but it would be difficult to deny that the participation by all the Polish forces in the Second World War bequeathed to the Polish people an indelible determination to survive which even the injustices of communism could not erase.

NOTES

1. This was by no means a uniform view, however. In July 1939, Clifford Norton in Warsaw wrote a long, sentimental letter to Orme Sargent in the Foreign Office extolling the virtues of Josef Beck, the Polish Foreign Minister. Norton, who was deputising for Ambassador Kennard, even praised Beck's assistance in the destruction of Czechoslovakia, 'regarded by Poland as an arm of Russia thrust along her southern border'. An unknown hand pencilled 'this is rather far-fetched' in the margin. (FO 371/23022: Norton to Sargent, 3.7.39.)

2. FO 371/23156 and FO 371/23022: Minutes of Inter-Allied Conference, 25.10.39; Evill to Foreign Office, 2.11.39; Zajac to Davidson, 31.10.39.
3. Zamoyski, A. *The Forgotten Few* (John Murray 1995), p. 58.
4. FO 371/24463: Minute to file, 9.1.40. Roger Mellor Makins CMG was educated at Winchester and Christ Church, Oxford; appointed to the Foreign Office 1928; promoted 2nd Secretary 1933; Acting 1st Secretary 1939; Acting Counsellor 1940; Counsellor 1942; knighted 1 January 1944.
5. Goddard, V., *Skies to Dunkirk* (William Kimber 1982), pp. 25–6.
6. FO 371/24463: Boyle to Makins, 16.1.40.
7. FO 371/24463: Collier to Mack, 23.1.40.
8. Zamoyski, p. 45; FO 371/24463: Minutes, Air Ministry/ Foreign Office meeting, 19.1.40
9. FO 371/24465: Strang to Boyle, 30.3.40.
10. FO 371/24466: Flt Lt N.R. Dobree to Air Attaché Paris, 27.3.40
11. AIR 2/4213: Report by Flt Lt Landau through Boyle, 29.3.40. All subsequent quotations are from this text unless otherwise noted.
12. FO 371/24466: Sikorksi to Chamberlain, 4.4.40; Chamberlain to Sikorski, 12.4.40.
13. FO 371/24466: Mack to Makins, 17.4.40.
14. AIR 2/4123: Boyle to Strang, 7.4.40.
15. Zamoyski, p. 62. Zamoyski also attributes Landau's report to the British liaison officer to the Polish Air Force and Station Commander at Eastchurch, Gp Capt A.P. Davidson, though there seems little doubt that he would have seen the report in any case.
16. Prazmowská, A., *Britain and Poland 1939–1943: The Betrayed Ally* (Cambridge University Press 1995), pp. 33–4.
17. Taylor, A.J.P., *From the Boer War to the Cold War* (Hamish Hamilton 1995): 'The Traditions of British Foreign Policy', pp. 9–12.
18. Prazmowská, p. 20.
19. FO 371/24480: Correspondence, 28.2.40–15.3.40.
20. CAB 85/16: Allied Military Committee, 1.5.40.
21. Cynk, J.B., *History of the Polish Air Force* (Osprey 1972), Chapter 1, *passim*; see also Zamoyski, pp. 44–56 – 'French Fiasco'.
22. Two excellent works which cover the French defeat of 1940 are: Guy Chapman, *Why France Collapsed* (Cassells 1968), and Alistair Horne, *To Lose A Battle* (Macmillan 1969); The DCAS, AVM Sir W. Sholto Douglas GCB KCB CB MC DFC, was

educated at Tonbridge School and Lincoln College, Oxford; RFC 1917; RAF 1918; Director of Staff Duties, Air Ministry, 1936–7; ACAS 1938–40; DCAS 1940; AOC Fighter Command 1940–2; AOC Middle East Command 1943–4; AOC Coastal Command 1944–5; AOC British Air Forces of Occupation in Germany 1945–6; Marshal of the Royal Air Force 1946; C-in-C and Military Governor, British Zone of Germany 1946–7; retired 1948; created First Baron of Dornock 1948; decorated by more than thirteen countries for his services in the Second World War; AIR 2/7196: Minutes, DCAS Conference, 25.5.40.

23. AIR 2/7196: Minutes, DCAS Conference, 25.5.40.

24. AIR 2/7196: Sholto Douglas to Peirse, 4.6.40.

25. AIR 2/7196: Porri to all departments, 24.5.40.

26. The enmity between the Russians and the Czechoslovaks was not as severe as that between the Russians and the Poles. Many of the Czechoslovaks interned by the Soviets were slowly released and allowed to proceed to the west. Some unfortunates were held in Siberian labour camps until the German assault on Russia began in June 1941, when they too were released and offered service in the Red Army (see: White, L.M. (ed.), *On All Fronts: Czechoslovaks in WW2 (Vol 1)* (East European Monographs, Boulder 1995); Kaspar, Miloslav F. 'Polish Campaign 1939', *passim*).

27. Bury, J.P.T., *France, 1814–1940* (Methuen 1985), pp. 255–6.

28. Čapka, J., *Red Sky At Night* (Anthony Blond 1958), p. 23; see also Darlington, R., *Nighthawk* (William Kimber 1985), p. 25.

29. Chapman, p. 41.

30. [VHA] MNO 5/810/1940: MNO report on conditions in France, 3.9.40.

31. Chapman, *loc. cit.*

32. Čapka, pp. 30–1; Darlington, p. 26. These accounts were dismissed by Miroslav Liškutín as 'silly propaganda nonsense'. (White, *op.cit.*, Liškutín, M.A. 'The Czechoslovak Air Force In War', p. 127.)

33. White, *op.cit.*; Kordina, *op.cit.*, p. 25.

34. White, *op.cit.*; Liškutín, *op.cit.*, pp. 127–8.

35. [VHA] VKPR 27/3/1/5: Report of French Campaign, 20.4.42. In addition to the 123 pilots, around another 100 men were employed in the combat zones as ground crew, bringing the full total to 220–40. (VKPR 25/3/1/3: Summary of events of the Czechoslovak Air Force overseas, produced in the summer of 1941.)

36. White, *op.cit.*; Kordina, Zdenek, 'The 1940 Evacuation of the Czechoslovak Armed Forces From France', pp. 63–80 *passim*.

See also ADM 1/10481: Admiralty Report on Operations AERIAL and CYCLE, 18.9.40.

37. CAB 65/7: War Cabinets of 18.6.40 and 19.6.40. See also Zamoyski, p. 38.
38. MNO 5/931/1940: Summary of Czechoslovak action in France, 4.9.40.
39. White, *op.cit.*; Němec, Jaroslav, 'The Crisis of the Czechoslovak Army in England in the Second Half of 1940', p. 86.
40. WP(40)281; Chiefs of Staff to War Cabinet, 24.7.40.
41. Figures quoted in Prazmowská, p. 26.
42. AIR 2/5153: Kalla to Air Ministry, 23.5.40.
43. AIR 2/5153: Boyle to Porri, 2.6.40.
44. AIR 2/5153: Porri to Boyle, 10.6.40.
45. AIR 2/5153: Beneš to Sinclair, 18.6.40.
46. AIR/2/5153: Medhurst to Sholto Douglas 3.7.40. Medhurst's anxieties about independence were soon justified. On 12 July, Newall wrote to the C-in-C Polish Forces (Gen K. Sosnkowski) informing him that the legal status of the Polish Air Force would 'be the same as that of the Polish land forces and the Polish Navy'. In reply, the General accepted the logic of having the Polish squadrons organised on RAF lines, but still the principle of Polish independence was established by this exchange (AIR/8/295: 16.7.40.)

ACM Sir Charles Edward Hasting Medhurst KCB CB OBE MC (1896–1954) was educated at Rossall, St Peter's at York and Sandhurst; served on the Western Front 1915–18; RAF 1919; RAF Staff College 1931–3; Deputy Director of Intelligence 1934–7; Air Attaché Rome, Berlin, Berne and Athens 1937–40; Director of Allied Air Co-operation 1940; Assistant Chief of the Air Staff (Intelligence) 1941; ACAS (Policy) 1942; Commandant RAF Staff College 1943–4; AOC C-in-C RAF Mediterranean and Middle East 1945–8; retired 1950. Medhurst was also awarded the Czechoslovak White Lion, Class II, in 1944 for services to the allied air forces.

47. Rajlich, J., Sehnal, J., *Slovenšti Letci* [Slovak Airmen] (Label 1991), p. 7.
48. AIR 2/5153: Conference minutes to DCAS, 3.7.40; DCAS to Medhurst, 6.7.40.
49. AIR 2/5153: Sholto Douglas to Medhurst, 5.7.40.
50. AIR 2/5153: Directorate of Organisation to Sholto Douglas, 6.7.40.
51. AIR 8/295: Newall to Gen Norwid-Neugebaur, 21.9.39.
52. AIR 2/5153: Medhurst to the Directorate of Organisation and other departments, 7.7.40.

53. AIR 8/295: Medhurst to Col B.J. Kweicinski, 16.7.40.
54. AIR 8/295: Minute to file by Medhurst, 18.7.40.
55. AIR 2/4600: Minute to file by Hollinghurst, 26.7.40.
56. FO 371/24467: Summary of correspondence, Air Ministry–Foreign Office, 28.5.40.
57. AIR 2/5093: Summary of correspondence, formation of Polish Inspectorate; 8.3.40 to 6.6.40.
58. AIR 20/5402: Report: DAAC to Director of Postings, 6.12.40.
59. FO 371/39481: Summary of correspondence, March–April 1944.
60. FO 371/47677: Review of *Robotnik*, 20.8.45; FO 371/39434: Report PWRC meeting, 21.1.44.
61. Quoted in Zamoyski, p. 195.
62. FO 371/47676: Peebles Town Councillor, 21.8.45; Kathleen Chapman to Foreign Office, 21.8.45; FO 371/47689: A. Aspinall to Foreign Secretary, 4.12.45.
63. Garlinski, J., *Poland in the Second World War* (Macmillan 1985), ch. 23 'The Last Soviet Offensive', *passim.*
64. AIR 8/1154: Air Ministry to all departments, 4.7.45.
65. AIR 8/1154; COS (45)442(0), 6.7.45.
66. AIR 8/1154: Cadogan to Brooke, 6.7.45; COS(45)442(0), 6.7.45.
67. AIR 8/1154: Foreign Office communiqué, 27.6.45.
68. FO 371/47676: Air Ministry to Foreign Office, 29.8.45.
69. FO 371/47677: Cavendish-Bentinck to Foreign Office, 5.9.45.
70. FO 371/47677: Cavendish-Bentinck to Foreign Office, 6.9.45; Foreign Office memorandum to all service departments, 8.9.45.
71. FO 371/47677: Burt-Andrews to Cavendish-Bentinck and Foreign Office, 5.9.45.
72. AIR 8/1154: Cavendish-Bentinck to Foreign Office, 5.10.45.
73. FO 371/47686: Interview, Sholto Douglas with Marshal Rola-Zymierski, 1.11.45.
74. FO 371/47686: Ms Alice Chatterson to Foreign Office, 6.11.45; and reply, 24.11.45.
75. AIR 8/1154: Sholto Douglas interview with Rola-Zymierski, 3.12.45.
76. FO 371/1155: 'Disposal of the Polish Armed Forces', 5.1.46; minutes, inter-departmental meeting, 21.12.45; Izycki to Tedder, 8.1.46. Mateusz Izycki had replaced Gen Stanislaw Ujejski as Inspector-General on 1.9.43.
77. FO 371/1155: Air Ministry memorandum, 17.1.46
78. FO 371/1155: Air Ministry/Foreign Office correspondence, 21-29.1.46.

79. FO 371/1155: Bevin to Stansgate, 29.1.46.
80. FO 371/1155: Correspondence, 18-20.2.46.
81. AIR 8/1156: Foreign Office to Warsaw, 6.3.46; Air Ministry circular, 12.3.46.
82. AIR 8/1156: Izycki to Tedder, 22.3.46.
83. AIR 8/1156: Polish Forces Committee; minutes, 4.4.46. The numbers in the Polish Air Force at that time were given as: 2,144 officers, 10,412 other ranks, 50 PWAAF officers, 1,123 PWAAF other ranks, and 185 apprentices – a total of 13,914.
84. AIR 8/1156: Air Ministry correspondence, 24.4.46 to 3.5.46.
85. AIR 8/1156: Correspondence, 17.5.46 to 25.5.46.
86. AIR 8/1156: Robb to Dickson, 7.9.46; AIR 2/9680; minutes, 24.6.46.
87. AIR 8/1155: GEN 125/24, 2.10.46; Izycki to the Polish Air Force, 16.11.46.

CHAPTER THREE

Czechs and Poles

PART ONE: 1940

We saw in Chapter Two how the Czechoslovaks came to be swept into the same category as the Poles during the hectic retreat from France in the summer of 1940. To British minds in positions of influence, neither party was wholly trustworthy, and they both came with too much pre-war political baggage. As for the French, it was clear that they had little time to spare to tend to the needs of the Slavs, or indeed to evaluate their usefulness. Both nationalities therefore arrived in Britain partly full of hope that their services would now be welcomed, and partly embittered at their experiences so far.

All of the exiled groups from Europe came to Britain at the worst possible time if they wished to be received with open arms. Britain in the summer of 1940 was suffering from a serious bout of 'Fifth Column fever', and *all* foreigners, no matter how devoted to the common cause they claimed to be, were treated with deep suspicion. The public had been whipped up to a state of near panic at the thought of hordes of German spies roaming the countryside and preparing the way for the Nazi legions to invade, for the popular rumour of the hour was that they had done so with great efficiency in the now occupied countries of Belgium and Holland. Indeed, in many Whitehall offices, that rumour was utterly believed to be a fact; therefore the formulators of domestic policy also sought to guard against the infiltration or activation of Abwehr agents whose nefarious talents might bring the Empire one step nearer to its doom.

Although anyone with a foreign accent was risking assault, arrest, or even worse if they spoke to the wrong person, some groups nevertheless had a slight advantage in those difficult first weeks

after the French collapse. The Poles, for example, were allies –
Britain had gone to war for them a year earlier, or so it was
believed – hence a Pole, if he had time enough to make his listener
understand that he *was* a Pole, stood a fair chance of receiving a
hearty slap on the back rather than a punch on the nose. Similarly,
the attack on Norway in April had stimulated much sympathy in
Britain, and their plight had received a great deal of good press
coverage, the Norwegians being portrayed as kindly, peaceful folk
caught up in an evil war not of their making. As for the French
– well, leaving aside the curious and often irrational relationship
Britain has had with France over the centuries, they were still allies
first and foremost, and they came to Britain on a tide of reasonable
goodwill generated by a largely positive press and the sublime
assurances of Winston Churchill that all would be well if the two
nations stood firm against the German menace.

These advantages were denied to the Czechoslovaks.
It has been noted earlier that in the War Cabinet of 18 June,
Anthony Eden had dithered over a policy of selective rescue,
offering to take Polish troops off French shores in preference to
Czechoslovaks. He was not alone in this policy of bias. Both the
Foreign Secretary, Lord Halifax, and the Chief of the Imperial
General Staff (CIGS), Sir John Dill, also made it plain where their
sympathies lay in regard to foreign support. But in the days of the
French collapse, Churchill's voice was repeatedly heard in the
War Cabinet urging whatever measures were necessary to save
as many foreign personnel as possible, irrespective of nationality
or political persuasion. He made it perfectly clear to everyone
that 'this should be regarded as an objective of the utmost
importance'. This statement, made on 20 June, effectively ended
any further talk of selective evacuation, and he spoke whimsically
of a British 'Foreign Legion' composed of anyone and everyone
who could be trusted to serve within it. 'It is unjust', Churchill
said, 'to treat our friends as foes', but although Halifax agreed in
principle, he sounded a cautious note by drawing attention to the
potential hazards of the policy, favouring 'a quick comb-out of
those aliens who were willing to fight for us'. Even so, he accepted
that there were strong political arguments for concurring with
Churchill's wishes.[1]

Halifax was speaking from experience, and to some extent
jogging Churchill's memory. A little over a month earlier, in
response to a statement by Halifax that the German sweep into
Belgium and Holland had been aided by native sympathisers,
Churchill noted certain groups then in Britain which he
considered worthy of close scrutiny. In his opinion, British fascists

and communists, all Italians, and Dutch, Belgian and Czech refugees 'should be behind barbed wire'.[2] Leaving aside the domestic element, fears were running high that these particular groups could contain active German spies or persons sympathetic to the Axis cause. Now, in late June, according to the then current estimates, upwards of 60,000 citizens of occupied states would soon be landed on British soil, a potential security problem of the first magnitude, hence Halifax's continuing alarm at the prospect even though Churchill had rapidly changed his tune.

But perhaps we should not be too harsh on Churchill. The realities of June 1940 meant that decisions needed to be taken with as much clarity of thought as possible, and this was the task assumed by the new Prime Minister. He had conceived a plan of rapid evacuation followed by an intense period of screening for undesirable attitudes, the primary criterion for rejection being the individual's unwillingness to serve under the allied flags. What remained after this process would be the 'unsuitable elements', and as he said in the War Cabinet of 24 June, 'arrangements could always be made to send them on elsewhere'.[3] He did not specify where 'elsewhere' was – though the probable destinations of the unwanted would have been Canada, Australia or the Isle of Man – but before most of the men had even disembarked, the agile mind of the Prime Minister had formed an army, chosen its complement, and shunted the rest off to an uncertain fate.

Within this pell-mell process, it was predictable that uncomfortable views would be expressed as earlier prejudices were dusted off. Gen Dill echoed Halifax's thoughts when he declared on 25 June that the Polish troops were 'generally of good quality' and could be supplied with rifles received from America, 'but the Czechs would have to be carefully sorted out before rearming'. Such words from Dill would have had little impact on Churchill, who considered his CIGS to be 'tired, disheartened, and over-impressed with the might of Germany'. Dill had been appointed by Churchill shortly after the latter's elevation to the premiership, but it was not long before he had acquired the nickname 'Dilly-dally' and been humiliated before the Cabinet when Churchill labelled him as 'the dead hand of inanition'.[4] Neither was Churchill particularly impressed with the perpetual caution of Halifax, the man A.J.P. Taylor described as the 'prince of appeasers'.[5] Halifax was a different matter to Dill, however. He was still the most senior figure among the *Munichois*, who, despite the waning of their influence, could still cause much trouble for Churchill in the early days of his leadership. For some time, therefore, at least until he was fully secure in office, Churchill had to treat Halifax with some care. Both men were finally removed in late 1941; Dill was replaced as CIGS by Alan Brooke, and Halifax was sent to Washington as Ambassador, Eden stepping into his shoes as Foreign Secretary.

Thus, although both Dill and Halifax voiced concerns in the War Cabinet, neither was ever likely to make much of an impression on Churchill, who already had his mind made up. But this did not stop the criticisms, and unfortunately for the Czechoslovaks, most of the deepest suspicions fell upon them. We saw earlier how Archibald Boyle, in his capacity as RAF Director of Intelligence, had attempted to stifle the proposal from Cyril Porri to form a Czechoslovak bomber squadron in Britain, declaring himself to be 'doubtful of many Czechs'. Boyle was also a member of the Joint Intelligence Committee (JIC), a body which met regularly to share inter-service information and allow MI5 and MI6 to keep abreast of any untoward developments.

The JIC was formed in 1936 out of the Inter-Service Intelligence Committee. It was a streamlining move, designed to minimise duplication of effort between the three main service departments, and also to keep central government informed on intelligence matters through the medium of the Foreign Office. By May 1940, both MI5 and MI6 had full access to the JIC, and representatives of both frequently attended meetings. The JIC was never a formulator of 'high policy'; rather, it debated issues which mattered in terms of overall security and made recommendations accordingly. As an instrument of power, therefore, it was fairly small-scale. But as a forum for attitudes, it was formidable. It stood as a general meeting place for those with connections to *real* power, and the relationships between those either directly involved with it or with the departments it represented created a powerful web of opinion-formers. Boyle was thus in a position to disseminate his views to a highly influential audience.[6]

On 30 May, three days before he issued his riposte to Porri, Boyle had attended a meeting of the JIC at which had arisen the question of employing aliens deemed friendly or otherwise. Someone had pointed out that aliens of any persuasion were not yet covered by security regulations in non-military areas – that is, within the civil service and industry. To rectify this, the Committee proposed that: 'all members of the Services and officials of Government Departments should be forbidden to employ enemy (i.e. German, Austrian and Czech) aliens in any circumstances'.[7] In the original document, the words 'and Czech' had been struck through in blue ink, but it is important to note that this amendment did not occur at the time, and neither was it an afterthought of the Committee before the paper was circulated and assessed. On 10 June, shortly before the evacuations began, the Foreign Office accepted these recommendations, thereby sending out the general signal to all government departments that Czechs were not to be trusted – indeed, they were to be officially treated as enemy aliens. Small wonder, then, that Boyle wrote what he did in answer to Porri's enquiry of 28 May. It also explains in part why the general 'anti-Czech' feeling was so widespread through the higher echelons of the services.

It was not until September that year, when 310, 311 and 313 Czechoslovak Squadrons were already formed and operational, that a blistering letter from the Home Office landed on numerous Foreign Office desks and came before the JIC. Referring to the earlier JIC memorandum, the Permanent Under Secretary of State, Sir Alexander Maxwell, soundly ticked off both departments for bracketing Czechoslovaks with Germans and Austrians, drawing attention to the fact that His Majesty's Government had recently concluded political and military agreements with the Provisional Czechoslovak Government established on British soil in July, and in a fine example of concealed rage, Maxwell suggested that 'it will, I am afraid, create grave difficulties if we treat our allies as enemies'.[8] Here is clear evidence that substantial sections of the power structure were prepared to write off the Czechoslovaks as belonging to a group of nationalities who were obviously under suspicion.[9]

However, the British had an uncomfortable precedent before them regarding Czechoslovak loyalty, both to their own cause and that of the allies. In January 1940, the Foreign Office had begun a series of inter-departmental meetings aimed at establishing a working procedure regarding the organisation of allied contingents on British territory. The requests had come from Sikorski for the Poles, and Edvard Beneš for the Czechoslovaks. Both intended to enlist nationals living in Britain for service with their forces in France. From the outset, the official British position was one of facilitation – they were prepared to assist with registration, travel arrangements and embarkation centres, but it was to be clearly understood that no military units could actually be created on British soil.

Almost immediately, the question of conscription arose, and with it some significant distinctions which threw the Czechoslovaks into a poor light. The spokesman for the Home Office, E.N. Cooper, insisted that 'some measure of compulsion was more necessary for the Czechs than the Poles', mainly because of the circumstances under which they lived in Britain. He argued that many of the Poles had been settled in this country for some time, and most had secure occupations, whereas 'the majority of the Czechoslovaks were refugees, some of whom had subversive tendencies'.[10] Speaking for the War Office, a Colonel Pigott suggested that a number of Czechs and Slovaks could be sent to Palestine to join the ranks of under-manned pioneer companies. Cooper concurred, adding that the Home Office 'were anxious to get rid of as many Czech and Slovak refugees as possible'.[11] A further sticking-point was the question of sanctions for refusal to serve. The Poles could threaten the withdrawal of rights of nationality, but the Czechoslovaks could not, because their representatives were not recognised as a legitimate government. In the end, it was decided to explore ways by which refugee benefits could be withheld unless men volunteered for service with the Czechoslovak Army and Air Force then in France.

It would be too harsh to conclude from this that the Czechs and Slovaks would literally be driven from British territory, but it is plain that they were not welcome and that men of influence were prepared to employ some unpalatable tactics to relocate as many as possible, preferably in uniform in the services of their 'national army'. But herein lies the essential problem, because men who had chosen to leave their homeland and make new lives elsewhere had no real reason to volunteer in its defence. Of the 2,000 or so potential recruits in Britain at the outbreak of war, a little over 10 per cent enlisted for service in France. Worse still, the Home Office concluded that 'evidence was accumulating that agitators had been at work among the refugees, a great many of whom seemed definitely opposed to the allied war effort'.[12]

These 'agitators' were mainly left-wingers who looked east to the Soviet Union for support. Czechoslovakia had the largest pre-war Communist Party in Europe, and although it also boasted a strong rightist element in its political spectrum, few actually imagined salvation at the hands of Berlin, preferring to look to Moscow for support. Anti-semitism was also a problem, as it was with the Poles, but in the main it was this polarisation of Czechoslovak politics which so perplexed the British and gave rise to a large part of the suspicion which dominated the period. If the Poles were distrusted because they had already been beaten and were no longer a relevant factor in the war effort – at least in the eyes of some senior officers – then the Czechoslovaks were distrusted because they were militarily untried, politically suspect, and appeared to be seriously lacking in morale and commitment. Within the space of a few weeks, large numbers of these 'enemies' had arrived in Britain, and attitudes simply do not change that quickly.[13]

This is but one dimension of a highly complicated relationship, for at its very core lay the uneasy political association between the British government and the émigré administration headed by Edvard Beneš. The British interpreted *all* the military agreements with the exiled forces in political terms, for two reasons. In the first place, active service in any theatre of war with the Western allies might be construed by an allied government as a right to sit at the peace conference when that day came, and this in turn might commit Britain to sustaining territorial claims, particularly in the east, which might inflame rather than placate the post-war environment. These lessons had been learnt at Versailles in 1919, and the British government had an absolute determination not to entangle itself in a similar net at the end of the present conflict. Secondly, active service by an exiled power might also be construed as conferring a right to influence strategic policy, and this too was rejected by the British, except in the case of the French and, to a limited extent, the Poles.

In the case of the Czechoslovaks, the second problem was a minor one. The force was too small for Beneš to realistically demand a voice in planning the allied campaigns, and both sides knew that. The attempts he made to take control of his own army and air contingents in regard to active roles were at best half-hearted, and therefore easy for the British to repel. Politically, however, the potential for conflict was enormous, and to fully understand the position of the airmen in Britain we must explore the diplomatic context in which they served.

The first obstacle to be overcome was the status of the Czechoslovak National Committee. All the other exiled powers had reconstituted themselves in Britain and had achieved some form of recognition of their legitimacy to represent their people trapped under German occupation. The Belgians and the Dutch still had colonial possessions, and the Norwegians and Poles had fully recognised governments-in-exile. Only the French stood outside this basic model, but that was because of the complications posed by the existence of the Vichy administration. Even then, de Gaulle was still regarded as the *de facto* spokesman for the fighting French. None of these considerations applied to the Czechoslovaks, yet without some principle of recognition they could not constitutionally raise an army on British soil and then use that force in defence of British objectives. These latter points were dealt with in part by the hastily sanctioned Allied Forces Act of 1940, but still the absence of a political agreement meant that the incoming personnel had no legitimate role to play in the wider engagement.

On 27 June 1940, Lord Halifax brought these issues to the notice of the War Cabinet. Until that date, the British government had kept the Czechoslovaks at arm's length, preferring to row in behind the French because it was they who had the formal alliance with Prague. After the Munich Agreement of 1938, Beneš had resigned his presidency and chosen exile in Britain, and even that came with conditions attached. He had to promise that he would take part in no political activity whatsoever, and in the mean time London got on with the slightly distasteful business of working with the new government in Czechoslovakia led by the ageing Emil Hácha. The rest of the politicians who had fled the country gathered in France and formed a Czechoslovak National Committee which was reluctantly recognised by the French as being 'qualified to represent the Czechoslovak *peoples*' – that is, not the Czechoslovak *state*. Even the addition of the 's' in 'peoples' reflected the desperately pedantic world of central European politics at the time, because the singular would have implied a Czech and Slovak unity which did not exist, Slovakia having declared independence in March 1939 and placed itself clearly within the orbit of the Reich.

It was the outbreak of war in September 1939 and the later defeat of France which saved Beneš from political oblivion. From the moment the first shots were fired, he claimed the moral high ground and declared Munich to have been a failure. He was greatly helped by a good press in Britain, and more particularly abroad, where he was seen as the victim of the weaknesses of the European powers. He had been fêted on a speaking tour in America in 1939, and he let it be known that he still considered himself to be the rightful leader of Czechoslovakia. The problem for Beneš, however, was that he was detested by the French and deeply distrusted by the British, who would have much preferred him to slink quietly away and not act as a permanent reminder of a failed initiative. Upon the occupation of France and the subsequent flight of the Czechoslovak National Committee to London, it became apparent to everyone that Beneš would seize the opportunity to rebuild his career.

This was not a pleasant prospect for the British. He had enemies aplenty inside the National Committee, and in its train came a host of ne'er-do-wells who covered the full spectrum of political affiliations, yet all claimed to be speaking for the people of Czechoslovakia. Some were interned, others closely watched. Beneš himself was briskly informed that if he wished to be the leader of a such a disparate group, he first had to demonstrate that he could command support from all sides, Slovak and Czech, communist and fascist, liberal and conservative. This was the position as the evacuees began to stream in from the French coasts, but it rapidly became obvious to the British that among them were a few thousand servicemen who technically had no government which could take responsibility for them.

It was this latter point upon which Halifax focused in the War Cabinet of 27 June. After outlining all of the various points which had previously militated against giving Beneš any recognition, he then disarmed his listeners by proceeding to massage most of them away as being irrelevant or redundant. The key phrase came in the middle of his argument, when he bluntly observed that the Czechoslovak personnel would have to be cared for 'whether or not' Beneš and his followers received any official recognition, so it was far easier to have him within the allied sphere of influence than without. He would be told that political unity was still to be his first objective, but if he could ensure a reasonable degree of stability then London would go so far as to recognise a Provisional Czechoslovak Government legally established in Britain, but in so doing they did not commit themselves to any territorial considerations whatsoever, either in terms of pre-war boundaries or postwar intentions. Beneš was jubilant. A political career which less than two years earlier had been in tatters had now been resurrected due to the fortunes of war, and as we shall see shortly, he had every intention of using his armed forces – and particularly his air force – to consolidate his position in time for the final victory.

But this was far from a purely one-sided agreement. The British also gained much by casting off their principles and allowing Beneš a foothold in the allied camp. Provisional status for his administration meant that in diplomatic terms he was only a temporary commandant, therefore he did not receive an ambassador, only a 'political representative', initially Robert Bruce Lockhart.[14] It also meant that he was not an ally in the strictest sense, and after a few manipulations of the lexicon he was described as being 'allied to the cause of His Majesty'. This status did not compel the British to consult him on any military or political matters whatsoever unless those issues directly affected Czechoslovak affairs. Furthermore, the British could now make hay in the field of propaganda because it could be made to appear that the terrible business over Munich had been put to one side and written off as an error of the previous administration under Chamberlain. Also, the new 'union' could be portrayed in the occupied territory as a genuine alliance against German aggression, perhaps stimulating the home Resistance into greater action than it had hitherto displayed. Lastly, and perhaps most important of all, any problems encountered with the Czechoslovak service personnel regarding military shortcomings could immediately be laid at Beneš's door, and given the rather grim British assessment of them before the French defeat, such an option was welcome indeed.

This attitude in part explains why the incoming air personnel were enrolled or commissioned into the RAFVR on arrival in Britain. The same tactic had been applied to the Poles in the early days of the war, but whereas the Polish Air Force had substantial political and military grounds on which it could legitimately claim the right to independent status, the Czechs had no such advantages. The British had every intention of minimising the opportunities open to Beneš to gain prestige and political influence. Furthermore, independence would allow him to press for the application of Czechoslovak military law, and the British were determined to avoid this as well. Given the amount of political, national and even religious disunity within the entire Czechoslovak group, freedom of jurisdiction in Czechoslovak hands was seen as a dangerous power to confer. The British decided to again minimise the limits to which men might be persecuted or intimidated simply because their beliefs or political persuasions did not coincide with those held by their superiors, and we shall see that this decision was almost certainly the correct one. These two reasons – political influence and jurisdiction – formed the basis of the British argument for installing the entire Czechoslovak Air Force into the RAFVR, much against the wishes of Beneš and his commanders. The battle ground was to be the construction of the Anglo-Czechoslovak military agreement.

The Czechoslovaks got their bid for independence in early. Having been granted a form of independence by the French, largely impotent though it may have been, quite naturally they looked to the British for similar terms. In a memo to the Air Ministry drafted on 18 July, three days before recognition was granted to the Provisional Government, they called for the 'rapid formation of Czechoslovak air establishments/air bases provided with British instructors and technical advisers.' These units would serve 'in co-operation with the RAF' – in other words, not as part of it.[15] Claiming one hundred victories for only twenty casualties in France – a highly unlikely statistic given the amount of action – they supported their argument by enclosing a copy of the French Agreement, Article 1 of which read: 'The creation of independent Czechoslovak fighter and bomber units is permitted within the framework of the French Air Force', together with the full retention of original rank. An added opinion was that language difficulties would make it impracticable for the men to be drafted directly into the RAF, thus independent bases and command would be the only sensible option. Ensuring that their ideas were not misunderstood, the memo ended with an unequivocal statement:

> This [French] Agreement in its completeness met the needs of the Czechoslovak Air Force and justified itself in practice. It would therefore perhaps be appropriate if the situation of the Czechoslovak Air Force in England were regulated by an Agreement of similar type.[16]

But the British were having none of this. Much of the spadework was still being done by Porri, and he had already been well briefed by the Air Ministry. He was told that in all future communications with the Czechoslovaks he was to stress 'the great practical convenience of enrolment in the RAFVR', and he was supplied with a rough draft of the proposed agreement that contained no mention of independent status.[17]

The baton was then taken up by the Allied Forces (Official) Sub-Committee (AFOSC) at its first meeting on 29 July. Turning to the demand tabled by the Czechoslovaks for independence, William Strang indicated the essential similarities to the agreement drawn up for the Poles but, he argued:

> The Provisional Czechoslovak Government will doubtless be content with a good deal less than the Polish Government. The Czechs are less obsessed with issues of prestige than are the Poles and are unlikely to put forward extravagant demands.[18]

He could not have been further from the truth. Prestige was *everything* to Beneš, and if Strang had been more sensitive to the deeper political history he would have known that.[19]

Porri also had an impact on these deliberations. He told the meeting that many of the pilots would prefer to remain under British command in British squadrons 'rather than be transferred to the Czechoslovak authorities in whom they had some reason to place only qualified reliance'. He added that morale might suffer should a policy of full independence be adopted. A subsequent minute, struck from the official record, reflects this opinion in unequivocal terms: '[Strang] said that, if necessary, pressure would be brought to bear upon President Beneš to obtain the concurrence of the Czechoslovak authorities with the existing arrangements', by which he meant compulsory entry into the RAFVR.[20] Any hopes that Beneš may have had for independence were effectively crushed by this statement.

The Czechs did not take this lying down. They wanted what the Poles were getting, so Beneš sent one of his senior foreign affairs advisers, Dr Hubert Ripka, to see Strang in person. According to Strang, Ripka 'attached the utmost importance for reasons of prestige to having a separate air force under their jurisdiction', but Strang – perhaps unwittingly confirming Bruce Lockhart's unfavourable impression of him as a lightweight – felt it best to side-step the question and refer Ripka back to the Air Ministry – not that he would obtain any satisfaction there either. The British then argued that the Czechs simply did not have the manpower for a fully independent air force, and that substantial British assistance would be needed to keep such a body operational. This was reasonable enough in itself, but as we shall see with the French, it was a principle which the RAF was prepared to bend if it kept the peace. However, the French were not the Czechoslovaks, and there was less political pressure involved, so in the end the RAF stuck by its decision and let the Czechs take it or leave it. With the only other option on the table being the dispersal of their pilots across the entire Royal Air Force, they took it.

Thus, the Air Ministry got its way. The Czechoslovaks went into the RAFVR, and there they stayed for the rest of the war. There was also the question of jurisdiction rights. Porri's argument that men might not have felt comfortable serving under Czechoslovak military law was not without substance, but the core of the matter lay in the multitude of different personalities and political views which the entire Czechoslovak forces contained. On the one hand, this made dissent in the ranks more likely; on the other, it raised question marks over the likelihood of the army and air components acting as a single body in pursuit of a single cause: the defeat of fascism.

As if to underline British concerns about Czechoslovak reliability, a major disturbance erupted immediately after the remnants of the land forces had encamped at Cholmondeley Park in Cheshire. Up to 550 men had mutinied, some claiming that Czechoslovak officers were displaying virulent anti-Semitism, others because they had communist sympathies and refused to fight a 'capitalist war'. This latter group had seen action as mercenaries in Spain, and most chroniclers of the event lay the blame squarely on them, but the British were appalled. The disorders were discussed in the War Cabinet of 26 July, and Beneš was coerced into sending the disaffected into the Pioneer Corps out of harm's way. Even so, it was omitted from the Cabinet discussions that conditions in the camp were of poor quality, a fact brought to the attention of the War Office by the British Council which paid a visit in the early days.[21]

Less well known is the fact that the mutiny spread to the air force contingent as well, and in this case the authority of Beneš to govern was seriously tested. In August 1940, Beneš received two reports which originated in the Czechoslovak squadrons based at Honington and Duxford. Nearly one-third of the entire air contingent gave its support to a series of grievances – some trivial, others not so – which in total threatened not only Beneš's precarious hold on power, but also the very existence of the Czechoslovak Air Force itself. One of the major bones of contention lay in the extremely high officers-to-men ratio with which the force had been lumbered after the retreat from France. For reasons examined in Chapter Two, the Czechoslovaks struggled to build a working system with one officer to every four men. Consequently, some officers were demoted to NCO, while some NCOs felt they should be officers, and other ranks declared that there were too many NCOs *and* officers, and that this impeded their progress. Furthermore, the British system of ranking was more restrictive than the Czechoslovak version, so there were fewer promotion slots available, less money being earned, and therefore dissatisfaction all round. In short, almost everyone wanted to be an officer, commissioned or otherwise.[22]

The senior officer who dealt with this was Gen Antonin Nižborsky. He chose to shift the blame onto the British, pointing out that nothing he could do would have any effect on their system of ranking. Essentially, he did nothing at all, but then what could he have done? Short of promoting everybody who demanded it, which would have been ludicrous, he had little choice but to turn away from the problem and hope it resolved itself. He was also faced with other complaints from the lower ranks which accused some officers of defeatism or malpractice while in France, and here he argued that no evidence existed to pursue the charges so no further action would be taken.

If Nižborsky believed that the problems would go away of their own accord, he was very much mistaken. Within two weeks he was writing to Beneš and warning of a potential total collapse of discipline if immediate action was not taken. Centred on the depot at Cosford, but including elements from the other two stations mentioned above, a list of demands formulated with the backing of some 450 pilots and ground crew was presented to Nižborsky. The five demands were: (1) The removal of Brig Gen Slezák as C-in-C and Inspector of the Air Force; (2) the replacement of other senior officers with active fliers, and not 'office types'; (3) the reassessment of individual abilities and skills to meet the new conditions of war; (4) a total overhaul of the officer corps, with new officers appointed based on qualifications and knowledge; (5) an investigation into the use of telephones for personal calls during the retreat from France, which, it was claimed, delayed or obstructed the transmission of orders and thus affected the evacuation, possibly even costing lives.[23]

Nižborsky illustrated these complaints with examples. He noted a 'significant lack of confidence' among the men because of the 'unacceptable behaviour of the officers', claiming that they did little but drink, gamble and make fools of themselves in front of the other ranks: 'The English military police brought back several officers at 3 a.m. and they were so drunk they had to be carried from the vehicles.' He then condemned the refusal of the rebels to obey orders, but added that they were aware that a formal mutiny would harm their cause in England and were determined to solve the problem peacefully and with as little fuss as possible. The accusations against Slezák were that he had promoted certain favoured men, threatened the rebels with courts-martial, and blatantly attempted to hinder the evacuation from France. Other officers, not named by Nižborsky, were accused of weakness, low moral fibre, defeatism and collaboration with the enemy, promising doubters that the Germans would permit their return to the Protectorate without punishment if they left immediately. Some politicians were also subjected to harsh criticism.

This time it was Beneš himself who responded, but after some considerable delay. Shortly before the signing of the Anglo-Czechoslovak Agreement in October, he penned a reply which aligned himself with the present leadership of the air force which, in his opinion, 'was not badly led'. Slezák had already been removed as a concession to the rebels, and Karel Janoušek installed as Inspector, but Beneš felt that one sacrificial head was

a small price to pay for stability. What he was not prepared to
tolerate was censure of his political judgement:

> With regard to the removal of politicians which during
> the French action did not show adequate abilities or
> understanding, if the writers of the Memorandum are
> sincere when they say that they give the President confidence
> in everything, they must have confidence in all political
> questions, including membership of the Government.[24]

Having scraped through on recognition with the pretence
of political unity – a charade clearly perceived by the British
government but ignored for reasons of convenience – and having
survived a substantial revolt in the army fuelled by political and
perhaps racial and religious tensions, a political rebellion in
the air force would have been the end for Beneš as the credible
leader of his émigré government. Addressing the complaints
made against the officers, he repeated Nižborsky's earlier defence
by requesting concrete information, claiming that misconduct in
France was 'clearly unsupported', that many officers had actually
assisted with some evacuation costs from their own pockets, that
at no time were officers compromised during the evacuation by
divided loyalties, either to the French or the Germans, and that
he would personally consider any reasonable and sustainable
grievance that was presented.

Four days after this despatch, the Agreement was signed with
the British and the Czechoslovaks. Much celebration greeted this
news, and a good many hot heads cooled down a little. But the
President's authority had been bruised; to forestall a mutiny, he
had had to sacrifice a brigadier general and nine other officers
to restore order.[25] Had mutiny occurred, then it would have been
almost certain that the British would have stepped in, dissolved
the entire air contingent – which barely had enough men to
function as a national group anyway – and selected the best pilots
and mechanics for dissemination across the RAF organisation.
Few had doubts about the real reasons for the trouble, and most
of the blame fell on a few agitators within the Cosford group.
Their aims were not military but political, but it was clear that
some air force staff had sufficiently angered the ranks while in
France to secure their mass support for what was ultimately a
political agenda.

Ironically, it was the sacrificed commander, Slézak, who
isolated the root cause of the problem. He clearly understood
that the British had organised the Czechoslovaks in such a way

as to remove all but the most trivial powers of discipline from them. The military agreement completely forbade the use of Czechoslovak military law, and although this applied to the other exiled forces to greater or lesser degrees, it particularly restricted the Czechoslovak authorities in the early months, when the process of settling down was proving so stormy. Slézak commented on the tendency of some of the men to disobey orders or foment discontent in the full knowledge that it was RAF practice to simply throw them out of the force into the Czechoslovak Army or the Pioneers. Thus some individuals – 'weaker elements', he called them – could manoeuvre a cushy number for themselves simply by turning in slapdash work, indulging in some political agitation against the establishment, or even delivering a bit of well-timed insubordination. In the face of such tactics, the Czechoslovak High Command was powerless. Where before the war it would have come down upon the offender with the full force of its own military law, now it had to sit impotently by and watch the British commanders usher the shirkers and the malcontents out of the ranks with little more than a censure. To Beneš, this was an urgent problem, and one which demanded a meeting with the British at the earliest opportunity.

The meeting of 16 January 1941 was convened primarily to discuss the issue of jurisdiction, but may have been motivated by difficulties in 311 (Bomber) Squadron. The then Director of the DAFL, AVM Alfred Collier, had earlier written to Kalla in response to a letter which highlighted a growing problem in the squadron. A number of men were refusing to fly on operations over occupied territory because (a) they feared capture, and (b) in the event of capture, they were concerned that their families would be punished. Kalla asked if the Air Ministry would consider permitting the offenders to be stripped of all rank, dressed in khaki and not RAF blue, and kept on the relevant station to perform labouring duties. Such a punishment, argued Kalla, would be mild if one considered that the men were essentially being charged with cowardice. Collier replied curtly that it was not British practice 'to conduct demotion in such a theatrical manner'. He added that the press might get wind of such a practice and label it as 'Gestapo tactics; that is, tactics against which Great Britain is fighting'. Rejecting the scheme without reservation, he rubbed salt in the wound by pointing out that all service within the RAFVR was technically voluntary, and that this differed from conscripted service and brought with it a relaxation of normal military discipline. In his opinion, discharge to other services was perfectly suitable.[26]

The Czechs retired to plan their next attempt at wresting somepower from the grip of the British. Beneš volunteered the view that since the Battle of Britain, the RAF was regarded as the elite military arm, therefore dismissal from the force was seen as little more than gross humiliation, punishment in itself. Seeking to block this loophole, Gen Sergěj Ingr argued for a compromise that would enable the Czechoslovak authorities to formally try an offender but leave the choice of punishment up to the British, and with this he was successful.[27] After sitting on the request for four months, the DAFL eventually granted permission for the establishment of Reprimanding Courts that would convene before or after the man's dismissal from the RAFVR. In effect, these would be little more than show trials, with the sentence already fixed by the British. As far as they were concerned, troublesome Czechoslovaks were a problem for the Provisional Czechoslovak Government, but only *after* they had been expelled from the RAFVR.

This argument over jurisdiction serves to illustrate much about the Anglo–Czechoslovak relationship in general, and the tensions within the Czechoslovak group in particular. Equally, it is important not to overestimate the effects of these troubles in the Czechoslovak Air Force during the autumn of 1940 and the early days of 1941. The threatened rebellions in the force and the command difficulties in 311 Bomber Squadron should not lead us to conclusions of cowardice or base weakness. Very few men in that squadron had ever seen combat in a bomber – one of the most terrifying jobs in the air war – and losses had been hard to bear and difficult to replace. Further, the knowledge that capture by the enemy could lead to the deaths or imprisonment of their families in the Protectorate forced some to either seek service in a fighter squadron or simply refuse to fly. In response, the Beneš government became heavy-handed, humiliating men before their peers and seeking the right to apply its own military codes towards these individuals. Understandably, the British refused.

Yet when 450 officers and men banded together and demanded the removal of certain officers from their midst, Beneš meekly complied. No doubt, what he might well have done was to throw the lot into the Pioneers or seek internment for them all, but to do so would have torn the heart out of his air force, and his prestige would have collapsed. He and his general staff (with at least the exception of Janoušek) felt able to browbeat a man who did not want to die for them, but in the face of organised revolt the Beneš regime was shown to be virtually powerless. As for the British, all they wanted was peace in the camp, as long as they remained the principal authority and the ultimate arbiters of justice. Perhaps it was as well for the Czechoslovak officers and airmen that they did.

PART TWO: 1941–3

In the main, there were only two issues which plagued the Czechoslovak Air Force throughout the period of exile in Britain during the war: recruitment and the quest for independent status. Both caused political and military difficulties between the Czechoslovaks and their British hosts, and also between the Czechoslovaks themselves, and neither was ever resolved to the complete satisfaction of either party. Of these two, recruitment was by far the most serious issue. Whereas the other exiled groups could draw men for air force replacement or expansion from a variety of resources – a large land force, a steady flow of escapees from Europe, or sympathetic support elsewhere in the world, particularly North America – the Czechoslovaks were forced to work hard for every man they placed in RAF uniform. They had a small contingent of men in the Middle East engaged on anti-aircraft and other duties (and this group rendered excellent service in the defence of Tobruk), but other than this potential source of further recruits, little else was at hand.

In mid-January 1941, Beneš wrote to Archibald Sinclair on the subject of air reinforcements. By this time, Beneš had a surplus of pilots, enough to form a third fighter squadron, but virtually no available ground crew with which to maintain it. He declared that the secondment of men from the land forces to fill the skills gap would be 'extremely difficult'.[28] Beneš was armed with a report from Ingr which dismissed any proposals to siphon troops from the army, claiming that recruitment here was also very limited and that 'we will need all types of war experience, not only from the air force, but also in all types of weapons in ground units back home.'[29] This was a weak spot for Beneš. He was constantly aware that 'back home' he would immediately have need of a viable and efficient military organisation to maintain order and resist any revolutionary action against his government, so he followed Ingr's lead and sent his letter to the Secretary of State. Sinclair replied two weeks later, again urging the release of troops from the army into the air force, insisting that there would be no third squadron unless the Czechs supplied their own aircraft hands.[30]

The problem was actually much worse than Sinclair realised. A comprehensive report prepared by Janoušek for Ingr had been circulated during the week before Sinclair's letter. In it, Janoušek described the situation as 'critical'. Even so, he fully accepted the need for a third fighter squadron to be formed as soon as possible:

> The argument for building a new fighter squadron is that, up to now, the Czechoslovak Air Force in France and here in England is our most powerful and political force in this war. Our army could not be fully evaluated because of the chaotic days in France [thus] the air force can be used for political and propaganda purposes whereas the army cannot.

Discussions regarding the formation of a third fighter squadron had actually begun in late 1940, it being clear to all parties that the large surplus in flying personnel would have to be employed in some fighting capacity. It was agreed that 126 mechanics and 100 troops for unskilled labour would be needed, and it was in this latter group that the shortfall was most keenly felt. The Air Ministry had offered some assistance with mechanics, but saw no reason to supply auxiliary troops when the Czechoslovak Army was inactive at Leamington Spa.[31] But at this point in January 1941, Janoušek identified a minimum requirement of 108 unskilled men to be immediately released from the army, requesting an urgent decision by Beneš if necessary.[32]

Sinclair's letter followed a few days later. Within a week of its receipt, Beneš had convened a top-level conference to discuss the matter. Stanislav Bosý, the Deputy Chief of Staff, revealed that the air force was 170 men short of the full complement, yet there were still 528 people of military age available for possible service, of whom 250 might prove suitable. Of these, 170 must go to the air force 'since it is not possible to consider weakening the land units.' Any recruits displaying 'lack of morale' could be sent to the Pioneers. Ingr countered that the Canadian government had not encouraged either Czechoslovaks or Poles to enlist in the British forces, but added that 'it is a matter of life and death' that more men be enlisted from whatever source. Beneš, still pushing for a third fighter squadron for political reasons, stressed that the army was in itself a symbol of political status, and that his main objective was a fully recognised Czechoslovak government. Without a credible military contingent, that aim was unlikely to be achieved easily. Ingr felt that any expansion or reduction of the air force would have no significant effect either way, but Beneš refuted this, insisting upon a third fighter squadron, with or without reserves. Slezák bluntly, said that if this was to be the policy, 'we have no choice but to transfer them from the army'. Ingr immediately reacted negatively, stating that neither the Air Ministry nor the War Office would even consider such a scheme. With this, Ingr was either being deliberately deceptive or was criminally ill-informed, for both of those departments were practically begging the Czechoslovaks to move men from the army into the air force. Some strong disagreement between the two followed, until Beneš closed the meeting with a request for more specific details on requirements and possible sources of personnel.

Beneš received his report swiftly, and with it came the shortages for February 1941: 311 (Bomber) Squadron was operating at only 66 per cent strength in flying personnel and at 80 per cent strength in ground crew. Both 310 and 312 Fighter Squadrons were up to strength in flying personnel, but were suffering from lack of ground crew, 310 operating at 85 per cent and 312 at a mere 50 per cent of the total establishment. The MNO totals for the whole force clearly illustrate that perennial problem which had faced them ever since the evacuation from France – too many officers and not enough other ranks. The air contingent showed a surplus of flying personnel (all of whom were either commissioned officers or NCO pilots) of 227, whereas the current shortfall of ground crew was 167. Should a third fighter squadron be created, the latter number would rise to 369, and this could only be made up with British assistance, rigid conscription, or by further depleting the establishment of the land unit. This last point Ingr flatly refused to contemplate. When Sinclair was informed, he replied:

> I am sorry that it has not been possible for you to release men from the Czechoslovak Army for service in your air force, and I agree that the figures you have supplied show that the number of men becoming available for air force service is unlikely to be large . . . The Air Staff must, I am sure you will agree, reconsider the question of forming a third fighter squadron, more especially as the men now becoming available will need considerable training before they can be regarded as fit for service.[33]

We should pause at this stage to reflect upon these meetings and consider the impact of the manpower shortages on the Czechoslovak Air Force. The whirl of reports, statistics and correspondence of January and February 1941 indicate that the excitement of the previous summer and autumn had passed into history, and that some harsh realities now had to be addressed. In the first instance, 'shortfall' does not refer to a literal absence of men in any given unit. British personnel had been posted to supplement the establishments where Czechoslovak nationals were unavailable, for without a full complement of ground crew a squadron would have been declared non-operational. As Sinclair stated, it was the policy of the Air Ministry to ensure that allied squadrons were 'whole' in terms of nationality, thus pressure was constantly applied to achieve that aim. Furthermore, each of the four squadrons was operating without any credible ground reserves, and this meant that rotation was not possible. Each man thus worked to his physical limit, and the effect on morale and efficiency was not unnoticed by the MNO. Yet even without adding reserves into the equation, the air contingent still relied on the presence of 240 (mainly British) support staff, which the Air Ministry wanted back. Not surprisingly, the idea of forming 313 (Fighter) Squadron was dropped as soon as the truth became apparent.

Also, the meetings of February 1941 revealed differences of attitude within the MNO which were serious. Janoušek and Slezák recognised the great importance of the air force for political, military and propaganda reasons, and in their view *any* source of recruitment was a valid one. However, Ingr – an army man if ever there was one – took the view that the existing force was overstretched anyway and that the land unit would lose all credibility if its complement was whittled away.

To meet the current, and future, manpower requirements, the MNO had little room for manoeuvre. There were only three feasible sources: overseas (specifically Canada and America); the Middle East contingent of the army, and whatever was left in Britain. The real hope was Canada. Early recruitment based simply on press releases was thoroughly disappointing, with only two Czechs, four Slovaks, one German and one German Jew stepping forward in 1940. The Czechoslovak Consular-General in New York, Col Oldřich Španiel, rejected the latter two and minuted London that 'more intensive propaganda activity' was needed, perhaps even a fully military mission. He also added, rather woefully, that the majority of people in Canada were Slovaks rather than Czechs, 'and on the whole we are talking a worker's element here'.[34]

Things were not going to get any easier, not least because the attitude of the Canadian government was at best cool, and the general attitude of the British government can only be described as indifferent. This is not to suggest that obstacles were deliberately placed before the interested parties, but rather that they were more or less left to fend for themselves. Both the Poles and the Czechoslovaks were keen to raise volunteers in North America, and early in 1941 had submitted formal requests through the British government to organise recruiting activity, yet the Canadian Defense Ministry promised only 'sympathetic consideration'. Another problem was the cost of the projected exercise, in that the Poles freely admitted that they had no available finances, the Canadians refused to contribute anything, the British Government felt 'unable' to sacrifice dollar reserves, and the War Office had expressed 'the strongest possible objections' to paying for the scheme. In committee, however, the Air Ministry advanced the view that the Poles 'were outstandingly good pilots', and that it would welcome additional recruits to counter any possible shortage which might occur in 1941, thereby leaving open the possibility that it might obtain extra manpower at virtually no cost and effort to itself.[35]

In essence, then, the Czechoslovaks had to rely upon sentimental appeals to people who had forsaken the nationality of their birth to fight for a country they no longer belonged to. Having found such people, they then had to bear upon themselves the not inconsiderable cost of transporting and training them to possibly sacrifice their lives in what was, after all, a common war effort. The Air Ministry, itself absolved from responsibility by the AFOSC decision, then moved relatively quickly to establish an agreement with the Czechs concerning Canadian recruitment. Yet even here we see the Air Ministry, while ostensibly presenting the Czechoslovaks with a solution to their problems, nevertheless acting in its own interests as well. At first capping the maximum number of enlistments at 100 every three months – 'to make good the estimated normal wastage' – it added the tempting offer that surplus volunteers might be enlisted at a further rate of 15 every three months, 'for service with British single-seater fighter squadrons', knowing full well that these men would speak excellent, or at least adequate, English.[36] Regarding expenditure, the Agreement euphemistically stated that all costs would be met from 'the credits granted by His Majesty's Government', which meant that the Czechoslovaks would pay eventually.

It seems clear from this that as a viable recruiting ground, Canada was effectively barren from the Czechoslovak point of view. Neither can it be said that the blame rested on the Czechoslovaks: it was more of a combination of the Canadian and British attitudes which stifled such chances there were for the émigrés to boost their dwindling numbers. In the main, the reasons were political and not military, and have much to do with Beneš's political machinations. On 19 April 1941, Churchill inspected the Czechoslovak Army at Leamington Spa, after which Beneš handed him a formal note essentially calling for full recognition of his Provisional Government. In this document, he clearly laid the blame at the door of the Foreign Office for the lack of full recognition, as a consequence of which the Czechoslovaks were considered as 'allies of the second category':

> The reasons invoked by the Foreign Office for the continuation of this policy were 'legal' difficulties. In fact, it is the remnant of the Munich policy. Our people here and at home feel it is unjust and a continuation of the Munich humiliation.[37]

Yet again Beneš had demonstrated his profound lack of touch when it came to the delicacies of British diplomacy, for the effect was not far short of catastrophic. Seeking to defend themselves, the men of the Central Department looked for allies of their own. The representatives of the Dominions were contacted one by one and sounded out for their views of full recognition for the Beneš government-in-exile. After much grumbling, Australia, New Zealand, South Africa and, after a long delay, Canada, reluctantly agreed. What matters here is that these mutterings of discontent were put on record, and could be used against Beneš if he persisted in accusing the Foreign Office of conducting 'a Munich policy' against him. In the savage world of exile politics, it is not wise to upset the servants of the host.[38]

The Canadians thus had no incentive and no obligation to extend anything more than indifferent assistance to the Beneš administration when it tried to recruit volunteers from North America. They had recognised the Provisional Government on 28 October 1940, more as an act of solidarity with London than a bold political stroke. Yet it was friendship cheaply bought, and this held good for all the Dominions. When the time came to actually do something constructive, especially regarding financial assistance, they folded their arms.

The Czechoslovaks reacted to the paucity of new blood in a desperate way by accepting back into their ranks some of the men thrown into the Pioneer Corps the previous summer. Within weeks, about fifty had been released and were used to fill the ranks of auxiliary ground personnel in Czechoslovak air units. When the Soviet Union was attacked in June 1941, the exodus became a flood. A 'considerable part' of the contingent sent to the Pioneers in 1940 was now seeking a return to the army, claiming they had been talked into revolt by agitators within Cholmondeley Camp, that they now sought 'forgiveness for their actions', and that unless they played their part in the war effort, 'their return home would not be a good or joyful one'.[39]

From the point of view of Janoušek, however, his air force gained nothing from this exercise. In early September 1941, he convened a meeting to discuss further recruitment and it was decided from the outset that the air force would be at a political disadvantage if it were shown to be receiving men who had earlier been thoroughly discredited.[40] It was accepted that only two realistic possibilities existed: either divert all the new recruits into the air force, or disband at least two of the squadrons in order to make the remaining two wholly Czechoslovak. The meeting was told that 311 Bomber Squadron had such a deficiency in ground crew that it operated with barely a third of the establishment enjoyed by British bomber squadrons, with the result that 'to ensure operations, the Czechoslovak ground crew work day and night in the worst possible conditions'. Touching upon the influx from the Pioneer Corps, it was noted that the army was now passing on men who were 'completely incapable' of adjusting to air force requirements, and because 311 was a fully operational unit, there was no time to spend on basic military training. It was better to receive no men at all from the army rather than substandard individuals. The only other option was to disband the small Middle East contingent and return them all to Britain for re-training.

We see here an air force in crisis. One squadron (313) was operating entirely due to British assistance on the ground, while another (311) was being worked to a standstill, yet powerful voices were refusing to erode the combat strength of the army any further. This situation had arisen simply because half of the Czechoslovak High Command persisted in looking ahead to the day of liberation, when a land and air presence might well be vital, and the other half concentrated on the conduct of the business in hand: fighting the war they were already in, and not a potential conflict at some undetermined date. Janoušek desperately tried to get them to understand that if they threw all their efforts into building up a crack air arm while they were in Britain and had all the resources at their disposal, this in itself would be a major advantage when the time came to return home. Foot soldiers could be found almost anywhere, but combat-toughened fighter pilots were worth their weight in gold.

It was a battle which Janoušek carried on throughout 1942, and all the while the numbers kept dwindling. From time to time Ingr permitted him to draft a handful of replacements from the army, but these tended only to replace existing vacancies and were never enough to facilitate expansion of any long-term training programmes. Whenever Janoušek approached Beneš for arbitration in the dispute, he received the inevitable compromise, for Beneš had no intention of pushing Ingr to his limits. It was at this point that the Air Ministry became involved, and there can be little doubt that Janoušek himself had brought the matter to the attention of senior officials within that department. He was a trusted man within British circles, and he would have been aware that to move Ingr from his position of intransigence, he would need powerful allies, thus we see a letter of great importance pass between Sinclair at the Air Ministry and Eden at the Foreign Office in early July 1942. The former wrote to the Foreign Secretary:

> I feel that I should let you know without delay of a serious
> state of affairs which has arisen and is bound to grow worse,
> unless corrected now, in regard to the Czech Air Force.[41]

He continued by outlining the present condition of the contingent: that it consisted of four squadrons with approximately 1,300 men, and that the units had, until that moment, been maintained at their established strength from the existing reserves and recruitment. He then added that these reserves were 'rapidly drying up, and unless more are forthcoming the squadrons will have to be rolled up and will gradually disappear'. He told Eden that all attempts to persuade the Czechoslovaks to release men from the army to meet the estimated wastage had failed:

> . . . but for reasons best known to himself, Dr Beneš is not
> prepared to allow this: all he has done so far is to instruct
> General Ingr in the Middle East to see if he can make any
> savings in men in the reorganisation of the Czech Forces
> there. This, however, will only provide about 100 men, which
> is totally inadequate to maintain the Czech Air Force at its
> present strength.
>
> I need hardly say how perturbed I am by the thought
> that such a gallant little force should be broken up,
> particularly in view of the valuable service it gave to the
> Royal Air Force at a time when we ourselves were short
> of trained pilots. Moreover, the political and military
> repercussions which would result from its disappearance
> would, I think, be unfortunate.

In the short term, nothing was done. The Air Ministry made its own enquiries and determined that a small force of around 200 could be taken from the Middle East 'sufficient to maintain the Czech Air Force at its existing strength for some four months'. Pressure was then brought to bear upon Beneš to the effect that if he did not agree to the transfer of the entire Middle East group back to Britain to make up the recruitment deficit, the Air Ministry would be forced to intervene and roll up one or more squadrons. This broke the deadlock, and in 1943, after the victory in North Africa, the force returned to Britain. Sadly for Janoušek, however, few were deemed suitable for air force training, so his lonely vigil for replacements continued. Out-ranked and out-argued by Ingr, and with little guidance from Beneš, it was a battle he could not win.

The net effect of this recruitment problem can be seen in the deployment patterns of the four Czechoslovak squadrons. In April 1942, 311 Bomber Squadron was moved from Bomber Command to Coastal Command, not because it was in any way inefficient, but because it was dangerously overworked and had enormous difficulty replacing operational losses. The three fighter squadrons also spent the majority of their time in quiet sectors, notwithstanding the year spent by 310 at Duxford during the Battle of Britain and the German bombing campaign which followed. A close analysis of the relative deployment patterns of all the smaller exiled contingents clearly shows that the Air Ministry gave them long periods of convoy patrol interrupted by much shorter periods in 'hot zones' like 11 Group in the south-east of Britain. This had nothing to do with distrust or military weaknesses. Rather, the RAF was well aware that recruitment for some of the forces was always going to be a problem, so any strategy which minimised losses was welcomed by both parties. In the case of the Czechoslovaks, that policy was continued long after D-Day when each of the fighter squadrons spent only one day on the Continent before returning to Britain, whereas all the other European groups accompanied the advancing allies across France and into Germany.[42]

There may also have been a political dimension to this. A more active involvement in the liberation of Europe might have given Beneš the opportunity to press for a seat at the peace table, and for the British that would have been a ghastly prospect. Furthermore, by keeping losses to a minimum, the policy also aided Janoušek in his struggle to maintain the force at fighting strength, and we know that he was by far the most popular member of the Czechoslovak High Command in British eyes.

He was in the perfect position to offset the restrictions placed upon him by his own leadership by speaking to the right men inside the RAF, and it is not beyond the bounds of possibility that he negotiated deployment policies which ensured that each man learned his craft and stood a fair chance of surviving the war to apply his skills at home. From the moment when he had replaced Slézak as Inspector-General, he had been advocating the careful cultivation of the air contingent as the basis of a postwar air force capable of defending the state. In that sense, he spent most of his war delicately balancing intake with losses, held back on the one hand by the desires of Beneš and Ingr to have the best of both worlds – an army *and* an air force, neither of which were ever fully up to strength – and helped by the RAF on the other hand by a policy which at least kept his valuable men away from the fiercest action for most of the time.

He was also closely involved with that other explosive issue: the quest for independent status. We know that in 1940 the RAF comprehensively blocked all attempts made by the Czechoslovaks to establish an independent force on the Polish model, and as far as the former were concerned, that was the end of the matter. But in late 1942, Beneš and his commanders conducted a full reappraisal of the situation and felt the time was right for another campaign. What triggered this resurgence is difficult to ascertain, as is a reason for the timing of the scheme. Beneš had won full recognition for his government-in-exile in 1941, largely at Eden's instigation and with the full backing of Churchill. Yet this did not make any material differences to his influence or position within the exile hierarchy. He received a full ambassador, Philip Nichols, and he was given greater air time on the BBC to address the homeland, but his ideas for postwar Europe and Czechoslovakia's place within it were still politely listened to by the Foreign Office, but always without any firm promise of commitment.

Even so, 1942 had been a good year for Beneš. His squadrons had performed admirably at Dieppe, and Reinhard Heydrich had been assassinated by British-trained operatives in June. Better still, the Munich Agreement had been repudiated by Eden in the House of Commons in August, and at last that dreadful stigma had been lifted – in public at least. So perhaps it was the combination of all of these successes which inspired Beneš to go back to the military agreement of 1940 and push for a full revision, but immediately he got off on the wrong foot by informing the British that the 1940 agreement had been concluded with an interim government which was now legally defunct and replaced by a sovereign administration, one which was fully entitled to independent forces. This was not a good strategy, for although he had a friend in Eden, his earlier outbursts against the men inside the Foreign Office meant that they were ill-disposed to do him any favours.

Together with his commanders, Beneš formulated a new agreement which gave much greater independence to his air force, and it is worth noting that he left the 1940 arrangements regarding the army entirely alone. To him, the air force was the supreme symbol of his resurrection as leader of Czechoslovakia and its future liberator, and aside from the men who served valiantly in the Middle East, the army had done nothing but train from the day it first set foot in Britain, not that this was its fault. The air force, however, had demonstrated its capabilities time and again, so his new vision of the future embodied full jurisdiction rights (which meant the application of Czechoslovak military law), the written promise of the British to make up any shortfalls in squadron establishments, and the right for his airmen to wear full Czechoslovak Air Force uniform. This last point was interpreted by the DAFL to mean that Beneš did not want his air force to return to Prague in a foreign uniform, and they were prepared to go some distance towards meeting that request, but the first two items were complete anathema to them. For two years they had fought running battles with the Czechoslovaks over jurisdiction and the practice of using British ground crew to shore up the Czech squadrons, and now here was Beneš taking a knife to barely healed wounds. This was going to be a bitter conflict indeed.

The ground crew question was the first point to be addressed. The DAFL commentary on the 1942 proposals reads:

> . . . it would be unfair to expect the Air Ministry to undertake such a commitment. There is little possibility of the Czechs obtaining substantial reinforcements for their air force, but rather than roll up any of their squadrons they will choose to draw upon Czechoslovak ground personnel as air crew, and will expect deficiencies thus occasioned to be made up by posting in British ground personnel. The RAF is also suffering from a shortage of ground personnel, and further it is contrary to the Air Staff's policy to man allied squadrons with British ground personnel.[43]

So much for that one. On the matter concerning full jurisdiction, the response was even more blunt:

The Czechs are a wasting asset and are already unable to
supply all the personnel for their squadrons. The position
will get worse as they have exhausted the possible sources of
recruitment and can only get new men by drawing them from
the Czech Army. The Czech Army are opposed to this course
and it is unlikely that they will produce many recruits. The
Czechs will therefore have squadrons which are partly Czech
and partly British, and it would not be satisfactory in their case
to have the Czech portion dealt with under Czech law.

This argument rested upon the principle that the other allied
squadrons were only permitted to apply their own military codes
when they had no British personnel at all, and that scenario
seemed as remote as ever in the Czechoslovak case in 1942.

Janoušek was aware that this would happen. From the very
outset he had been warning Beneš and Ingr that, try as they
might, they would not be able to shift the British from a position
based on as many political grounds as military. Furthermore,
he was directly against the application of Czechoslovak military
law, which he considered a potential cause of 'dissatisfaction
and embitterment' if men were forced to serve under it. A close
reading of the papers suggests that Janoušek had actually been
excluded from the preparations of the draft document, and his
many negative commentaries on it seem to bear this out. Indeed,
on one occasion he attacks the whole proposal as having been
prepared by 'an officer who does not know and cannot know the
realities in which the Czechoslovak Air Force lives and fights'.
This was almost certainly aimed at Ingr, indicating that the long-
running feud was far from over.[44]

Janoušek was distrusted by Beneš and disliked by Ingr, but as
far as the British were concerned, he was the best and most able
Czechoslovak officer associated with the air force. His men knew
him and trusted him, and he in return was never reckless with
their lives nor fought any battles except against Germans. But
although he was in his element with his own air force and the
wider field of the RAF, he was responsible to men who had many
personal and political scores to settle, and in the case of Ingr, a
man who had come down sharply in the world. At the time of
Munich, he was at the head of some thirty-six divisions of regular
troops, or nearly half a million men if reserves are included. In
Britain, he presided over less than five thousand, and it hurt.
It is not an easy thing to lose an army; still less easy to have one
simply down tools and throw in the towel, but in fighting hard to
maintain even that little bit he had left, Ingr seriously weakened

Gen Vuillemin (left), C-in-C of the French Air Force, on inspection in 1940.
(*Imperial War Museum C626*)

Gen Charles de Gaulle (centre) inspecting Free French pilots in 1941.
(*Imperial War Museum CH3856*)

Dutch Fokker T.VIII float-planes on patrol in 1940. Following the German invasion of Holland in May 1940, nine of these aircraft and their crews successfully escaped to England. (*Imperial War Museum CH1161*)

Dutch Navy pilots photographed soon after their arrival in the UK in 1940. (*Imperial War Museum CH1044*)

A group of Polish armourers in the classroom, 1940. (*Imperial War Museum CH1138*)

George VI inspecting the men of 300 and 301 (Polish) Bomber Squadrons, 1940. (*Imperial War Museum CH2024*)

A Czechoslovak airman in national uniform. (*Imperial War Museum CH1132*)

Czechoslovak air and ground crews of 311 Squadron, Coastal Command, beside a Liberator at Beaulieu in 1943. (*Imperial War Museum CH10689*)

Flying beer to the troops in Normandy: ground crew of 332 (Norwegian) Squadron fill a Spitfire's converted fuel tank with beer at Tangmere, July 1944. (*Imperial War Museum CH13488*)

Flt Off Wustefeld with Spitfires of 350 (Belgian) Squadron, October 1944. (*Imperial War Museum CL1364*)

Rear Adm Riiser-Larsen (Norway, left), meeting a pilot of an Anglo–Norwegian fighter-bomber wing in Belgium, 1944. (*Imperial War Museum CL1529*)

Polish air chiefs with their pilots in Belgium, 1944. From left to right: Flt Lt Krakowski; Flg Off Urban; Flt Lt Golko; AVM Izycki (C-in-C-of the Polish Air Force) and Air Cdre Kwiecinski (Polish Air Attaché). (*Imperial War Museum CL1533*)

President Edvard Beneš of Czechoslovakia with senior commanders. Karel Janoušek, the Czechoslovak Inspector-General, is in centre frame. (*Imperial War Museum CD3838*)

Allied air chiefs or their representatives in Belgium in 1944. From left to right: Rear Adm Riiser-Larsen (Norway); Col Savic (Yugoslavia); Col Van Berkelom (Holland); Grp Capt Schebal (Deputy Inspector General, Czechoslovakia); Grp Capt Kinatos (Greek Air Attaché); Air Lt Col Huang Pun-Yung (Chinese Air Attaché); Air Cdre Kweicinski (Polish Air Attaché); AVM Cassimatis (Greek Air Ministry); Col Hecksher (Brazilian Air Attaché); AVM Izycki (Poland) and Air Cdre Wouters (Belgian Inspector General). (*Imperial War Museum CL1527*)

Jubilant French airmen of 342 (Lorraine) Squadron back on French soil, 1944. (*Imperial War Museum CL1463*)

Czechoslovak airmen at a mission briefing. (*Imperial War Museum HU40538*)

the one fighting arm which was out there winning medals and shooting down Germans.

As for the DAFL, it was not remotely interested in political games or bruised egos. All it cared about was maintaining the Czechoslovak Air Force at fighting strength with little or no interference from anyone. In an unnecessary document – unnecessary because it addressed no particular points and was in fact little more than a stream of consciousness tacked onto the critique examined above – someone at the DAFL took the time and trouble to record his thoughts with almost bullying frankness:

> The whole conception behind the Czechoslovak's desire to have more autonomy pre-supposes that the Czechoslovak Air Force is developing and expanding, and it seems that the Czechoslovak Air Force aspires to a position of importance which is not relevant to its size.
>
> We have always recognised the Czechoslovak Air Force as a political necessity; at the same time we cannot but regard it as a military luxury.
>
> The Czechoslovak Air Force is but a handful of personnel some 1,500 strong, hardly sufficient to man one small RAF station. Moreover, it is a wasting asset, for there seems to be not the slightest hope of obtaining recruits. Not only is expansion out of the question, but it is doubtful whether we shall be able to maintain it at its existing strength. The Czechoslovak Air Force has always been dependent upon the RAF, and this dependence is increasing and is likely to increase simply through lack of personnel.
>
> This request of the Czechs may be primarily a political one, because according to our information, many of the changes which would be consequent upon the introduction of the revised Agreement would be bitterly resented by some sections of the Czechoslovak Air Force. Although national feeling runs high in Czechoslovak subjects, it is curious that the Czechs think more highly of RAF decorations than their own. It is also noted that quite a number of Czech personnel do not wear the arm badge 'Czechoslovakia' because they like to be mistaken for RAF personnel.
>
> The Czechoslovak Air Force has been treated sympathetically and generously by the Air Ministry; its status as an RAFVR Air Force has given the Czechs many advantages and facilities which have had to be denied to other Allied Air Forces. The Czechoslovak Air Force would obviously be the principal loser if it withdraws from the RAF, although of

course, from our point of view the administrative problems
and complications following the withdrawal would be out of
all proportion to the size of the Czechoslovak Air Force and
the scale of its effort.

It looks very much as if having reaped a bumper harvest
in the Royal Air Force, the Czechs now wish to walk out
in search of other fields in which to sow. Perhaps we have
been too kind to the Czechs, but then we have had Munich
thrown in our face.

The Czechoslovaks suffer from a very exaggerated
inferiority complex, which is especially in evidence when
dealing with big neighbours, in particular with the Poles,
and they are always striving to go one better than their
neighbour. We have, however, found that it has been a
principle with them to ask for more than they think they will
get and they often undertake what it is not in their power to
accomplish. We cannot offer them much more; they have
as much independence, if not more, than most of the other
Allies, but as they are not self-sufficient, they cannot run
themselves by themselves.[45]

This was heavy stuff, even by Air Ministry standards, and it
should be clearly understood that the points made about some
men choosing not to wear the armband 'Czechoslovakia' and
preferring RAF decorations over Czechoslovak national awards
have been vehemently denied by veterans alive today. Even so, the
document throws much light on other RAF attitudes concerning
the Czechoslovak Air Force, and to describe them as a 'luxury'
was perhaps the worst of them. In the service of their homeland,
their government and the Western allies, over five hundred Czech
and Slovak airmen died, none of them luxuriously.

The author of this document was probably Sqn Ldr Hugh
Seligman, the head of the Czechoslovak section in the DAFL.
We cannot be certain because the document is unsigned,
but other evidence points to it originating from his office.
However, this is not to say that these views represented his own
personal opinions because Seligman would not have had the
authority to circulate such a paper so widely within the Air
Ministry without his superiors having read and approved it
first. We must therefore conclude that many, or perhaps all,
of the observations received the agreement of several senior
commanders, maybe even Frank Beaumont, who was then
the Director of the DAFL and who three years earlier had
championed the Czechoslovak cause so fervently.

None of the points raised in the critique or the above document were shown to the Czechoslovaks themselves. Indeed, had Beneš, Ingr or even Janoušek read the above, most likely a serious incident would have occurred. Yet the files give no indication that the papers ever left the Air Ministry save for one place, the Foreign Office, and here Beneš had no friends left any more.

The Foreign Office became involved in what should have been a strictly military matter because the Czechs had built in a diplomatic element. By insisting that the 1940 Agreement had been signed with a now defunct body, Beneš was throwing down the gauntlet to the men of the Central Department. In effect, he was saying: 'Recognise me now as the President of the Czechoslovak Republic and not some cast off from the failed politics of yesteryear.' To underline his position, he selected a minor incident from January 1943 involving an equally minor document, a Protocol redefining the financial arrangements between the two governments which had been signed by Sir Alexander Cadogan and Hubert Ripka. This, claimed Beneš through one of his envoys, breached Article 64 of the 1920 Constitution whereby only the President of the Republic may sign such an instrument, and to 'repair the damage done', the amended Anglo-Czechoslovak Military Agreement would need to be concluded between the respective heads of state, namely Beneš and King George VI. The Foreign Office was aghast at the thought of this little man, described by one historian as 'scarcely taller than a dwarf', demanding royal assent for so trifling a contract. Philip Nichols tried hard to convince the Czechs that diplomatic agreements of this nature were generally conducted at inter-governmental levels, but they would not be moved.[46]

The Foreign Office called for the Air Ministry's view, and we have seen what that was, in all its candour. With the papers came instructions. Jack Ward minuted:

> The Air Ministry, who were not aware that the Czechs were going to take the matter up with us diplomatically, would be glad if we could stall as long as possible on this proposal, which they assert is a purely political, prestige-hunting move by the Czechoslovak Government which would not be endorsed by a free vote of the Czechoslovak personnel.[47]

He added that the Air Ministry found it considerably easier to deal with allied air personnel who were in some capacity part of the RAF, and he concurred with the suggestion that the line of refusal should emphasise the danger to the men if they fell into enemy hands wearing the uniform of the Czechoslovak Air Force. This was because, as expressed in a later communication to the Air Ministry, 'the German Government have declared on various occasions that in view of their doctrine of the extinction of the Czechoslovak State before the outbreak of the present war, they do not recognise the reconstituted Czechoslovak forces as lawful combatants under international law'.[48] Clearly, the Foreign Office thought it better to frighten the Czechoslovak Government into withdrawing the scheme rather than persuading it to adopt it.

Yet there was also frustration in Ward's view of the matter. He pointed out to the Air Ministry that the argument that the 1940 Agreement had been improperly concluded implied that it had also been invalid for the three years during which it had been in force, and this alone meant the Czechs had acted in bad faith. He added: 'It seems unlikely that [they] realise the full implications of their own argument, and their real motive is doubtless to find a pretext for the conclusion of a 'Heads of State' Treaty which would mark in the eyes of the world their present status as a fully sovereign Allied Government.'

The buck was then passed to Philip Nichols, who took the matter up with Jan Masaryk, the Czechoslovak Minister for Foreign Affairs. Masaryk was American on his mother's side, and tended to be more easy-going with the British attitudes than some of his more nationalist colleagues. As son of the revered Tomaš Masaryk, the founder of the Czechoslovak state, he was the man to whom the British usually turned when things with Beneš were getting messy. The opinions of the Foreign Office and the Air Ministry – the latter in greatly sanitised form – were presented to him for review, and Masaryk promised to reply 'in due course'.

He kept his word. Having received the documents in August 1943, he did indeed reply 'in due course', but it took him a whole year to do it. Why there was such a delay is not possible to state with any certainty at present. The files contain no reference to the matter until August 1944, when Masaryk wrote to Nichols stating, 'I have now been asked by my Government to approach you again on this matter,' and he continued to outline the correspondence of the previous year. This seems to indicate that the one-year delay was caused by a genuine silence, and not simply absence of evidence, but in any case it was far too late and the momentum had been lost for ever. Most minds were now focused on the titanic battle then taking place for the liberation of Europe, and it is no surprise that the Foreign Office responded somewhat sluggishly, reminding the Air Ministry in mid-August that the matter had reappeared.

The DAFL was in no mood for this at all. The papers were passed from desk to desk until the Deputy Director, Alan Dore, wrote to the Director of Personal Services:

> These proposals are obviously political, and I know that the Czech Air Force had no hand whatsoever in drafting them. We have had an unofficial talk with Air Vice-Marshal Janoušek . . . who told me quite privately that in his opinion the Czechoslovak Government has merely brought the matter up again for national prestige.[49]

This clearly demonstrates that Janoušek was distancing himself from the whole scheme, though we know that he at least had a hand in some of the amendments. However, given the shambles it had become, perhaps he was more than justified in raising his hands and disowning the whole affair.

From that point in the late summer of 1944 until November, the revitalised proposals for independence were gradually whittled away until almost nothing was left. All serious consideration of the major points ceased, and the DAFL's focus fell upon the request that the Czechoslovak airmen should be permitted to wear their own national uniforms. This was toyed with by George Venn at Personal Services, but he came to the conclusion that it would 'highly incorrect' to sanction such a drastic modification of the King's uniform. A new compromise was then discussed. Dore put forward the idea that Czechoslovak cap badges and buttons could be substituted for their RAF variants, and he wrote to Venn suggesting that 'in all probability they would be content with this'. Venn rejected this too. There is some slight evidence that the matter went as high as Sinclair for a decision, and in October 1944 Dore wrote to the Foreign Office with the badges and buttons scheme seemingly fully approved. The twist, though, was that the Czechs could only modify the uniform in this way after they had left Britain for Czechoslovakia.

If we think back to Ingr's bold vision of full independence in the autumn of 1942, of the sceptical comments and cautious warnings of Janoušek, of the savaging the proposals received at the hands of the British, of the long and presently inexplicable delay in seeing the matter through to a conclusion, we arrive at a handful of nickel buttons and a sewing kit, and even that was not to be used until they each had one foot on the plane home. Yet still the torment was not at an end. Another month slipped

by then D.L. Stewart at the Foreign Office replied to Dore with
a summary of Masaryk's views: 'I confess our first reaction was
to wonder whether your proposal would really satisfy the Czechs
but [it] apparently went down quite well.' He also said Masaryk
was pleased but had a further request: '[He] at once asked me if
it would include badges of rank.'[50] According to Stewart, Philip
Nichols seemed to think that, because the contingent would be
out of the country anyway and this extra concession would mean
'a good deal to the Czechs', there would be little problem in it
being approved.

Nichols was wrong. Perhaps as a diplomatist he failed to
understand the service perspective of the King's uniform. Only
five days passed this time before Dore replied: 'I am not at all
happy about this.' Admitting that he had been 'very surprised' by
this extra request, he added, somewhat obviously:

> This would simply mean that both officers and other ranks
> would cease to hold Royal Air Force ranks and would be
> known by their Czechoslovak equivalents . . . If the Czech
> Foreign Ministry is going to press for inclusion of badges of
> rank also, then I think we shall have to reconsider the whole
> subject . . . You must admit that it is difficult to imagine
> a more ridiculous situation than to have a body of men
> serving as officers and other ranks of the Royal Air Force and
> wearing a uniform which bears no resemblance to that of the
> Royal Air Force apart from the material of which it is made.

Even from a distance of nearly sixty years, the indignation is
almost tangible. It certainly amazed Stewart, who minuted: 'I did
not think this affair could become even sillier than it was before,
but it has succeeded in doing so.'[51]

The whole sorry affair was wound up officially with a note
from Nichols to Masaryk in which the former stated: 'My
Government, after careful consideration, much regretted that
they could not, at this stage of the war, solve the practical and
jurisdictional problems arising'.[52] This was not true, because
such problems as there were could have been solved if the will
had been there to do so, but neither the Foreign Office (which
had little interest in the business anyway) nor the Air Ministry
(which did not want to be bothered with it right from the start)
had any intentions of moving an inch to accommodate the
Czechoslovak desires.

Except, of course, for the right to wear their own badges
and buttons. In December 1944, Patrick Dean wrote Nichols

a final line on the matter. Recalling that the Air Ministry had refused to grant the concession over ranks, he added that the Ministry had enlisted the aid 'of some of the Czechoslovak Air Force officers' to approach Masaryk and persuade him to drop the idea of full independence in favour of the badges and buttons. Who these officers were is not recorded; in fact it was all done 'with the greatest secrecy'. Dean suggested that Masaryk be told of the official view of the Air Ministry, but stressed that the officer involvement should be kept strictly confidential.[53] This seems to imply that the Air Ministry was up to murky tricks here, sending officers to do its spadework with the Czechoslovak Secretary for Foreign Affairs. Perhaps this was so, and perhaps it also proves that the British belief that many if not most of the men in the force would have recoiled from independence was valid after all.

PART THREE: 1944–5

The long and somewhat tortuous debate over the independence proposals of 1942 threw into stark relief the real relationship between the Air Ministry and the Czechoslovak Air Force in Britain. Yet we must be absolutely clear on one vital point: at no time were the ordinary men and officers of the force implicated in these various disputes during their time in exile. In fact, it has become clear through interviews with veterans that they themselves had no idea that this wrangling and pedantry was going on at the higher level. Even the bitter views of the Air Ministry were primarily directed towards the Czechoslovak High Command and the Beneš government; and as far as the RAF at Group level was concerned, the four squadrons conducted themselves with honour and courage throughout the war. No, these arguments were about two men – Beneš and Ingr – who continually pushed for more even though they knew full well that their chances of success were slight, but in so pushing merely irritated their hosts who for their part believed they had fulfilled all that could be reasonably expected of them.

Besides, in late August 1944 a new crisis had developed, something significant enough to relegate the squabbles over independence to the back of the stage. Acting on instructions received from London, Moscow and local commanders, a force of partisans and state troops in Slovakia turned against German divisions ordered into the country to quell rebel activity. It was a bloody affair that achieved only limited success. Although the rebels managed to hold on to central territories and the Red Army launched a massive offensive along the northern borders, huge German reinforcements crushed the uprising by mid-October at a cost of thousands of lives, both military and civilian.

However, at the start of the uprising, Beneš called for immediate RAF assistance with bombing strategic targets and dropping supplies to the partisans. As with all other communications from the European exiles not of a strictly military nature, the Air Ministry passed the request to the Foreign Office. Early in September, Frank Roberts wrote to the War Cabinet and told it unequivocally that Slovakia was in the Russian zone of the war and any effective help should come from Moscow, not London. This sounded the keynote for the British response: it was always going to be a matter for the Soviets, but how to make this fact plain without alienating the Beneš administration would be the primary task. The Chiefs of Staff replied the following day, aligning themselves with this policy and totally dismissing long-range bombing operations, which, they said, were purely a matter for the Russians. The reactions of the other two major allies were also tentative. The Americans did no more than recognise belligerent rights in Slovakia and assumed that all combatants were under the command of the Czechoslovak government in London. From Moscow, only silence.[54]

Ingr wrote directly to the War Cabinet on 27 September and all but pleaded for allied reinforcements. He said that an uprising in the Protectorate was now imminent and would begin on a signal from London, therefore he needed arms for 10,000 men to be despatched within six nights and the further preparation of supplies for another 50,000–60,000 men within two weeks after the action began, all with the appropriate ammunition, food and medical stores. Eight days later, the Chief of the Imperial General Staff, General Alan Brooke, curtly replied that it was still a matter for the Russians, that all air operations should be carried out by them, and the implication was that future supplies should be a Russian problem also.[55]

A day later, the views of the Special Operations Executive were expressed. It maintained that hitherto the Czechoslovak government had offered 'little co-operation' in SOE's attempts to organise an effective resistance group in Bohemia and Moravia, but now that the war had progressed favourably for the allies, the Beneš administration suddenly wished to 'pursue the task of promoting such an organisation . . . to avoid the unenviable position of being the one nation which was not internally prepared for liberation'. The report dismissed the claim that the Slovakian action had happened 'at the behest' of the Czechoslovak government, and insisted that responsibility rested with the Russians alone. One crumb of comfort for Ingr, however, lay in SOE's belief that the people of Bohemia and Moravia would nevertheless look to the West for help 'and expect their arms and assistance to be delivered by us and not the Russians'.[56] The Chiefs of Staff Committee minuted in response that all risings must be supported by advancing allied forces, and since the west was not in a position to assist, all material aid must come from the Russians. The final official decision was that it was a matter for the Soviets to provide active aid, and that the West would continue to encourage the Czechoslovaks by supplying small-scale sabotage groups in the Protectorate.[57]

An exasperated Beneš tackled Nichols about this wall of intransigence, and the latter wrote to Roberts on 23 October, who then passed the letter to the War Cabinet. Beneš was disinterested in the argument that all risings should be supported by advancing Russian troops, but he made it clear that there was a political dimension to the problem which was being virtually ignored:

> The President seemed inclined to allow it to be inferred that he would draw his own conclusions from our attitude on this subject; i.e. that we were content to see Czechoslovakia pass within the political sphere of the Soviet Union. He rehearsed, once again, the reasons why his policy had always been, and would always be, to seek assistance and support from both the east and the west, and why it was in the interests of [Britain] that this should be Czechoslovakia's policy. I replied with some warmth that if he were to draw the conclusion that we were disinterested in Czechoslovakia's future and that we were quite content to see her enter definitely and permanently into the Soviet sphere of political influence, he was completely mistaken.[58]

One can see from this why Beneš was so aggrieved, and see also how he came to the opinions that he held. He had received not one particle of evidence to suggest that Nichols was as good as his word, and the constant insistence that it was a Soviet matter must surely have convinced him the Britain was finally washing her hands of the entire Czechoslovak 'problem'.

Only one hope remained for Beneš – the immediate transfer of his total air strength to the zone of operations. Perhaps wisely, he enlisted the help of his Inspector-General. Janoušek approached the Air Ministry with caution, acknowledging that any decision 'would largely be governed by the reply from the USSR'. But still he asked for at least minimal preparations to begin at once, these being the placing on standby of enough ground personnel to keep the squadrons operational, and the provision of sufficient supplies for a month's hard fighting. But time was running out for the rebels in Slovakia. Janoušek's plea was only received at the DAFL on 23 October, and by that time the German reinforcements were spreading havoc across the land.

The Red Army continued to maintain a desperate front in the Carpathian Mountains, and although the uprising itself had been suppressed, the Soviets still needed all the help they could get. In mid-November, Masaryk again asked for the return of the squadrons, and he claimed that the Russians had promised material support and given their full consent to the transfer. It seems unlikely that Masaryk was lying, though no substantiating document has yet come to light to prove the case either way. If he *was* lying, then he laid himself open to a charge of serious misrepresentation. Given the nervousness felt by the British regarding Soviet attitudes, the result would have been the complete destruction of his credibility. Sinclair was brought up to speed on the matter by Portal, and Sinclair himself wrote to Masaryk with his rejection, arguing that the squadrons were 'playing an important part in our theatre of the war and we should not be able quickly to replace them'. On the date of this letter, 310 and 313 Fighter Squadrons were both at North Weald, while 312 was at Bradwell Bay. During the month of November, 310 and 313 flew eleven escort missions for bombing raids on Germany, while 312 flew twelve.[59] Apart from training, the rest of the period was largely idle. In other words, they were hardly racing across Europe in support of the liberating armies, so it is difficult to accept that they were somehow indispensable and could not be released given the will to do so.

In any case, Sinclair gently placed most of the emphasis on the problems of supply and maintenance in his letter to Masaryk, but Portal was far more frank. He told Sinclair that the Czechs barely had enough men to run one-and-a-half squadrons by themselves if the British personnel were removed. He also doubted the plan in itself, seeing 'no sound military case' for the transfer. He then ended in a vein which is sadly reminiscent of the tone used by the DAFL in 1943:

If the Czechs are set upon transferring their forces then it seems to me that the proper course is to transfer the responsibility of maintaining them from the RAF to the Russians. It would be up to the Russians to provide aircraft and all the other things needed to maintain the squadrons; on the other hand, we should be rid of the commitment at the cost of finding three squadrons' worth of pilots and 1½ squadrons' worth of ground personnel, which would be difficult but not impossible. [Either they] stay where they are or [go] over lock, stock and barrel to the Russians. I do not expect that the Czechs would welcome this alternative since in practice it would probably lead to the virtual disappearance of the Czech Air Force for a considerable time. They would probably be well advised to continue the present arrangements which at least keep the Czech flag flying at no very great cost to themselves.

It seems that Portal was sorely tempted 'to be rid of the commitment', but although his views seem to indicate an utter indifference to the fate of the Czechoslovak Air Force, or even the military situation in Slovakia, in essence his was a realistic view at the time. But there is still this impression of 'the tolerated guest' about the Air Ministry's dealings with the Czechoslovak air contingent. Yes, it would have been acceptable if the British had not been inclined to trouble themselves overmuch about a very small force and its limited role in a gigantic war effort; but the language employed and the tone of its delivery frequently conveys the sense of irritation at having to deal with them at all, as if they should sit patiently on the south coast and wait until the end of the war before kicking up any more fuss.

The denouement came in two notes, one from Sinclair to Masaryk, much distilled, which highlighted the problems with the maintenance of communications, and the other from Nichols to Eden, which recorded the former's conversations with Masaryk and his reaction to the news that Britain was not going to grant any requests whatsoever:

He heard me in silence and his manner betrayed that the answer we had returned was not unexpected. He showed that he appreciated the arguments even if he could not share the conclusions.[60]

With this, the Beneš government's first attempt to get its air force home came to an end, and it has to be said that, in the main, the attitude adopted by the British government and the Air Ministry was a reasonable one, given the practicalities of the time. It was perfectly true that the Russians were in the best position to assist the Slovak rising, and even if three squadrons of Spitfires had been flown to that zone, maintaining them would have been almost impossible. To rely on men who had worked on the machines would have meant that only one or, at best, two squadrons would have functioned in any effective sense, and even these would have been totally dependent on spares flown through uncertain communications routes from Italian bases.

Yet it is also possible to see these admittedly valid reasons as little more than smoke to obscure the truth of the matter: that the Air Ministry simply did not wish to incur the extra work at a time when the war was entering its final phase. To transfer the whole contingent to the Russian zone would have meant a complex and laborious demobilisation on the British side, but to send the units east as a detachment of the RAF to fight with the Soviet armies would have raised numerous political complications far in excess of the potential benefit to the war effort. It was therefore easier to do nothing and use logistics as the basis of a negative argument. But one thing of great importance emerges from this episode: the attitude of the British regarding the return of the Czechoslovak Air Force to the Slovakian theatre sent all the wrong signals to Beneš and his government. By continually advising them to seek aid and permission from the Russians, the British were, at this late stage in 1944, making a rod for their own backs. For when less than a year later they were falling over themselves to give assistance to the Czechoslovaks, the latter effectively snubbed them in favour of their Russian allies.

By the middle of April 1945, Marshal Koniev's First Ukrainian Front had penetrated deep into the eastern half of Czechoslovakia, while Patton's Third Army had advanced into the western areas. This prompted calls from the Czechoslovak government for the immediate transfer of the army units to the western sectors in order to participate in the imminent liberation. Nichols, writing to Eden, relayed and endorsed proposals from Hubert Ripka that such a transfer be made together with a token force of air force pilots and their machines from Britain. Ripka had suggested that the effect on morale 'would be out of all proportion to the actual number of airmen concerned'. There had obviously been no response because a week later, on 25 April, Ripka wrote to Nichols and again called for the 'immediate despatch' of all possible army and air force units to the fighting front in western Czechoslovakia, insisting that such a move was 'essential for home morale'.[61]

In what by then seems to have been its customary practice, the Air Ministry lingered a while before replying. In fact, it waited until the war was almost over in Europe before the matter was taken up by Beaumont at the DAFL. He had been approached in late April by Janoušek, who had urged the immediate transfer of at least the three fighter squadrons, minus their British personnel, to the liberated territories. To save any fuss about demobilisation, the units could move as a detachment of the RAF and then, when the war was over, a new Anglo-Czechoslovak Agreement could be negotiated. Writing on 5 May 1945 to AM William Dickson, then Assistant Chief of the Air Staff (Policy), he suggested that the transfer could take place reasonably effectively if they had a three-month pack-up of spares to be going on with; and, perhaps as his trump card, he let it be known that the Foreign Office approved. But he also noted that 'there may be complications with the Russians with regard to the employment of these squadrons in Czechoslovakia'. This was a mistake, for if he really wanted to get anywhere with the plan, it would have been wise to keep the Russian factor at the lowest possible profile. As it was, he had let the genie out of the bottle.

Dickson rejected the plan at once. His leading point was that 'we can hardly be a party to the despatch of this Czech force into an area which is under Russian military occupation without having an assurance that the Russians approve', and he also pointed out for good measure that they would have to fly through American air space, so they would need to concur as well. He then took pains to distance himself from the apparent goodwill of the Foreign Office, telling Beaumont rather curtly to busy himself with RAF matters concerning the squadrons, and to let Janoušek know that when he had the agreement of the Russians, his men could go home.[62] Reasonably enough, the Air Ministry was prepared to wait for the Foreign Office to give the go-ahead to the plan, but of particular importance here is the insistence that it should be the responsibility of the Beneš government to provide evidence of Soviet concurrence, and it was this condition which became the keynote of almost everything which followed.

The situation in Prague was complex. Beneš and his government were already there, having made the journey via the Soviet Union and through the newly liberated territories in the east. He had left Janoušek and a handful of other officers in Britain to supervise demobilisation and repatriation. Fearful of another scenario similar to the one which had paralysed Poland at the war's end, he was determined to minimise Russian influences at all costs, except for provoking a coup. There were powerful communist elements in Czechoslovakia from the military and political wings, and his position was always delicately balanced between having enormous numbers of Red Army troops on his soil and a natural desire of the people to see their men in the fighting forces come home to a hero's welcome.

Prague was officially a Soviet zone; the Americans had agreed to that, and the British had agreed with the Americans. In the eyes of the Foreign Office, this meant that the matter was virtually removed from British hands in so far as executive decisions were concerned. All that needed to be done was: (a) secure Russian approval for the repatriation; (b) let the Americans know; (c) let them work the logistics out between themselves. All the British had to do was wave goodbye at the appropriate moment. This, at any rate, was the plan, and everything now rested upon the Soviet attitude. Letters to that effect were issued swiftly. Alec Randall in the Foreign Office informed Hubert Ripka that the RAF would give the green light as soon as the Russians signalled their consent.

But Ripka was not happy with that at all. The request for the transfer, he said, had come directly from President Beneš in Prague, and since the President would not dream of acting against his government's interests while still in the Soviet zone of occupation, the latter's approval could therefore be taken for granted. The Foreign Office reacted positively to this. A meeting took place on 17 May, when this argument was thrashed out with the DAFL, and all seemed content that Ripka's assessment of the situation in Prague was sound enough. British caution prevailed, however, and it was felt prudent to be absolutely clear that the Russians would not object. Philip Nicols, due to leave for Prague as the British ambassador, was told that the Beneš government should obtain Moscow's 'formal agreement'. This meant their agreement *in writing*, and this also proved to be another mistake. For if the British government had been sufficiently assertive and simply sent the Czechoslovaks home, much of what followed might never have happened.

Even the hitherto sceptical figure of Dickson aligned himself with the view that the Russians had approved the transfer by virtue of their silence. Indeed, he was positively sanguine. He thought the three-month detachment plan to be a good one too, allowing the British to maintain influence over the Czechoslovak Air Force while at the same time providing a useful firewall against any accusations that the British were supplying a foreign power in the heart of Eastern Europe; after all, as a detachment the Czechs would still be a part of the RAF. Embracing the political dimension, he added:

> Moreover, I suggest that there is nothing that the Russians want more than for us to be difficult in helping the Czechs. The former are offering equipment to the Czech Army with both hands, and they will be delighted at anything which will tend to make the Czechs turn more and more to them for help. The Czechs do not want to divorce themselves from the RAF at this stage and have asked for three months grace in which to consider the return to Czechoslovakia all of their units, [though] they are most anxious for the fighter squadrons to return and remain there while deliberations are proceeding.[63]

The irony in this last sentence is exquisite: after five long years of struggling for independence, convenience (and perhaps political expediency) had forced a change of heart, and now the last thing the Czechoslovaks wanted was to be separated from the RAF.

This was the position on 25 May, approximately five weeks after Ripka's initial request for the return of the squadrons. And yet deep in Whitehall, some minds remained uneasy about the lack of definite Soviet approval. A week went by, and perhaps there was much finger-tapping and pencil-chewing in the Foreign Office because by the end of May doubts were beginning to surface. The focus was not so much upon whether or not the Russians agreed to the transfer, but under what circumstances the fighter squadrons were to return. If, for example, they returned with RAF markings on the planes, would that arouse Soviet suspicions that the British were emphasising their relationship with the Czechs? But if they returned with Czech markings, would that give the Soviets a chance to treat the contingent as fair game? As Jack Ward noted in a long minute on the subject: 'I believe that the Russians have already collared the Czech Army, but that we still have a chance for the air force.'[64] Such doubts were enough to force a retreat to the original position. The Russians must give their absolute and unconditional approval before a single kitbag was packed.

Meanwhile, six hundred miles or so to the east, the frustration was increasing. Men within the Beneš government thought the British were deliberately stalling to force the hand of the Soviets, and in a broadcast from Prague in early June, Beneš had raised the stakes by promising his airmen that they would

be home soon. In England too, the levels at which the problem
was being discussed were also raised. The Chiefs of Staff
Committee drafted a report for Churchill on 7 June with a brief
synopsis of the problem, placing emphasis upon the fact that an
immediate postwar association with the air force would provide
'a valuable connecting link with the Czechoslovak Government'.
Churchill had recently issued his 'standstill' order regarding
Royal Air Force strength in Europe, meaning that there must
be no immediate depletion of numbers, hence the Committee's
decision to refer this matter to him. After declaring that 311
Liberator Squadron was no longer required as a service unit,
and that the three fighter squadrons were 'efficient fighter and
ground attack units', the Committee decided that 'the loss to
our fighting strength will not be appreciable' if they returned
in the near future.[65] On the same day, the Air Staff issued a
note for general circulation to all relevant departments within
the Air Ministry supporting the proposals, and although both
bodies still emphasised the need for Russian concurrence, it was
accepted that a postwar agreement with the Czechoslovaks could
be politically useful 'at a time when they will be in many respects
under the dominating influence of the USSR'.[66] Finally, again on
the 7th, Nichols sent a despatch for Cabinet distribution which
reviewed the military situation in Prague. Marshal Koniev had
received the Freedom of the City, and again Beneš had called for
the swift return of his air force.[67] On the 8th, the Air Staff drafted
an annex to the Committee's report recommending the transfer;
and on the 11th, the COS report, together with the Air Staff
annex, was sent to Churchill.[68] On the 13th he wrote above the
document: 'Let them go back forthwith.'[69]

Once the great man had spoken, the ball was now in play.
On the same day, Dickson issued a general directive stating that
the Prime Minister and the Chiefs of Staff had decided that the
four squadrons were to return at once, and therefore all the
relevant directorates should prepare. The detachment scheme
would still apply, 'but the Russians will not be told for the present.
To them, the move will appear as the permanent return of the
Czechoslovak Air Force to Czechoslovakia.' As always, the parcel
was tied with the now familiar ribbon, 'everything subject to
Russian agreement'.[70]

We might pause at this moment and consider the final
couplet of this directive. On the one hand, the Soviets were to be
deceived; on the other, they were expected to give their consent
to this deception, albeit unknowingly. Having lost its value as a
military arm, the Czechoslovak Air Force had now completed its

transformation into a political tool once again. The British were not remotely interested in whether or not the contingent would be a viable force in its homeland, because the opportunity to claim a stake in a Central European country presently occupied by the armies of the Soviet Union was now of far greater importance. Furthermore, 'Russian agreement' was rapidly becoming something of a diplomatic unicorn – sought by many, seen by none. No evidence has come to light during this study which proves conclusively that the Soviets made any pronouncement on the subject, negative or otherwise, and all the contemporary evidence, circumstantial though it is, indicates that what little interest they had in the matter was generally positive.[71]

Oddly enough, when something which approached consent *did* finally appear, the British refused to believe it. On 13 June, Seligman wrote to Christopher Warner and told him of a letter, apparently received by the US 5th Army in Plzeň, which stated that the new Red Army commander in Prague – named as Major-General Paramzik – had confirmed that the Czechoslovak government now had 'full and unrestricted access' to Prague airport.[72] An extract, over Paramzik's name, found its way on to Seligman's desk:

> Will you please inform the Allied Supreme Council that the High Command of the Red Army have ordered that British aircraft carrying military or civilian persons may fly without restriction and are to land at Ruzýn aerodrome near Prague. The aircraft so landing are guaranteed an unrestricted return flight.[73]

When Janoušek heard of this, he claimed that it gave *carte blanche* to the Czechoslovak Air Force to return immediately. Seligman commented: 'He was quite emphatic about this, but we do not altogether share the view, although it is true to say that this is the first occasion on which we have seen anything resembling a permit of any sort from the Russians for Czechoslovak personnel to land in their own country.' Warner then transmitted a message to Nichols in Prague:

> Authority has now been received for transfer of Czech air squadrons to Czechoslovakia with their aircraft as soon as satisfactory evidence is received that Russians agree. Air Marshal Janoušek has endeavoured to convince the Air Ministry that they have already done so, but the letter from the Major-General of Red Army Prague Command . . . which

he produced as evidence, appeared to the Air Ministry
clearly to refer to flights of courier aircraft since it referred
to return flights from Czechoslovakia as well as flights in.[74]

One might be forgiven for thinking that this was taking caution to
excess. All parties well knew that the move could never have been
accomplished in one straight hop from Britain to Czechoslovakia,
and that a substantial degree of ferrying of stores, effects and
personnel – civilian and military – would be involved. Even the
most critical reading of Paramzik's 'permit' forces the conclusion
that all these aspects had been covered, and perhaps the only
food for pedants lies in the phrase 'British aircraft', which could
be interpreted as aircraft manufactured in Britain or aircraft with
British markings – a distinction which would have affected the
proposal to livery the planes in Czechoslovak colours and symbols.
Nevertheless, this was not the point which Warner focused upon,
and in closing he informed Nichols that a three-month pack-up of
spares would be supplied:

> It must, of course, be obvious both to the Russians and the
> Czechs that the former will be able to reduce the squadrons
> to impotence, if they so desire, by refusing them aviation
> spirit and by declining to agree to their being supplied
> from here with the major replacements which will gradually
> become necessary. The Air Ministry calculate, however, that
> even in this event the air squadrons should be able to do
> an adequate amount of flying for a period of about three
> months to have a good propaganda effect.[75]

It is possible to defend the rather cynical position adopted here
by the Air Ministry, given the huge problems that were developing
in Poland at the time, but the way they were going about it
handed all the winning cards to the Russians who, when all is said
and done, hardly had anything to do with the situation at all.

But Karel Janoušek cared nothing for the politics just then. As
far as he was concerned, he and his men could go home at
last after more than six years in exile. Emboldened by the
prospect, he asked that all three fighter squadrons be completely
re-equipped with brand new Spitfire IX HF(E) aircraft so that
they might not have to participate in the victory parade in tired
machines. This, thought the Air Ministry, was a good idea. Almost
at once, however, it was pointed out that this might offend the
Russians, since they had been denied these very planes at a late
stage in the war, and it took another couple of weeks before a

compromise was reached – one full squadron would be so refitted and the others given a thorough makeover. In the event, it was at last decided that *all* the squadrons should receive new machines, but over a staggered period finishing in early August 1945.

Amid all this confusion, politics surfaced again. Nichols had been busy in Prague still trying to secure cast-iron Soviet consent. He had then been told that all Red Army units were scheduled for withdrawal during the first two weeks of July, and that Beneš and his ministers 'were loth to approach the Russians for they did not consider the latter to have any authority in the matter'. One purpose of his note was to ask if this withdrawal obviated the need for Soviet approval anyway, although he had heard that a request was shortly to be made to Marshal Koniev for his forces to supply aviation spirit once the squadrons returned. Surely, it was argued, Russian agreement would be implicit if the answer was positive.[76] The Czechs themselves also insisted that the military command in Prague was 'wholly Czechoslovak', and the delay was making matters worse, not better, in their relations with the Soviets. At last, on 18 July, Dickson gave the 'go' order. On 7 August, all three fighter squadrons would return to Prague in mixed livery, the crew all wearing RAF uniform, with prominence given to their own national ranks and service badges. As it happened, a one-week delay was caused by bad weather, but at 2 p.m. on Monday 13 August 1945, all 54 Spitfires landed at Ruzýn airport in blazing sunshine, having twice flown low over the city in close formation.

The squadrons were reviewed prior to departure by AM Sir John Slessor on 3 August. In a speech originally drafted for Portal, he paid a handsome tribute to the officers and men of this gallant little force and made useful references to a desire for postwar collaboration and friendship. After they had gone home, a week-long party got under way, during which everybody who mattered mounted the podium and recited glowing tributes and heartfelt thanks to the RAF and all it had done to keep the nation's hopes alive during the years of occupation. Present throughout this week of celebration (in which, it is said, the pubs ran dry of beer, leading some hotels to import emergency supplies from southern Germany) were an outstanding array of Royal Air Force commanders, many of whom received the Order of the White Lion from the hands of the President. Nichols returned a detailed report of this event also, drawing Ernest Bevin's attention to the valuable opportunities afforded for high-level discussions between British and Czechoslovak officers. As far as the Ambassador was concerned, this did much 'to serve the interests of His Majesty's

Government', and the jolly atmosphere 'demonstrated that the mutual respect and good fellowship established under war conditions . . . are still potent factors in the relations between the two countries'.

So it had all ended in handshakes, backslaps, medals and smiles all round. In that last week of August 1945, the Czechoslovak Air Force was the nearest it ever came to being a true ally, at least in British eyes and those of the Czechoslovak press. All the quibbles and niggles of five long years of war were put aside or forgotten amid the swirl of parties and speeches, but as we shall see, the bonhomie was not to last long. The seeds of disaster had already been sown and were starting to germinate. The British, by constantly seeking Soviet approval, had given time for powerful anti-Western blocs to develop inside the Czechoslovak military, although it should have been perfectly easy to understand why Beneš did not want to go cap in hand to the Soviets and ask their permission for his air force to return to its homeland. Such an action would have been contrary to his hunger for prestige and all his beliefs about the sovereignty of his country. The British had fooled themselves into believing that the Russians cared about what this tiny country did or did not do with its equally tiny air force, and by concentrating on that instead of supporting their ally to every last degree, they came away with nothing.

Things began to go sour early in September. The British had confidently expected negotiations towards an new air agreement to begin as soon as things began to settle down in Czechoslovakia, but then came sudden news of a major upheaval in the organisation of the Czechoslovak Air Force itself. The new Director of the DAFL, Air Cdre Ferdinand West, informed the Foreign Office that Janoušek had been removed as C-in-C and replaced by Slezák, who had now been openly proclaiming his communist sympathies:

> It seems that the Headquarters of the Czechoslovak Air Force in Prague has been almost entirely re-staffed. Those Czech officers of high rank who held appointments in the RAFVR have been dispersed and, in nearly every case, are filling relatively unimportant posts.

So the wheel had turned full circle, and the man who had deposed the hated Slezák in 1940 now found himself pushed aside in favour of him. West continued:

> I gather this internal trouble is largely political and Janoušek has been accused of being too Anglophile in his tendencies

and not sufficiently appreciative of the Russians. Extreme
leftists have even labelled him as a Fascist and anti-Jew leader.

Another telegram, this time from Nichols, told London that 'the
Russians are displeased that most personalities holding executive
positions in other ministries are those with wartime experience
in England and who possess no undue communist tendencies'.[77]
Beneš was already losing control of his armed forces, and now
we may glimpse the Soviet strategy regarding the return of the
squadrons in August, for it would have been counter-productive
to place any obstacles in the way of the transfer when the overall
aim was to get the men home and then begin the process of
discarding the 'dangerous' elements. The delay merely enabled
them to strengthen their power base throughout the summer.

London was shaken by this news, but by no means was all hope
lost. It now became absolutely vital to secure a re-equipment
deal with Prague before the Soviets completed the process of
absorption. The omens looked favourable. No one had raised
any objections to the supply and maintenance of the squadrons
under the detachment plan, and senior pro-communists within
the Czechoslovak Ministry of Defence had let it be known that
sixty Spitfires might be the first item in a substantial order to
follow soon. The focus now shifted to the organisation of a
full expedition with the authority to negotiate on behalf of the
Czechoslovak government. Janoušek had been sent from Prague
to wind up the Inspectorate in London, but he dropped by at
the Foreign Office and led it to believe that he would head the
Mission when it came. In return, London told Prague to bait the
hook with a promise of assistance 'on a generous scale' if the
Mission arrived with full negotiating powers. Nichols returned
with a firm date, 9 December, when a team of senior air force
officers would arrive with a long list of requirements and plenty of
money to spend.

What followed then was a series of postponements. Christmas
came and went, and what few communications there were hinted
that the Russians were also preparing a list of their own. The
promise of a 'substantial gift' of equipment to the Czechoslovak
Air Force from Moscow chilled British hearts, but then out of
the blue a new date for the Mission was floated: 6 February 1946.
More to the point, the Czechoslovaks had requested another
pack-up of spares to maintain the existing Spitfire squadrons, but
as a minute stated: 'we cannot go on indefinitely sending supplies
until the policy and financial aspects of the matter are settled'.
Within days, however, another postponement had been called.

By late February, a sense of urgency was creeping into the despatches – not panic exactly, but something close to it, as it became apparent to all that the last chance of holding on to a position of influence was sliding away. The Air Attaché in Prague, Gp Capt G.M. Wyatt, was informed that preparations were nearly complete, yet he should not delay any longer, 'but approach the Czechs in the strongest possible terms and press them to send an Air Mission'. As more bait, the Air Ministry suggested that he tell it at once that any discussions now would not commit it to a final decision, and to perhaps hint that growing shortages of materials meant that action sooner rather than later might be in their favour.

Wyatt replied quickly, having consulted Nichols, and both were agreed that there was 'practically no chance of persuading the Czechoslovak Government to discuss future equipment' at that time. The reason given was that the impending elections in Czechoslovakia made it likely that the government would not 'risk discussions on this subject with us until Russian intentions are clearer'. Within five days, however, Wyatt telegraphed again and told London that a Mission would be despatched soon, but Janoušek 'frankly disliked the idea of heading a Mission whose function was to sever rather than enhance connections with the RAF'.

After yet another short postponement, the Czechoslovak Air Mission finally arrived in Britain and convened on 3 April 1946. Janoušek was its leader, but Slézak was not among the team. Swiftly discussed was the supply of 72 Spitfires, 24 Mosquitoes, 4 training aircraft and enough bombs, ammunition and auxiliary equipment to sustain ten days of fully mobilised combat, all at the knock-down price of £354,000. This the Mission accepted with thanks. Then, amid many fine speeches, the sad duty of the Committee was to formally end the Anglo-Czechoslovak military association which had begun in the awesome chaos of the summer of 1940. It was agreed by all parties that on 30 June 1946 the Czechoslovak Section (RAFVR) would cease to exist as a legal and political entity, and the supporting agreement would be terminated. All that remained to be done was for the Czechoslovak government to ratify the re-equipment plan and then a new relationship could begin.

Janoušek and his team returned to Prague with the draft of the new agreement in his pocket. The Air Ministry could do nothing but wait upon events. Five weeks of silence passed. Then, in mid-May, a top secret telegram arrived from Wyatt which indicated that new Soviet aircraft, possibly as many as ninety, were flying in from Russian bases and being positioned under hangars in aerodromes across the Republic. In a state of some alarm, he admitted that all 'previous direct and indirect enquiries regarding Russian equipment . . . have always received indefinite and evasive answers'. He contacted Janoušek who told him that the draft Agreement had yet to reach the Cabinet for discussion. Wyatt noted: 'The delivery of Russian aircraft at this time may be a Communist pre-election gambit, for the people are being told the aircraft are a gift from the Russians.' Janoušek told him that unofficial sources said otherwise, that a high price was being charged, and that, in any case, the general staff were now said to be uninterested in purchasing British aircraft.

In early June, the Air Ministry lost patience and told Wyatt to ascertain whether there would be firm orders or not, and to set 31 July as the deadline, after which the aircraft would be supplied to another buyer. If Wyatt replied, the document has not survived, but a note from him to the Air Ministry sent on 2 September 1946 confirmed that the agreement had still not yet been signed.[78] From that date onwards, the files are silent. As for Karel Janoušek, he was later declared to be 'an enemy of the people' and served eleven years in prison.

NOTES

1. CAB 65/7: War Cabinets of 20.6.40 and 21.6.40.
2. Gilbert, M., *Winston S. Churchill: Volume 6, 1939–1941* (Heinemann 1983), p. 342.
3. CAB 65/7: War Cabinet, 24.6.40.
4. See Alex Danchev's essay 'Sir John Dill and Winston Churchill', *Journal of Contemporary History*, Volume 22 (1987).
5. Taylor A.J.P,. *English History, 1914–1945* (Oxford 1988), p. 473.
6. For glimpses into the formation and work of the JIC, see West, Nigel, *MI5* (The Bodley Head 1981) and *MI6* (Weidenfeld & Nicolson 1983); Glees, Anthony, *The Secrets of the Service* (Cape 1987) and Andrew, Christopher, *Secret Service* (Heinemann 1985).
7. CAB 81/97 (JIC(40)86): Memorandum, 30.5.40. The document was signed by Cavendish-Bentinck, J.H. Godfrey, F.G. Beaumont-Nesbitt, Archibald Boyle and H.I. Allen.
8. CAB 81/98: Home Office to Foreign Office, 14.9.40.
9. It is reasonable to assume that the document referred to Czechs *and* Slovaks: (a) because very few official documents bothered to make the distinction, using the term 'Czech' to

mean Czechs and Slovaks, and (b) because Slovakia, technically
at least, was perceived to be in the Axis camp anyway.

10. FO 371/24365: C/1419/1419/62 et al: 26.1.40. The original
    text is reproduced here. In the circulated draft of these
    minutes 'had' was replaced by 'reported to have'.

11. Ibid. Again, 'get rid of' was replaced by 'emigrate' in the final
    text.

12. FO 371/24365: Inter-Departmental meeting of 11.6.40.
    Figures based on War Office data collected from
    'recruitment drives' organised on behalf of the Czechoslovak
    Legation in London.

13. The attitude of the JIC changed very slowly indeed. Towards
    the end of 1940, when the invasion scare was over, the
    Committee considered one of a series of intriguing papers
    entitled 'Rumours of a Military Nature Intended to Mystify
    and Mislead the Enemy'. These were suggestions put forward
    by the various service and security departments to the Inter-
    Service Security Board (ISSB) for realistic assessment. If
    considered feasible, the 'rumour' would be made public.
    One such rumour was designed to scare the Italians by
    threatening to bomb Vesuvius, 'to see what would happen',
    in the hope that the awestruck peasants would panic and
    demand protection from the government. To this idea, the
    ISSB concurred. Another involved fifty Nazi rats which had
    been infected with bubonic plague prior to being dropped
    over England on rat-sized parachutes. The rumour, aimed at
    weakening German public morale, would suggest that these
    rats had gone missing in Germany, and that the authorities
    were falling over themselves trying to find them. To this, the
    ISSB said, 'we have no comment'. Finally, MI5 had suggested
    spreading a tale of ten Luftwaffe pilots who had baled out
    over Britain and been interned. Pledging to strike back
    against their former masters, they were now flying Hurricanes
    in Polish squadrons operating from Britain. Said the ISSB:
    'We are not enamoured with this rumour . . . particularly the
    reference to the Polish squadrons in the final sentence' (CAB
    81/97: (JIC (40) 386), 23.11.40).

14. Sir Robert Hamilton Bruce Lockhart (1877–1970) was an
    author, diplomat, spy and *bon viveur* who narrowly escaped
    execution at the hands of the Bolsheviks for supposed
    conspiracy in 1918. He was attached to the British Legation
    in Prague, 1919; lived and worked in Central Europe
    throughout the 1920s; appointed British representative to
    the Provisional Czechoslovak Government 1940; became

head of the Political Warfare Executive 1941; knighted 1943, and remained close friends with Beneš and Jan Masaryk until their deaths. His opinion of the Foreign Office at this time was not favourable, for he told his diary that it was 'a decrepit, indecisive and cautious collection of tame cats' (Bruce Lockhart, R.H. *Diaries Volume 2*, entry for 1.6.40).

15. AIR/2/5162: Memo from Czechoslovak National Committee to Air Ministry, 18.7.40.

16. AIR/2/5162: 18.7.40: Summary of the Franco-Czechoslovak Air Force Agreement.

17. AIR 2/5162: Internal Air Ministry Memorandum, 21.7.40.

18. CAB 85/19: Minutes AFOSC 29.7.40.

19. Strang had no love for Beneš. In the final days of the Franco–German conflict, he had become angry with Beneš as the latter attempted to force his own concerns onto the agenda. Bruce Lockhart claimed Strang was 'slightly hysterical', and shouted: 'Doesn't he realise the fate of the world – [of] the British Empire – is being settled in the next forty-eight hours?' (Bruce Lockhart, R.H. *Diaries Volume 2*, entry for 13.6.40). In a much more depressed tone in a later entry, Bruce Lockhart complained that Strang had 'never once consulted [me] about Czech matters or shown the slightest interest in them. I insist always that the Czechs can help us during the war. But no one listens. No one cares.' (ibid., entry for 1.7.40). By the same token, Bruce Lockhart had no love for Strang either: 'He is a poor creature – gutless and second-rate. The young men like Roberts are good but suffer from the inaction and caution of their superiors' (ibid., entry for 25.5.40).

20. CAB 85/19: Minutes AFOSC, 29.7.40.

21. CAB 65/7: War Cabinet, 26.7.40. For further reading on the Cholmondeley Park mutiny, see the works by White, Liškutin and Dagan listed in the Bibliography.

22. VKPR 52/1/1/19: Letters of complaint from Honington and Duxford, 6.8.40. The desire for status even extended to former police officers who also wanted their civilian ranks recognised.

23. VKPR 23/1/2: Nižborsky to Beneš, 26.8.40.

24. VKPR 23/1/2: Beneš to Honington and Duxford, 21.10.40. The draft was prepared by him, but the final document was signed by Nižborsky.

25. MNO 8/2167/1940: Minute to file by Nižborsky, 10.10.40. The names of the officers, who were sent to the army at Leamington Spa, appear in this file but are not relevant to the present study. A small number of other ranks were also transferred.

26. MNO 13/67/1941: Collier to Kalla, 9.1.41. One case in point which received more than enough attention from both the Czechoslovak and British points of view, was that of an NCO pilot who, in December 1940, twice refused to go on operational flights over Belgium and Germany. Given the opportunity to think the matter over, he was again ordered on a mission, and again refused. He had applied twice for transfer to a fighter squadron (a not infrequent request from 311 in the early years) and had twice been refused. Given that a front-line fighter pilot's life expectancy was slightly less than two weeks at this stage of the war, this seems to indicate that the man was no coward. He was, however, demoted in the manner described by Kalla. Some local papers heard of this, and Collier's anger is clear from his tone when he told Kalla that the Air Ministry had only come to hear of it through the press coverage, hence his reference to 'Gestapo tactics'.

27. Ingr was C-in-C of the Czechoslovak Forces in Great Britain. In the First World War, he initially fought with the Austro-Hungarian Army until captured in Russia, thereafter changing sides. Promoted to Brigadier-General in 1933, he remained in the Protectorate until June 1939 when he was summoned by Beneš to the west. He was an implacable opponent of the pro-communist Gen Ludvík Svoboda who operated in the east, and as a result he was branded 'an enemy of the Soviet Union' *in absentia*. He became Czechoslovak Minister at The Hague after the war, and remained in exile in the west after the Communist coup of 1948.

28. MNO 14/366/1941. Letter from Beneš to Sinclair, 14.1.41

29. VKPR 25/1/1/3: Report by Ingr, 5.1.41.

30. VKPR 26/1/1/4: Sinclair to Beneš, 28.1.41.

31. VKPR 26/20/11: Slezák to Ingr, 3.12.40. In this report, Slezák also noted that 312 (Fighter) Squadron was eighteen men under strength in auxiliaries, and noted that British pressure required the Czechoslovak Air Force to be fully established in all capacities by 31 October 1942. It was a requirement destined never to be met.

32. MNO 13/232/1941: Janoušek to Ingr, 20.1.41.

33. MNO 14/601/1941: Sinclair to Janoušek, 11.3.41.

34. MNO 11/4222/1940: Španiel to the MNO, 24.10.40.

35. CAB 85/20: AFOSC Minutes, 4.3.41.

36. MNO 17/2023/1941: 'Agreement regarding Recruitment for the Czechoslovak Air Force in Canada and the USA', 30.5.41 (See also VKPR 25/2/1/3.)

37. FO371/26394, Beneš to Churchill, 19.4.41.

38. FO 371/26394: Roberts to Malkin, 22.4.41. See also the general correspondence in this file through to July 1941.

39. VKPR/25/3/1/3: Confidential report by Nižborsky to the MNO, 7.7.41. Nižborsky's tone in the document could be described as politely derisive.

40. VKPR 25/4/1/3: Meeting, 3.9.41. This discussion was for commanders within the Inspectorate only. Ingr was not present, nor were any of the political leadership.

41. FO 371/30850: Sinclair to Eden, 5.7.42.

42. Brown, Alan, *The Czechoslovak Air Force in Great Britain, 1940–1945* (PhD, University of Southampton 1998) for a full examination of the statistical data relating to squadron deployment.

43. AIR 2/5162: Memorandum on the Proposed Revision of the Czechoslovak Forces Agreement.

44. ČsL VB 215/CIII-2e/1/212: Remarks, etc., Janoušek 16.11.42.

45. AIR/2/5162. This document formed page 3 of the critical examination of the new proposals, and was entitled: 'The following general conclusions may be of interest.'

46. AIR 2/5162: Nicols to Eden, 8.6.43.

47. FO 371/36377: Ward, minute to file, 23.6.43.

48. AIR/2/5162: Unsigned minute from Foreign Office to Air Ministry, 7.7.43.

49. AIR/2/5162: Minute from Dore to Air Cdre George Venn CBE, 23.8.44.

50. AIR/2/5162: Stewart to Dore, 23.11.44. Czechoslovak officers and airmen in the RAFVR wore their national badges of rank on their sleeves and RAF badges of rank on their shoulders. In a separate moment of thought, Stewart wrote: 'It is astonishing that the Czechs can take this seriously, but it is all to the good that there is a chance of their being satisfied'. (FO 371/42300: Minute to file by Stewart, undated.)

51. AIR/2/5162: Dore to Stewart, 28.11.44. See also Stewart, minute to file, 4.12.44.

52. FO 371/42300: Nichols to Dean, 18.11.44.

53. FO 371/42300: Dean to Nichols, 7.12.44. Dean urged Nichols to keep the matter close to his chest because the officers were most concerned that their involvement would come to the notice of their superiors. It seems fair to presume that Janoušek had a hand in this, but the evidence is tantalisingly sparse and thus prevents any solid conclusions.

54. CAB 121/360: Chiefs of Staff to the War Cabinet, 5.9.44; Halifax to Foreign Office, 8.9.44.
55. CAB 121/360: Ingr to War Cabinet, 27.9.44; Brooke to Ingr, 5.10.44.
56. CAB 121/360: SOE to War Cabinet, 6.10.44. SOE's attitude towards the Czechoslovaks generally was not particularly warm. In his studious account of Heydrich's assassination, Callum MacDonald traces the relationship between SOE and the Czechoslovak Intelligence Service and demonstrates that Beneš was clearly culpable of using agents who were often ill prepared and unsuitable for covert activity to further his political interests rather than achieve any measurable success against the Germans. Before the assassination of Heydrich in May 1942, SOE attempted to place twenty or so agents in the Protectorate, most of whom were caught and killed, while some defected to the Nazis and severely dented SOE's faith in the Czechoslovak resistance. One, Karel Čurda, betrayed Heydrich's assassins and was hanged as a traitor in 1946 (MacDonald, C., *The Killing of SS Obergruppenführer Reinhard Heydrich* (Macmillan 1989), *passim*). After Heydrich's death, SOE continued to train and supply Czech agents, but again the success rate was minimal, and again some surrendered voluntarily to the Germans. Essentially, the Czechs were on their own after that and SOE confined itself to intelligence gathering rather than active subversion (Foot, M.R.D., *S.O.E. – The Special Operations Executive, 1940–1946* (BBC 1984), pp. 199–203). Bruce Lockhart also supplied the Foreign Office with periodic resumés of Resistance activity in the Protectorate covering a wide range of subjects, including morale, prices, Gestapo activities and food shortages. There were, however, some doubts concerning the truth and sources of his information at times. In January 1943, he met the head of MI6 (Maj-Gen Sir Stewart Menzies), who suspected that the Czechoslovak government in London was 'touching up or even faking reports', and Bruce Lockhart admitted that he had often seen reports supposedly sent from the Prague Resistance when he knew from own sources that communications had ceased due to Gestapo activity. It was felt that Moravec and perhaps even SOE had had a hand in the deception (Bruce Lockhart, R.H., *Diaries Volume 2*, entry for 20.1.43). Bruce Lockhart's summaries may be found throughout the FO 371 correspondence series.
57. CAB 121/360: COS Committee, 7.10.44.

58. CAB 121/360: Nichols to Foreign Office (Roberts), 23.10.44.

59. AIR 27/1683 and AIR 27/1695: Operational record books for 310, 312 and 313 Fighter Squadrons, 1–30 November 1944.

60. AIR/8/1257: Nichols to Eden, 13.11.44; Sinclair to Masaryk, undated.

61. CAB 121/360: Nichols to Eden, 18.4.45; FO 371/47139: Ripka to Nichols, 25.4.45.

62. AIR 2/6947: Minutes, Beaumont to Dickson, 11.5.45; Dickson to Beaumont, 12.5.45.

63. AIR 2/6947: Pearson-Rogers to Dickson, 25.5.45.

64. FO 371/47139: Minutes to file, Gatehouse and Ward, 30.5.45. Ward also commented on COS 120, arguing that the paper was governed by paragraph 12, which acknowledged that political uncertainties might make it difficult to recommend long-term postwar rearmament policies for Czechoslovakia, Poland and Yugoslavia. The latter's requirements had been met according to the 50:50 agreement with the Western allies supplying the air and naval forces, and the Soviets supplying the army. It was within this context that he proposed targeting the Czechoslovak Air Force for future development with Western equipment.

65. AIR 2/6947: COS Committee report for the Prime Minister, 7.6.45. Churchill had declared on 17.5.45 'that no weakening of the Royal Air Force in Europe shall take place until further notice'.

66. AIR 2/6947: Air Staff Directive, 7.6.45. The note was also copied to Churchill.

67. AIR 2/6947: Telegram, Nichols to Foreign Office, 7.6.45.

68. COS (45) 379: Air Staff Annex, 8.6.45.

69. CAB 121/360: COS Committee report, 11.6.45.

70. AIR 2/6947: Dickson, General Directive, 13.6.45.

71. For example, the personal bodyguard which had been supplied by Stalin and had been with Beneš since 16 March was replaced by Czech troops on 4 June as part of the general hand-over of military command in the Republic (VHA 20-15/2 (2872) 1945, minute to file, 4.6.45).

72. Sir Christopher Frederick Ashton Warner (1885–1957) was educated at Winchester and Magdalen College, Oxford; Captain of the Royal Fusiliers 1914–18; Foreign Office 1920–23 and 1928–51; promoted Counsellor 1942; knighted 1943; head of the Northern Department 1945; Ambassador to Belgium 1951–5.

73. AIR 2/6947: Seligman to Warner, 13.6.45.

74. AIR 2/6947: Foreign Office to Prague, 15.6.45. This telegram

was copied through the Air Ministry, including Sinclair. Nichols was also informed that the basic administration in preparation for the move would take approximately ten days. Warner then included a short reminder that to the Soviets *and* the Americans, the contingent was returning under the 'detachment' plan. The reason that the Americans were now being deceived was to avoid complications of supply and maintenance under COS 120, for if the Czechoslovak Air Force was designated an independent force of a friendly allied power, then the Americans would have been entitled to a voice in its future.

75. Ibid. Nichols replied on the 18th and solemnly informed Warner that information he had received from the Czechoslovak government seemed to indicate that they did not believe that the Soviets would 'render them impotent'. He also noted that Czechoslovak officials 'seemed confident of obtaining satisfactory evidence within the next day or two'. (AIR 2/6947: Nichols to Foreign Office, 18.6.45).

76. AIR 2/6947: Nichols to Foreign Office, 3.7.45.

77. FO 371/47141: Correspondence, 27.8.45 to 5.9.45.

78. AIR 8/1257: Correspondence, 23.2.46 to 2.9.46.

CHAPTER FOUR

The Free French

Politics also stood in the way of another group of exiles to arrive that summer. For the French, however, the scenario was a complete contrast to that of the Czechs and the Poles, both of whom had witnessed the total occupation of their countries. In France, the situation was very much different. Northern France was under German authority, yet the southern regions were permitted to establish a government based at Vichy. No one disputed the fact that this government would at all times have to bow to the wishes of Berlin, but its very existence caused a schism in Anglo–French relations and was the source of much bitterness within the French air contingent itself. Whereas the Poles and the Czechs might argue over purely political issues, debate largely focusing on how their societies should be reconstructed after the war was over, the French had to decide whether or not France still existed as a free country or as a vassal state, and at the very core of this dispute was Gen Charles de Gaulle.

One historian has described the France that went to war in 1939 as 'a deeply conservative, defensive society, split by social conflict, undermined by a failing and unmodernised economy and an empire in crisis'.[1] There is much in this view which historians of the Third Republic would recognise as accurate. Since the devastating defeat by Bismarck's Prussia in 1870, France had fought against herself with every weapon at her disposal, even descending briefly into civil war during the battle for Paris. Not once did the country have anything more than temporal political stability. Before 1914, not once did the people unite against any external threat, except to pursue the bitter desire to exact revenge against the hated Germans and recover the lost provinces of Alsace and Lorraine. With that aim achieved in 1918 after the sacrifice of millions of casualties, France then pressed for a 'peace' plan which would have reduced Germany to little more than an agricultural backwater had the provisions of the Treaty of Versailles not been gradually whittled away by the other powers, foremost among which was Britain.

Anglo–French relations had been rocky at best for most of the interwar period, and there seems little doubt that the 'alliance' which existed between them on the eve of war in 1939 had more to do with strategical pragmatism rather than a genuine catalogue of shared interests and policies. If France fell, Britain would be in range of captured French airfields; if France resisted, Britain would throw a measure of her weight into the balance, as she had done in 1914. Either way, Britain could not afford to stand by and let France fight alone. But this did not necessarily mean that an Anglo-French coalition would be plain sailing. Staff talks began very late in the day, and at all times the shame of Munich and the haunting prospect of another calamity permeated every attempt to galvanise both governments into spirited preparation. In the spring of 1939, the British tentatively requested details of the French air preparations for defence of the home territory. These were supplied in overview format, and the strategic thinking revealed that France would deploy her air power to meet a simultaneous attack by both Italy and Germany. The system was designed to be wholly subordinate to the orders of the land force commanders, though all intelligence would be shared. France's only standing air defences were the metropolitan forces in the north-east, held primarily in readiness to defend Paris, and the other three 'air armies' were to be mobilised only in the event of hostilities.[2]

A Supreme War Council had been swiftly established when war began in 1939, but the lack of activity in the west meant that the early adrenaline swiftly dissipated. When at last the Germans did attack in May 1940, all the problems of allied warfare soon emerged. As David Irving phrased it: 'The British found the French undisciplined and temperamental; the French found the British pedantic and pigheaded.'[3] By the time it was apparent that France could no longer resist, relations were at an all-time low. Mutual recriminations reached their zenith at Dunkirk. Only a small proportion of the quarter of a million men rescued were French. Adm Darlan complained that the British had scrambled for safety at the expense of his countrymen, claiming that the British had only one thought when faced with annihilation: 'To the boats!'[4] Whether or not this individual's opinion represents the true state of affairs, we can be certain that in the wake of the

Dunkirk disaster, little fabric of the 'alliance' remained, at least in spirit. In practical terms, however, both powers were now in the same position: one mistake would mean destruction, possibly for all time. In a poisonous atmosphere of defeat and distrust, and with accusations of incompetence flying back and forth, concerted, level-headed action was difficult indeed to realise.

As the French prepared to fight the rearguard action in early June, and Churchill shuttled to and fro in a vain attempt to inspire them to fight on, Dowding famously argued that no more British aircraft or pilots could be sacrificed for what was obviously a doomed campaign on the Continent. At first Churchill overruled him, promising the new French premier, Paul Reynaud, that a few more planes could be spared, but then the C-in-C of the French Air Force, Gen Vuillemin, all but brushed aside the contribution of the RAF as 'tardy, inadequate, but nevertheless of value'. One can imagine the fury which this unleashed in British quarters. Gen Hastings Ismay called it 'nothing short of outrageous', adding:

> We have thrown no bricks at them despite the fact that they let down our Expeditionary Force; and they, without one word of gratitude for the help we gave them in evacuation and in air fighting, do nothing but sling mud at us.[5]

It was against this grim and malevolent background that French troops and airmen began to arrive in Britain.

We have seen already how strained were the arrangements between the French and their Slav allies, and almost from the start the same rancour pervaded attempts to come to a working arrangement with their British hosts. One of the first problems to be encountered was the embarrassingly small number of French air personnel who had chosen to leave their home territory. The Chiefs of Staff report of 24 July estimated that only 2,000 Frenchmen had been counted off the boats, and of these only a very small number were airmen. In August, Medhurst recorded his thoughts on the French. After a mild lament that the RAF had been lumbered with the job in the first place, he somewhat loftily noted that Churchill had 'given an undertaking to General de Gaulle that he shall have an air force, wholly French in character, and that we are to maintain it'.[6]

At the time, a small French unit comprising all the available trained pilots and mechanics had been hurriedly formed at RAF Odiham in Hampshire. Plans were being laid to equip them with British aircraft before they proceeded overseas, and the remainder of the 200 or so French airmen in Britain would then receive accelerated training before they too would be posted abroad to replace wastage. This scheme to post the trained men overseas indicates the essential difference between the French airmen in exile and the other European nationalities forced to regroup in Britain. As far as the Free French were concerned, they were still very much in the war despite partition of their country, but to understand the complexities of their situation, we must first review the political issues of the hour.

In a superior work which examines the entire wartime relationship between the Free French, the Americans and the British, C.E. Maguire makes the point that Charles de Gaulle was the only senior Frenchman left standing in June 1940 who was prepared to fight on.[7] It was de Gaulle who, almost by act of will, brought the Free French movement into being, who defended the British action against the French fleet in Oran, who was bold enough to openly blame the French military leaders for their own defeat, and who was prepared to accept, albeit reluctantly, that he needed British assistance if France was ever to be restored. Churchill was aware of this, and he welcomed de Gaulle as the one positive dividend from the catastrophe of the summer. But this did not mean that he liked the man. Anecdotes abound which illustrate that the relationship between the two was difficult and frequently sour. Described by Churchill in 1940 as 'a lanky, gloomy Brigadier', de Gaulle apparently possessed a God-given ability to rankle Churchill with almost his every word and gesture. Richard Collier told the tale of an interrupted meal at Chequers when the Frenchman insisted on speaking to Churchill on the telephone as the latter sat down to dinner. 'Cheeks crimson, napkin crumpled', Churchill took the call and returned after ten minutes in a boiling rage. 'Bloody de Gaulle!' he cried. 'He had the impertinence to tell me that the French regard him as the reincarnation of Joan of Arc. I found it very necessary to remind him that we had to burn the first!'[8]

Beyond the bluster lay the stark fact that each needed the other in the desperate hours of 1940, yet this co-operation came at a hefty political price. De Gaulle's position was tenuous indeed. In order to prevail, he must first reduce the profile of the Pétain government and demonstrate that it had no popular support; but the Vichy administration, despite being openly aligned with Berlin, had still been democratically installed, making it a legitimate government irrespective of what anyone thought of it. Maguire draws our attention to the important fact that, had Britain and any future allies been victorious without the Free French maintaining at least the illusion of an alternative government, then France's empire might have been part of the prize.

Thus it was vital for de Gaulle to form an acceptable alternative government and to maintain its sovereignty, but this in itself brought with it a host of thorny complications. De Gaulle had to simultaneously ridicule the Vichy regime as a puppet of the Nazis while avoiding being accused by it of being a tool of the allies. This was no easy balancing act. De Gaulle had to be on his guard at all times not to give the appearance of merely doing Churchill's bidding, unless there was some vital French interest at stake. Furthermore, it often suited his purposes to give the impression of being deliberately obstructive and difficult if it would add to the aura, real or imagined, of a tough, single-minded man who was fighting for France with a little help from an ally in need of friends.

We must therefore not be too harsh on de Gaulle, at least in regard to his actions during the first two years of the Free French movement. He had virtually no money, little support, and almost no men with which to rebuild his national forces. Throughout the summer of 1940, a steady trickle of Frenchmen found their way to Britain, but more than a few of these opted to serve with the British Army rather than sign up with de Gaulle. Others sought repatriation to France, for they saw in de Gaulle a destructive rather than creative force, which would be used to impose a rightist government on France once the war was won – *if* it was won. As with the Czechoslovaks, however, many of whom disliked and distrusted their self-appointed leader, Edvard Beneš, a good number of Frenchmen who threw in their lot with de Gaulle were fighting for *France*, not for him. As far as they were concerned, any political issues would be resolved after the defeat of Germany. De Gaulle was astute enough to realise this, promising that all of France would be given the opportunity to decide her future when the moment arrived.

The British also stood to gain by having de Gaulle on board as a more or less willing accomplice in the prosecution of the war. Although the prospect of real military assistance was unlikely in the short or even medium term, the presence of de Gaulle offered hope that resistance in France would be stiffened. This was also a factor in Britain's recognition of the Provisional Czechoslovak Government. In both cases, the political leaders – despite what the Foreign Office might think of them – would act as rallying points for Resistance groups in the occupied territories. Also, and again as with the Czechs, the British needed someone to administer the exiled forces for them, and it was infinitely easier to 'appoint' a nominal superior to do the job rather than assume full responsibility themselves. This was certainly the case with Beneš, and to a considerable extent with de Gaulle, too.

But to return to the moment of formation: the Free French suffered from an inferiority complex. They were embarrassed by their country's defeat, by Britain's continued resistance, and by the pitifully small numbers who had volunteered to serve with them. In Maguire's words, they 'over-reacted when questions of sovereignty or culture were involved'.[9] As a result of de Gaulle's determination to show that France still lived as a sovereign power, he insisted at all times that he should have total control over the troops and airmen who escaped to Britain. If a French serviceman presented himself to a British recruiting office, he should at once be referred to the Free French authorities, who would decide whether they would take him or not. There was nothing unusual in this – it was standard British policy with all of the exiled groups to refer them to their national representatives if they applied to serve with British forces – but de Gaulle could cut up rougher than most when his own men were involved.

De Gaulle was therefore not interested in forming Free French squadrons in Britain, at least to begin with. Every available man would have to be under his command and where he wanted him. He had a war to fight, he needed money and he needed men, so the easiest way to acquire them was to 'liberate' French colonies hitherto untouched by German forces. Some declared for him at once, others – such as Gabon – after a fight. But in the summer of 1940, the target was Dakar in French West Africa. That is why the trained men Medhurst referred to were being swiftly transferred out of the country, to join the forces being assembled for OPERATION MENACE. We know that this turned out disastrously for the allies, and according to Maguire, 'this undermined any confidence that the British military had in the Free French'.[10]

Medhurst was concerned about de Gaulle's absolute insistence that all French personnel should be sent to him. On 20 July he wrote to Sinclair and Newall wishing to set down 'the facts of the situation' as he perceived them. He had been informed that de Gaulle had commanded the formation of one fighter and one bomber squadron in the Middle East, though he pointed out that de Gaulle did not have the men to form full squadrons at all, only flights. The real problem was not overseas, however, but at home. Medhurst reminded his superiors that when the situation in France was deteriorating, the RAF had solemnly promised that all French personnel who wished to fight on could do so with the British forces, if they could manage to escape. As a result, many of the early exiles had signed up with the RAFVR. But Medhurst then drew attention to a recent pronouncement by de Gaulle:

> He has been insistent that any Frenchman who has left French territory for the purpose of continuing the struggle against Germany [is] to be regarded as his servant and should first receive his permission to enter British service. Without this permission [he] might be regarded as guilty of disobedience to his leader.[11]

Medhurst was right to flag this as a major policy problem for the British, for in every other case the allied governments were told firmly that if a man chose not to serve with them, they had no right compel him by any means. Now de Gaulle was essentially threatening every Frenchman with desertion or even mutiny if he did not rally to the Free French, and Medhurst was concerned that the General might insist that all French personnel be released from the RAFVR, possibly against their will.

The answer to his query was despatched swiftly. On 24 July, all air attachés and overseas commanders were informed that if any Frenchmen applied for service with de Gaulle's Free French Air Force, British officers should 'encourage only those whom you consider trustworthy, physically fit and qualified to take their place immediately'.[12] Everybody should be encouraged to serve with de Gaulle rather than the RAF, but they would temporarily enrol in the RAFVR until further notice. This in effect let the Air Ministry off the hook, for it knew perfectly well that very few of the men volunteering for service with the Free French were capable of taking up arms at once, and those who were only partly trained would be of little use in Africa, so they would automatically be sent to England as RAFVR personnel for further training. Those who *were* directly appointed to serving units would still be enrolled in the RAFVR – and thereby Britain would uphold her promise – but de Gaulle would nevertheless have his men under his command with minimum interference from the British.

A hidden dividend for the British in this arrangement was that they could be satisfied that all French personnel were going to be employed in some way or another, either directly with the British forces – despite de Gaulle's dissatisfaction – or with the

Free French. For again, as with the Czechs, the Home Office had
sounded the alarm that some French personnel lately arrived in
Britain were attempting to evade military service and settle down
as civilians or political refugees.[13] British policy on this issue
was strictly enforced: no aliens, friendly or otherwise, would be
permitted to take up residence in Britain unless they had been
resident in the country before the outbreak of war. Anyone who
was demobilised from his national contingent for reasons of
age or incapacity would be granted temporary residence until
the war was over, at which point he would be handed back to
the relevant government. The only exceptions to this rule were
those persons whose nationality would have made life difficult
for them if they had been compelled or strongly persuaded to
serve in their national forces. A perfect example of this lay in
the case of the Sudeten Germans, who technically came under
the control of the Czechoslovak authorities, but with a few
limited exceptions they did not want them anyway. Austrians
and 'anti-Nazi' Germans were also two groups for which special
arrangements were made, and in many cases these people were
enlisted into the Auxiliary Military Pioneer Corps (AMPC),
always the British Army's last resort for its miscreants, misfits and
ne'er-do-wells.

To be fair to the French, not many of their number tried
to side-step the restraints. Besides, there were at least a few
from *all* the exiled groups who tried to disappear into civilian
life soon after arrival. But the French issue was complicated
still further by the intense political feelings among the men
themselves. An interesting though largely disregarded report
was enthusiastically sent to William Strang early in August 1940
by Medhurst and Porri at the DAAC. Compiled by an unnamed
officer from the intelligence section at Coastal Command, it
purported to show the true picture within the Czechoslovak,
Belgian and French contingents.

It was said that 70 per cent of the French evacuees understood
the British action against the French fleet at Oran, thus on
balance it seemed that the majority at least could be persuaded
to fight on the allied side. Even so, this still left nearly a third with
a deep resentment that could be manipulated by propaganda
or agents working against the common cause, therefore careful
screening would be necessary before French personnel could be
trusted in service. Furthermore, it was revealed that the French
were also politically divided between royalists and republicans.
The former group were well represented among the sailors – a
point of interest to remember when we consider the formation

of 340 Free French squadron – while the fewer republicans were split between loyalty to de Gaulle and resignation to accepting the realities of defeat exemplified by the Vichy government. The report argued that propaganda must be intensified in Vichy France to force it to become anti-German, and the rather gloomy conclusion drawn by the investigator pointed to a general distrust of politicians and parliament generally. 'Nothing could have been more rotten than the Third Republic,' were the alleged words of one sailor. 'A king could hardly do worse; he might even do better.'[14] Lastly, the report noted that anti-Semitism was at a very high level – again, nothing unusual in the wider context of the exiled groups as a whole, but a further disturbing indication that the racial policies of the Third Reich were not as reviled as some would like to believe.

Frank Roberts and Jack Ward at the Foreign Office chose to ignore most of the recommendations and observations contained in the August report, not through reasons of disbelief – though Ward commented that the writer displayed 'a violent prejudice' – but because there was very little in practice which could be done to make the situation any different.[15] Thus, by the end of the summer of 1940, as the Battle of Britain was being fought in the skies over south-east England, both the Air Ministry and the Foreign Office had concluded that the French, Czechoslovak and Polish contingents would all need careful attention as the process of 'shaking down' began in earnest. The political volatility and prejudicial assessments of each group's fighting capabilities had left their mark, and it mattered not that Polish and Czechoslovak squadrons were already in action against the Luftwaffe, and that they had scored numerous victories and suffered casualties in the fight for the common cause. For, as we have seen, the attitudes formed in the early part of the war, often without any hard evidence to sustain them, had a habit of lingering on into the middle years when – as one would reasonably suppose – all doubts might have been cast aside.

By August 1940, about a hundred French airmen were enrolled in the RAFVR awaiting training, and some twenty or so were in action with RAF squadrons. By the autumn, that number had increased to 350 as stragglers made their way from the liberated territories and from Vichy France. The November report produced by the Chiefs of Staff on the allied contingents contained the estimated numbers of foreign service personnel then in Britain, and the figures put the whole issue into perspective.[16]

Force	Navy	Army	Air	Total
Free French	2,750	1,080	350	4,180
Polish	1,750	17,450	8,500	27,700
Dutch	2,400	1,570	270	4,240
Czechoslovak	0	3,470	1,250	4,720
Norwegian	1,000	1,410	3*	2,413
Belgian	0	780	165	945

*(see note 16)

This is a good indicator of why de Gaulle was so sensitive about the utilisation of his air personnel. His total forces ranked third on the list of displaced allies, narrowly behind the despised Czechoslovaks and a long way short of the Poles his superiors had treated so shabbily. In all, the allied forces numbered 44,198 men of all ranks, but the supposedly senior ally, the French, could only contribute less than 10 per cent to this tally.

The French forces in Britain therefore had much greater political significance than merely being a military presence, at least until the allied victory in North Africa. An agreement was reached with de Gaulle in early August which covered all the major points listed above in regard to training and recruitment, and it was swiftly decided that RAF Odiham, near Basingstoke in Hampshire, would be the central depot for the French air personnel. The French had a few aircraft of their own for training and navigation purposes, but both the equipment and the men were technically on loan to the RAF until de Gaulle had need of them. Morale was described as 'good', but in the language of the Chiefs of Staff, this was the equivalent to 'average' in layman's terms. Their abilities, however, were described as 'very satisfactory', and the intensive training delivered to them at Odiham led to about fifteen pilots and fifty other ranks being declared fit to join the crews selected for OPERATION MENACE in September 1940.[17]

The fact that morale was not especially high is no surprise, given the context into which the French volunteers had been propelled by the sorry events of that summer. Worse still, Britain was unsure whether or not she was at war with unoccupied France in the south. In early July 1940, the new French government issued a warning that any British aircraft within a 20-mile limit of French territory would be shot down as hostile, a threat to which the British immediately responded in kind. Boyle justified the action to the Foreign Office by arguing that the Germans might try to use French aircraft to steal a slight advantage, but everyone knew that Vichy was going to comply fully with the terms of the armistice. The Pétain government issued orders for all French Air Force planes and pilots to concentrate in North Africa for demobilisation; many obeyed these orders, though some broke ranks and flew to Gibraltar. These were the men who came to Britain in the early autumn.

What matters, however, was the rancorous atmosphere which all this distrust and confusion created. Medhurst noted in September that there were 'very strong political reasons why we should make every effort to stimulate the morale of these young men'. Attempts by the French to form their own air training school had foundered due to the lack of instructors, but Medhurst suggested a scheme whereby the French and Belgian contingents could pool their expertise and train pilots for their own national forces. The RAF was willing to supply the equipment, and Adm Muselier for the French and Col Wouters for the Belgians both signified their approval. All three parties moved quickly, despite arguments from some quarters that the proposed use of resources would slow up the training of British pilots. It was vital, retorted the Chiefs of Staff, that a spirit of alliance be engendered between the allied forces if the process of integration were ever to succeed. Permission for the scheme was therefore granted within days of Medhurst's suggestion.[18]

The Franco-Belgian Training School at RAF Odiham had a short but successful life. It was in full operation by December 1940, and had rapidly produced fifteen French and six Belgian fighter pilots, all of whom had joined RAF squadrons and together destroyed four enemy aircraft in combat. But it had become apparent that many of the French volunteers had less experience than had been expected, and though an average of 165 flying hours was being chalked up at Odiham, some courses were delayed because basic training was deemed necessary in some cases. Even so, Dowding expressed his satisfaction with the quality of the pilots produced, and the COS report for February 1941 recorded the improvement in morale as 'considerable'. By May, however, the experiment was at an end. The Chiefs of Staff informed the Cabinet that the facilities at Odiham were urgently required for other purposes, but in truth the object of the exercise had been to get as many French and Belgian pilots in the air as quickly as possible to improve morale, and that had been achieved beyond doubt. Further training could be handled by the RAF alone, or by the allied contingents themselves, but the Franco-Belgian collaboration demonstrated to everyone concerned that the desire to continue the struggle was very strong indeed, and in itself this was a worthwhile dividend.

The French also had other things in mind by the winter of 1940/41. Adm Muselier wrote to the Air Ministry in November exploring the possibilities of forming a Free French fighter squadron in Britain, and Collier at the DAAC wrote to Sholto Douglas to explain the position: 'The Free French authorities have noted the frequent references to Poles and Czechs in the British press and feel that their own personnel in England is rather left out of the limelight.' A cynic might have made much of this rather pouting grievance, but Collier stuck to the practicalities. It seemed that the French felt they could supply the pilots but not the ground crew, therefore any squadron would have to be dependent on British technicians to keep it in the air. More to the point, they also requested that the squadron should never fly over French territory, 'because of the risk to their lives if they land'. This obviously irritated Collier, for he bluntly recommended that the scheme be scrapped unless higher powers overruled him in view of the proposal's political implications. Within days, that was exactly what happened. Both Sholto Douglas and the Vice-Chief of the Air Staff, Sir Wilfred Freeman, comprehensively rejected the plan after Medhurst threw his weight into the balance. The former head of the DAAC (he was by this date Director of Plans) sympathised with the French request, but argued that such a squadron could not be considered unless they were willing to supply their own ground personnel. He suggested forming French flights within British squadrons, but if de Gaulle would not accept that, then any future Free French pilots should be sent to the Middle East. In short, no one was prepared to countenance the establishment of a Free French fighter squadron in Britain to satisfy what appeared to be nothing more than de Gaulle's hunger for prestige.[19]

The matter fell into abeyance until the summer of 1941. Muselier contacted the Air Ministry again and assured it that sufficient ground crew had been found to form a fully operational Free French fighter squadron at the earliest opportunity. He had manipulated his available manpower by drawing technicians from the Free French Navy who had once served with the French Naval Air Arm, and hence had some experience of working with aircraft. Muselier also baited his hook with an implied threat that it would also be possible to use these men to establish the core of a Fleet Air Arm, something the British would not accept at any price because overall control by the RAF would be seriously weakened, if not negated altogether, so it was reluctantly decided to agree to the proposal, but with conditions attached. In the first place, the French had to undertake to operate the squadron as an integral unit and submit to the overall policy of allied command. Secondly, they were not to use the squadron merely as a pool of trained reserves for topping up their forces in North Africa. If they concurred with these wishes, formation could proceed.[20]

Boyle, Muselier and a number of other French officers met at the end of June to discuss officially the creation of 340 (Free French) Fighter Squadron. The meeting heard that the French could eventually supply enough pilots to make the plan viable. Already they had 10 men serving with RAF squadrons, a further 93 in various stages of basic flying training, 41 in fighter OTUs, and another 35 about to begin initial training at stations across the country. Muselier promised to maintain the squadron in Britain, and he calculated that after a year the men seconded from the Navy would be replaced by fully trained operatives, thus making the squadron a wholly integral unit entirely compatible with RAF standards. It would still technically be a naval squadron, but one 'placed at the disposal of the RAF'. This was typical French wordplay, creating the impression that their independent status was sacrosanct, and that they were somehow doing the RAF a favour. The Air Ministry representatives probably rankled to hear it – especially after the Admiralty voiced concerns about the naval connections – but it was the best they were going to get. One problem was removed, however. Muselier withdrew his objection to his aircraft flying over French territory, but it is unlikely that this concession signalled a real change of heart. Other allied squadrons – notably the Czechs and the Poles – had brushed aside concerns for their safety over enemy territory by retorting that it was an acceptable risk of war, so it is hardly likely that the French would have stood alone in their refusal, driven as they were by the desire to increase their column inches in the British press.[21]

Much still remained to be done before 340 Squadron could take its place in the line. Sholto Douglas formally agreed to its formation in August 1941, but he insisted that a British commander should take charge while the squadron was shaking down and dependent on British ground staff acting as instructors and technicians. De Gaulle also stirred the pot by nominating Adm Muselier as the French commander, and not Gen Valin, the C-in-C of the Free French Air Force. This was to emphasise the major contribution being made by the Navy to the project, but this jangled nerves in the Air Ministry, provoking it to ask for assurances that the squadron would be subject to RAF law, and not that of the French Navy. Then, in October, the whole plan was thrown into jeopardy because of supply problems, British commitments to Soviet Russia being cited as the reason. The RAF had undertaken to send 170 Hurricanes to Russia in October, and a further 200 in November, all drawn from existing RAF squadrons as Spitfire replacements became available. The French were not pleased, but Sholto Douglas stood his ground. The Belgians had also recently proposed their own fighter squadron, but both would have to wait until Stalin had been sated with Hurricanes.

By early October 1941, the mists were clearing. Sufficient aircraft would become available within four weeks, and 340 Squadron would form at Turnhouse on 7 November. Yet the party was spoilt almost as soon as the invitations were sent, for in a brief minute to the Air Ministry, Muselier confessed that he had been unable to find the ground crew after all. If 340 was to function as an operational unit, the British must supply the maintenance echelon for at least the first six months. Now this was guaranteed to irritate the British; the agreement had been that the French would have their national squadron and all the glory which came with it, but now it seemed that the RAF must supply the essential staff while the pilots wallowed in the attention and de Gaulle gained another feather in his cap. We have seen how sensitive the British could be in regard to allied squadrons that were incapable of operating as fully national units, the particularly bitter row which erupted over just such an issue with the Czechoslovaks standing as the worst example. And yet even before the essential preparations for 340 had been completed, another storm had begun to brew, this time between the French themselves.

It began in mid-October with a summary to the Air Ministry dealing with 'trouble and discontent' at the School of Technical Training, St Athan. The naval ground crew which Muselier had promised were cited as the cause of a host of minor personal grievances which had totally disrupted the already fragile unity of the various French service arms. 'There is a good deal of rivalry between the Air Force and Naval personnel,' ran the report. 'They are obviously not mixing at all, and do not even appear to be on speaking terms with each other. The whole spirit of the Free French unit at St Athan is therefore very bad . . . and unless a solution is found it will have a very bad effect on the spirit of the fighter squadron.' It was apparent that numerous differences in pay and rank between the Free French Navy and Air Force were to blame – the Air Force crews receiving less money for what they perceived to be equivalent status – and although the worst of the squabbling was skilfully smoothed over by a French officer, Commandant Jubelin, the roots of the dispute were actually political, and it was to get a lot worse before it got better.

Jubelin had impressed some of the British so much that he was nominated as the French commander of 340 Squadron when it formed; indeed, this was seconded by Valin, but ultimately rejected by the Air Ministry due to his age (thirty-four) and lack of operational experience. Valin himself also came in for criticism for allowing such a disparity of pay and conditions to develop in the first place. He was immediately requested to personally guarantee that all rates of pay would be equalised for equivalent ranks where French personnel were stationed on an RAF base, and for good measure he was reminded that men from all three services came under RAF law. He agreed to the conditions on 23 October, and the British reasonably assumed that formation could proceed.

On 31 October, Sholto Douglas, then AOC Fighter Command, approved the selection of Sqn Ldr Keith Lofts as the first CO of 340, with two flight commanders from the Free French Air Force, Flt Lt Duperier and Flg Off Mouchotte. This sparked the next furore. De Gaulle and Muselier both recorded their anger at the choice, claiming that they had not been consulted on the appointments and that there were no navy pilots in the original establishment of flying personnel. De Gaulle had been persuaded by two navy pilots named Scitivaux and Laurent that the Air Ministry had deliberately sought to keep the Free French Navy at bay in the composition of the squadron, but Fighter Command fiercely replied that the Free French had overestimated their own influence in the construction of 340 and as far as the RAF was concerned, pilot selection was a question of suitability, not political preference.[22]

It was in the midst of this unsettled atmosphere that 340 (Free French) fighter squadron was formed at Turnhouse on 7 November and mounted on Spitfire IIa aircraft. Its ground crew was composed of sixty men from the Free French Navy and a further twenty-five from the air force, but the inter-service tensions had not gone away despite the good reasons for unity which 340's existence should have engendered. In less than a week, Valin was writing to Archibald Sinclair and warning him that the problems in the ranks might lead to a complete seizure of communication between the two services, leading either to the collapse of the squadron as a viable unit, or to the complete replacement of all personnel by naval technicians. Valin asked Sinclair that if things got any worse, would the British step in with an emergency cohort of ground crew. The reply he received from Sinclair was an emphatic 'no'.[23]

Things bumped along for a while, and though 340 was declared operational on 29 November, little flying took place during the early winter months. The time was spent on defensive patrols along the northern coasts, but the continuing hostility among the ground crew echelons meant that servicing times were extended. The morale of the pilots was described in the 19th COS report as 'very good', but that of the ground crews as 'mixed'. Then, in mid-January 1942, Valin lobbed another grenade into the pot. He informed the Air Ministry that he did not have sufficient ground crew to form the Free French flight 'Alsace' in the Middle East, and he requested that the entire ground crew then presently with 340 Squadron be transferred to the Western Desert at once. Muselier was also lobbying him for the return of his sixty-five men at the earliest opportunity. Valin asked if the RAF would be prepared to rapidly install a replacement ground crew in 340 Squadron, 'as it was important from the political aspect to keep the squadron in existence in the United Kingdom'.

When this news reached Sholto Douglas, he made his views crystal clear in a letter to H.G. Crowe at the DAFL: 'I am not at all anxious to fall in with General Valin's wishes. In the first place, I feel that I have been "led up the garden path".' He went on to reiterate that the original agreement with the French rested upon their promise that they would supply the ground crew, 'but now that they have got their squadron, they wish to go back on their undertaking. I feel that I have been "bounced". I don't like this sort of dishonest dealing.' He accepted that Anglo-French collaboration on the squadron might work in practice, and he used his own experience of this with 313 (Czechoslovak) Fighter Squadron which relied entirely on British ground crew. But in the French case he was not prepared to back down: 'I find the Czechs much easier to deal with than the Free French who, as you will I think agree, are very difficult and touchy people.' He instructed the DAFL to tell Valin that no one was going back to the navy, or being transferred to the Middle East, and if the French objected he would ask the Air Ministry to disband the squadron at once and disperse the pilots:

> In actual fact – though you need not say this – this is the course that I would prefer, as I only agreed to the formation of the squadron to please and encourage the Free French movement. I should not be sorry to convert it to a British squadron and spread the pilots around other British squadrons – where in fact many of them have done very well in the past.

On 22 January, the DAFL relayed a sanitised version of this to
the Spears Mission, the channel of communication between
the British and the Free French. Crowe suggested that Valin
recalled the French pilots from the Middle East and allowed
them to fly with British squadrons, for it seemed unlikely that the
necessary maintenance staff would be found. After a few days, the
Spears Mission returned with Valin's opinion. As far as he was
concerned, the North African theatre of operations was more
important, therefore the best option was to disband 340. This
would (a) let the navy have its men back; (b) solve the problem
of the friction between the two services in 340; (c) ensure that the
pilots would remain operational with the RAF, and (d) release
the 25 French Air Force mechanics, who could then make up the
shortfall in the Middle East.[24]

The fate of 340 Squadron was thus hanging by a slender thread
before it was even three months old. Conscious of the awesome
political fall-out if the squadron were to fold, irrespective of
who ordered it, the DAFL sent its own representative to 340
Squadron with a brief to determine the facts. J.A. de Laszlo
travelled through the winter weather from London to Ayr and
spoke with Lofts, who was still commanding the troubled unit.
Together they compiled reports which threw into high relief not
only the immediate problems with 340 Fighter Squadron, but
also the deeper issues which plagued the Free French movement
as a whole. For Lofts, the main problem was the high number
of NCOs. The better rates of pay available for the extra stripes
meant that both the air force and navy wings continually
promoted their men 'regardless of their efficiency', leaving the
squadron with enough NCOs to administer 3,000 men. The navy
men constantly demanded a return posting, and air force NCOs
refused to take orders from navy NCOs, and vice versa. The few
men who belonged to the Fleet Air Arm tended to ignore both.
Some tactless desk-hand had also posted a number of Tahitians
to 340, and they complained bitterly about the Scottish weather
and refused to work outside in the cold. One by one, men were
finding their way out of 340 and were being replaced by British
maintenance men, and according to Lofts, this British presence
was 'the backbone of the squadron'.

De Laszlo took a slightly different view. He named and
shamed two individuals whom he considered guilty of fomenting
discontent across the station, mainly because they were 'both
angling for a cushy job in French HQ in London'. He explained
that the high number of NCOs was causing innumerable
disciplinary problems because of their refusal to take orders

from each other. This was wrecking the confidence and morale of the lower ranks to the point where men simply refused to do any work, safe in the knowledge that they were unlikely to be punished. The earlier promise by the French to equalise pay had indeed been honoured, but instead of raising it to meet the standards of the navy, they lowered it to the levels of the air force. Even so, de Laszlo described the morale among the pilots as 'extremely good', but the ensuing difficulties on the ground meant that 'the most serious trouble' was likely to break out soon unless something was done.

Lofts had clearly had enough, and by early February 1942 he was on his way to a new posting abroad. The moment seemed right for the man of the hour himself to pay a visit to 340, and de Gaulle's appearance in the biting cold of mid-February produced a brief moment of comic irony. Writing his own report for the Spears Mission, Sqn Ldr Skepper told how, after the officers had consumed warming drinks 'in lavish quantities', de Gaulle stood on a podium near him and lectured the men on the importance of maintaining good communications. 'Unfortunately there was a heavy wind blowing,' noted Skepper, '[and] I was unable to hear what he said.'

Some time later, de Gaulle granted Skepper the pleasure of one of his long monologues, in which he criticised British and American tactics. Wrote Skepper: 'I suggested to the General that it was a great pity that he did not know English better so as to be able to explain his theories to important government officials, to which he replied that as he had been unable to make the French nation realise the value of his opinions, it was hardly likely that he would have any influence on the English.' If ever there was a stray note which completely captured the essence of a flawed alliance, Skepper's memories have served history well.

In early April 1942, 340 Squadron moved south to Tangmere and began fighter sweeps over northern France. It was a cherished hope of some at the Air Ministry that the promise of serious action would dispel the gloom. The new station commander, Grp Capt Appleton, constantly reinforced the point that life as a front-line squadron was much rougher than Scottish patrols, but he urged the pilots to remember that the evidence showed that allied pilots shot down over enemy territory were unlikely to be treated differently to any other RAF man. But it still seemed impossible to improve morale and discipline on the ground, and the differences went much deeper than petty squabbles over pay and ranks. The divisions which had plagued the Third Republic since its forced inception at the hands of the Prussians way back in 1871 still had resonance in 1942. Republicans and royalists taunted each other, and those who still nursed anti-British grudges after Oran quarrelled with Gaullists and spread defeatism. Soon after the move to Tangmere, Valin made an appearance and bluntly told the men that they 'were not giving complete satisfaction'. He threatened them with courts of enquiry, demotion, and even expulsion from the squadron if they did not pull their weight and give maximum effort to the cause of France. He laid the blame squarely on the NCOs of the Free French Navy. Skepper, who accompanied Valin, saw men lounging about and reluctant to attend to their duties unless forced by officers. In his report, he noted that 'it would seem improbable that any reasonable form of discipline can ever be established in this squadron' unless the RAF dictated practice and the French applied a heavy hand.[25]

Appleton was either insensitive to these problems or simply unaware of them. By his own admission, it seems to have been the latter, for in a report made to the DAFL he declared himself satisfied with the work of the squadron and had observed no significant difficulties. Quite possibly, however, he was not permitted to see the worst of the internecine battle simmering beneath the surface. The testimony of the British Engineer Officer indicates that the French kept their problems to themselves, leaving the British out of any discussions concerning the ground crew or their grievances. The French themselves admitted that they tended to attach too much importance to the matter of rank. A central problem was that many NCOs had failed their trade tests, but were nevertheless good NCOs for their leadership qualities. On the other hand, many airmen had qualified with high scores in the RAF examinations, leading to the absurd position that the lower ranks were telling their seniors what needed to be done and how to do it. Supervision of routine maintenance work and engineering activities was therefore impossible, so the DAFL ordered the squadron (a) to select the best NCOs and push them through further trade testing; (b) to remove three senior NCOs described as 'not a good influence on the squadron', and (c) to post nine others to distant duties when suitable replacements had been found.

Earlier in the month of April 1942, political discussions had been advancing towards a new treaty of alliance with the French. The rushed document of August 1940 had substantially outlived its use and relevance, but the British were still determined not to give their reluctant ally too much room for manoeuvre. The problems in 340 Squadron resulted from the control de Gaulle expected to wield over all of his forces, the Air Ministry noting that he and his acolytes promoted and demoted individuals without any reference to the appropriate RAF authorities, something upon which the British insisted with all the other allied forces. More often than not, men were rewarded with an enhanced rank according to their political views and acceptability within the Gaullist clique, and it was felt that this practice had contributed to the difficulties which plagued 340 Squadron from the day of its formation. In the new Anglo-French agreement signed on 1 May, this loophole was neatly filled by inserting a clause committing the French to nominate airmen for promotion and then place their recommendations before the RAF, the decision of the latter body being final. It was a hard-won point. De Gaulle resisted this apparent loss of sovereignty for some time, but the British stood firm, the net result being a slow but consistent improvement in the morale and discipline of 340 Squadron.[26]

In the air, however, 340 was making a name for itself. The move south had raised the pilots' spirits, and the operations summaries for the period show how the workload of the squadron had increased enormously. Between November 1941 and March 1942, the squadron had flown a total of twenty-six sorties while in Scotland, whereas within a month of moving to Tangmere, that number had increased to 189, most of them over the French coastline. The success rate had also boosted morale. In six weeks, 340 had accounted for 9 enemy aircraft destroyed, 2 probables and 2 damaged. In return, the French suffered five men missing and one serious injury. By mid-summer 1942, a total of 1,611 operational hours had been flown, though by then the scores for and against were more or less even. Twelve pilots were decorated by de Gaulle for outstanding service; but perhaps more importantly, most of the problems within 340 Squadron had either been resolved or were in the process of resolution.

One niggling issue would not go away, however. Still the tension between the Free French Navy and Air Force continued, though not so much on the ground by October 1942, but at the higher levels. At the time, 340 Squadron contained fifty-three naval personnel, three of them pilots, and the French authorities wanted these men back in the navy for further training. This would place a further strain on the maintenance resources of 340, for although the squadron had been in existence for some time, the initial ratio of air force to navy personnel had been 30:69. That dependency on the naval arm had scarcely decreased by the autumn of 1942, standing at 37:55, with a further 28 air force men due to arrive in four months after training. The DAFL reacted assertively, pointing out to the French that the shortfall would have to be made up by posting RAF mechanics to the squadron, which in itself broke the agreement to keep the unit as a national entity. Word came through that Muselier's successor, Adm Auboyneau, would argue that because 340 had been consistently described as an RAF squadron, he was no longer bound by the agreement to keep it flying with his men. In desperation, the DAFL requested the French to withdraw the mechanics over a phased period, replacing each one man-for-man with trained air force personnel. The reply from the French was non-committal.

A dark situation had become a crisis by November 1942. Frank Beaumont, then in charge of the DAFL, wrote to Sholto Douglas at Fighter Command and warned him that if the Free Free French Navy went ahead with its proposals without replacing the men, 340 Squadron would almost certainly fold. The best-case scenario would be to concentrate all the Free French Air Force mechanics into one group and post surplus pilots to British squadrons, in effect reducing the unit to one viable flight. Sholto Douglas disagreed with this calculation, and he could see no satisfactory alternative to sending in RAFVR mechanics if the French Navy persisted. As far as he was concerned, the political damage would be very serious, but it had to be the French and not the British who would shoulder the blame in that eventuality.

On 18 November, the formal request from the French for the transfer of all the naval men landed on Beaumont's desk He wrote immediately to Sholto Douglas, noting that the French Navy had also demanded the return of the one naval pilot still flying with the RAF, a Lt Claude, then with 118 Squadron. Quite obviously, the Free French Navy was determined to sever all its connections with the RAF, and Sholto Douglas authorised the emergency transfer of RAF mechanics to make up the deficiency, even if that weakened existing RAF units. Angrily, he minuted that the postings out of the squadron could take place as soon as possible, and under no circumstances would naval personnel be permitted to rejoin the unit, 'in order to avoid further trouble'. The change in personnel happened on one day, 1 December. Out went the navy men, and in came fifty-three RAF mechanics hastily removed from reserve squadrons across the length and breadth of Britain. Within days, a DAFL report on 340 Squadron noted that 'discipline among the ground personnel has improved'.[27]

It had taken over a year of intense argument between the administrative divisions of two air forces and one navy to bring peace to 340 Squadron, and although in that time the unit had acquitted itself with honour, doing what it was formed to do, the real battles had taken place across desks and conference rooms. The story of 340 serves to illustrate the extremely irritable alliance between the British and the French. Sholto Douglas in particular was deeply incensed by the latter's refusal to uphold previous agreements and its inclination to play political games both with the RAF and, ultimately, the lives of men under his command. The RAF did not give up in its struggle to have its own men in 340 replaced by French mechanics, but it was victory in North Africa and the subsequent release of personnel for other duties which finally enabled the squadron to approach full national integrity, not a change of heart by the French authorities.

In March 1943, the squadron was withdrawn from the southern sectors and returned to Scotland. Officially, this was described as a routine rotation, 340 being long overdue for a rest. However, DAFL documents show that there were other motives involved. By this time, 340 had a pilot surplus amounting to eighteen men fully trained on Spitfires, but instead of posting these men for service in British squadrons, it had been decided to keep them in a quiet sector to maintain the reserve pool. Two new French squadrons had also been formed in 1943. In January, 341 Squadron had been created out of personnel who had served in the Western Desert; and in April, 342 Bomber Squadron formed at West Raynham, again with men made available from the Middle East campaign. In both cases, it was felt that the new units would need time to adjust to the war conditions in Europe, therefore losses might be higher than normal. By keeping 340 on convoy patrols in Scotland, any unexpected pilot wastage could be made up relatively quickly.

For the rest of the war, 340 Squadron continued to play its part on a variety of fronts. The unit moved south again in 1944 and provided fighter cover to the Normandy landings, ending its days as an RAF allied squadron on 25 November 1945, when it was formally transferred to the French Air Force. Throughout 1944, further French squadrons were created, the last being 347 Heavy Bomber Squadron, which formed at Elvington on 20 June. None of the new units, however, suffered anything like the trauma experienced by 340, for by April 1943 the Free French movement was being guided towards extinction as de Gaulle made a reluctant peace with Gen Giraud and the unified French Committee of National Liberation replaced the old authority.

There had been a long-running political conflict between de Gaulle and Henri Giraud. The latter owed his position to the assassination by a French student of Adm Jean Darlan in December 1942. Darlan had been Vichy's representative and commander of its forces in North Africa, but he had thrown his lot in with the allies after the landings in November. His reward for ordering the cessation of resistance to the allied thrust was to be appointed High Commissioner for French North Africa, much to de Gaulle's disgust. A few weeks later, Darlan was dead, and Giraud was named as his successor. Giraud had become a rallying point for the anti-Vichy, anti-de Gaulle faction in French politics. He enjoyed extensive American support, and was described by one historian as 'the perfect superior – indulgent, affectionate, adored by his men because he listened to their complaints and laughed at their jokes'.[28] He was a complete contrast to de Gaulle, and therefore he represented a serious threat to the latter's bid to speak for the whole of France. But de Gaulle was confident that he could dispose of Giraud and absorb his forces, hence he moved his headquarters to Algiers in May 1943. Not long after this, the two groups merged into the French Committee of National Liberation – a marriage of convenience rather than shared objectives. This 'dual command' was announced on 21 June, but yet again another period of bitter in-fighting commenced as de Gaulle openly tried to attract Giraud's men into his own camp. Giraud did not last long, however. Faced with an opponent who used every tactic in the usurper's handbook, he was virtually forced to resign as C-in-C in April 1944. Thus, like it or not, from the middle of 1943 all French forces were, if in name only, fighting under a unified command. The conflict of loyalties which had afflicted 340 Squadron so profoundly did not attach itself to the new squadrons which followed. Also, from the point of view of the RAF, the new influx of trained personnel greatly relieved the manning problems with which the old Free French Air Force had been plagued.

Reviewing the situation in April 1943, a DAFL report noted that many of the North African contingent would rather fight with the British than the Americans. Looking far ahead to the day of victory, it was thought that the utilisation of French crews in offensive operations against the occupied territories would leave a beneficial impact on morale, a major side effect being the sound impression service with the RAF would have on the men once the war was won. This is not to suppose, however, that the British had read the new fusion of French forces correctly. A memorandum from the Minister Resident in Algiers – the future Prime Minister,

Harold Macmillan – described the forthcoming merger as being 'good for all concerned'. He argued that 'the more de Gaulle is forced out of his personal mystique and Fuehrer principles, the more he is likely to switch over on to another popular line'. According to Macmillan, de Gaulle's brand of 'concealed fascism' would be mollified by the association with Giraud, leading to an altogether more fruitful alliance. 'De Gaulle has continually bitten the hand that has fed him,' he concluded, and warned that any renewed attempt by the French to sit on the Combined Chiefs of Staff committees should be resisted at all costs.[29]

We know now, of course, how wrong Macmillan had been in his assessment of the coming new order in Algiers. De Gaulle was far too shrewd a manipulator to allow his quest to be thwarted by Giraud, but at the time the union was greeted with something approaching jubilation in Britain. Medhurst, by now the Assistant Chief of the Air Staff (Policy), proposed 'the complete Frenchification' of all existing squadrons, thereby releasing those RAF men still engaged in making up the numbers. Even so, he was not in favour of building up a large French air force in Britain, preferring instead to concentrate all their available forces in North Africa. Consequently, the training of crews on British air stations for service in the Middle East and the Mediterranean proceeded at an urgent rate through the early summer of 1943. Still looking ahead, DAFL reports note that at some stage the entire French contingent in Africa would eventually arrive in Britain as plans for OVERLORD advanced. The Air Ministry went so far as to produce a propaganda leaflet, dropped by the thousand over the occupied territories, extolling the virtues of the new united air arm and its future role in the liberation of France.[30]

From the administrative point of view, the potential to construct a truly united and rejuvenated Free French Air Force posed certain problems not encountered before. The Air Ministry called for a single Free French Air Force headquarters, and to keep the training regime fully compatible with RAF standards. Moreover, Free French Air Force law would only apply in cases where the relevant squadrons were uniquely French. One of the first moves was to appoint a liaison officer with direct access to both authorities. The man chosen was Wg Cdr Rock de Besombes. Here was an officer most trusted by the DAFL, and one can imagine the relief in British hearts when he reported that his superiors had no objections to the entire Free French Air Force being regarded as part of the inter-allied air pool being assembled for OVERLORD. Indeed, the prospect of taking part in the liberation was wholly welcomed, and for the British this enthusiasm paid a useful dividend as it kept the French away from the tentacles of America. For by 1943, British policy was slowly shifting into a postwar mode, and the need to maintain satisfactory relations with the French after victory in Europe was bubbling to the top of the agenda.

Preparations for OVERLORD continued apace during the autumn of 1943. The expected influx of French air personnel from North Africa was provided for in the establishment of an Aircrew Reception Centre at Filey, Yorkshire. The DAFL report which detailed the training and redeployment plans noted that the Free French Air Force headquarters had been 'most co-operative' with the RAF concerning procedures for selection, medical inspection and trade-testing in advance of the posting to Britain. In fact, the French had requested extra representation in the target force. The new chief of the French air staff, Gen Bouscat, let it be known that the morale of his men was excellent, and on the last day of 1943 the Foreign Office received what it described as 'excellent news'. President Roosevelt had met briefly with de Gaulle to discuss the forthcoming operations and present political dimensions. During the conversation, Roosevelt 'told de Gaulle straight that he had formed at first a bad impression of him, but he now thought that he had been mistaken, and the allies would certainly play the game with him if [he] would act fairly and frankly in return'. The euphoria was short-lived, however, because the French immediately tabled a new request for a seat on the Combined Chiefs of Staff Committee. Brushing this aside, Churchill remarked that if the request were granted, 'the Brazilians, Mexicans and the Chinese would immediately demand equal representation'. More than a touch of hyperbole, for sure, but this gives us a sense of how Churchill regarded the alliance with the French. As we shall see, his mood did not change.[31]

Churchill's refusal again increased the tension between the FCNL and the British, but the conflict was now entirely political, and had no visible effect on the military alliance. When OVERLORD was launched in June, there were a total of twelve French squadrons in the RAF target force, and four of them – 329, 340, 341 and 345 – provided fighter support over the French coasts. So great had the action been, several French pilots were listed as 'tour-expired', and before replacements could be found, several RAF pilots were rapidly drafted in to make up the shortfall. By the time of the liberation of Paris, a grand total of thirty-five French squadrons were in existence under British, American or Soviet control, and almost immediately the question of the hour turned towards the postwar scenario. As with all the allied forces except the Poles, the British endeavoured to secure peacetime rearmament contracts, but in order to win these they had to find some means of removing the vast differences of opinion which still lay between themselves and the French.

Early in February 1945, Churchill was informed of the proposal to push ahead with French rearmament under the COS 120 scheme, the initial plan being to equip and train ten Free French Air Force squadrons as soon as possible. He replied: 'I cannot believe that there is any hurry in this matter. We have a lot of things to settle with the French before we devote ourselves to helping them become a great air power after the war is over.' Uppermost in Churchill's mind was the question of French political stability as the Vichy regime was mopped up and the new order, symbolised by de Gaulle, struggled to take its place. De Gaulle had entered Paris on a tidal wave of popular sentiment, but he by no means commanded the support of everyone; and besides, the Resistance felt equally entitled to a share of power, and it had a strong communist element at its core. The Air Ministry's view was much more pragmatic: 'If we do not get in now, the United States will,' ran a comment sent to Eden. He in turn wrote to Churchill and implored him to think again, pointing out that French squadrons trained and equipped by the Americans already outnumbered their British counterparts by a ratio of 18:12. If the British dallied in pursuing rearmament, vital contracts could be lost. Furthermore, the Americans were shaping up to *give* the French a large number of operational aircraft once Japan had been defeated. Within a week, Churchill had reconsidered, and a note from Eden to all departments simply read: 'You can now go ahead.'[32]

The French had also indicated a desire to build Mosquitoes under licence from the British. Apart from the material benefits, the RAF supported the plan because it would help reflate the French air industry – 'useful in the interests of stability' – and it would deflect them from the temptation to build German aircraft and components, both of which were lying around in some abundance. The French were keen to despatch a negotiating mission to Britain in the spring of 1945, mainly to discuss rearmament plans, but also to examine new technology then at the development stage. Despite persistent requests on their behalf to get things moving, they were told that the mission should be delayed pending an Anglo-American decision on how much knowledge should be disclosed to them.

If this sounds like an odd way to treat an ally, we must consider a comment made in a Chiefs of Staff report to the War Cabinet in the middle of February 1945: 'French security is doubtful, and there is a decided risk that any information which we give to the French might find its way to the enemy.' The report therefore recommended withholding any disclosures of a sensitive nature, but it equally counselled against showing them only currently operational equipment which might well become obsolete in a couple of years. To do so, decided the chiefs, would be to create an opportunity for 'lasting grievance'. A final element in the calculation involved the Soviets, for it was felt that whatever was shown to the French would, reasonably, be demanded by Moscow too, and that would never do. They were aware, however, that Russian engineers had been very active in Germany, collecting Messerschmitt jet engines like postage stamps, so in the final analysis the Soviet question was of little importance.[33]

In any case, nothing could be done without the concurrence of the Americans. The problem was relayed to Washington for the attention of the State Department, but for some weeks the wires were quiet. In the mean time, the French grew impatient. A telegram from the SHAEF mission in France to the Foreign Office warned that they were preparing to scrap the deal completely unless progress was made soon, provoking a mournful comment from Jack Ward that the Americans had 'a theoretical stranglehold' on the entire plan, adding that they also possessed the industrial muscle to supply the French with Packard-built engines at a loss if they so desired. Although similar to the Rolls-Royce variants in power and performance, the Packard engines would be a much cheaper alternative – a mighty incentive to an industry rebuilding itself after five years of war.

The British then found themselves in a position to which they were to grow accustomed as 1945 wore on. As with the question of Polish resettlement and the return of the Czechoslovak squadrons to Prague, what the Soviets might or might not do proved to be a cause of frustration and indecision. Uppermost on the agenda in March 1945 was the issue of whether or not the Russians should be told of the French licence scheme. If they asked the French whether they (the British) should tell the Russians, the French might say yes or no. If they said yes, they might tell the Russians before the British did, thereby making the British look furtive and shifty. If they said no, the British might find themselves in the awkward position of having to refuse their advice, having asked for it, or run the risk of being seen to make a secret agreement with one ally while excluding another. The final decision was almost the stuff of legend in regard to British foreign policy making – a 'wait and see' policy would be adopted, with neither party being told about anything. Perhaps in the end it was the right approach, for two days later the US State Department delivered its verdict regarding the Mosquito plan. The answer was 'No'.[34]

The full details of the refusal reached the Foreign Office later on the same day. The Americans argued that they as well as the British had the right to benefit from the postwar rearmament programmes, and the scheme to build Mosquitoes under licence in France would not further the interests of Washington. With a rather limp excuse tacked on for good measure, they declared that they had undertaken 'a considerably extended programme' of arming the French, and while they had no objection to the British securing contracts with Belgium, the Netherlands, Norway and Denmark, any extension of productive capacities to meet the needs of the French would weaken the combined efforts to continue the war against Japan. Regarding the redevelopment of the French aero-industry, they curtly replied that the personnel might be better used to ensure the final defeat of Germany. The British were not amused by this. In a swift reply, Eden noted that he had been under the impression that Washington had had no objections in principle to Britain's rearming of the European allies; indeed, his ministers had told the relevant parties that no obstacles were foreseen in securing American concurrence. In other words, the British now looked very foolish, and a parting shot from the Foreign Office rather petulantly pointed out that the Russians had not breathed a single word about their own plans for Eastern Europe.

As always in cases like this, the truth was not very far from the myth. A rumour which first circulated in Whitehall before the American verdict, and which was confirmed a few days later, concerned the Americans' offer to the French of a substantial number of A20 Boston aircraft, with other types to follow. William Pearson Rogers, writing to Jack Ward, noted: 'This rather confirms, as we have always anticipated, that the Americans will not hesitate to unload on to the French their surplus material and obsolete aircraft with little regard to the real needs of the French rearmament plan.' Ward agreed, and in his marginal notes he wrote: 'The Americans are becoming market conscious [though] they would doubtless contend that these aircraft were allotted for purposes essential to the war, whereas we British serpents were only thinking of the post-war period.'[35]

In fact, Ward knew this assessment to be true, yet this did not soothe the uncomfortable knowledge of what postwar realities would be like with the Americans calling the plays. While the French squadrons were still in action over Germany, all three of the Anglo-French postwar plans had been stalled or rejected by Washington. The plan to immediately reinforce French air strength by ten squadrons under COS 120 had been put on hold pending the final defeat of Germany; the plan to send an air mission to Britain to study technological developments had been rejected by the Americans (and, as we have seen, questioned by the British themselves), and the plan to allow the French to build Mosquitoes under licence had been swept aside because it interfered with Washington's own scheme of showering the French with redundant aircraft. This was not a healthy beginning for the 'special relationship'.

Roughly a month later, four days before Hitler ended his own life and that of his Third Reich, the Foreign Office learned that the Americans had been deadly serious in their plan to thrust their surplus stock upon the French. Ward received notice that a total of 128 Boston aircraft would soon be in French hands, and that they would also be used in areas of British responsibility, hence the need to warn the French that no help in maintenance or spares could be expected from London. This was not pique, but practicality. It was clearly apparent that America was going to allocate aircraft to the allies, 'more or less as they see fit', while at the same time dictating rearmament terms to Britain. Jack Ward minuted: 'The Americans are having it both ways, strangling our attempts to help the allies while doing what they please themselves. But then Lend-Lease was an American scheme, and we must pay for indirectly, if not directly.' A comment to these thoughts reads: 'All the more reason for going ahead with our Mosquito project regardless of American objections.' Apparently, Sir Stafford Cripps had urged upon Churchill the need for just this assertion of British independence, but the Prime Minister demurred.

Worse still, the French themselves refused to believe that the licence scheme had been spiked by Washington, and chose instead to lay the blame at Whitehall's door. The French Air Minister had 'flown into a passion' upon hearing the news, and loudly declared that it was quite obvious that the British did not trust his nation or his people, and that it was an insult that they should be denied access to new types and developments. Ward described the whole fiasco as 'lamentable', and the final, ludicrous exchange took place when, upon hearing the news that the proposed mission had now been cancelled, someone at the Air Ministry told the French attaché that if only his superiors would come to this country, 'we have a good deal of interest to show them among the items not actually on the secret list'. The attaché's reply was not noted, which perhaps is just as well.[36]

In the event, many of the squabbles were resolved when the French took up their role as part-occupiers of German territory. The dissipation of forces plus the need to restore their own national defences led them to a compromise whereby American aircraft were accepted in the short term and a limited rearmament contract was signed with the British as well. Several hundred Vampire FB.5s were built under licence from 1950 for two years, and a few more were assembled from imported parts until indigenous designs became available in sufficient numbers to form the core of the new French Air Force. But it is difficult to escape the lingering thought that the difficulties in the Anglo-French alliance during the Second World War had almost nothing to do with military prowess or the right to adopt a superior position, even though Churchill was resolute in his determination to restrict the influence they had on the conduct of the war. Rather, it was all a question of prestige, honour, and not a little of the mutual contempt and distrust which has thousand-year-old roots. On the other hand, Central European leaders have long tried to split the Anglo–French entente when it has existed, and whether it was Bismarck, the Kaiser or the Bavarian corporal, somehow the irritable neighbours have always managed to pull through. A strange relationship indeed.

NOTES

1. Overy, R., Wheatcroft, A., *The Road to War* (Macmillan 1989), p. 142.
2. A useful survey of the French air defences in the summer of 1939 may be examined in AIR 2/2916 (War Organisation of the French Air Force). Aircraft types and likely deployment in the event of active service are also featured.
3. Irving, D., *Churchill's War* (Veritas 1987), p. 281.
4. Irving, p. 308.
5. Colville, J., *The Fringes of Power* (Hodder & Stoughton 1985) p. 150.
6. AIR 2/5212: Minute to file, 24.8.40. Medhurst also mentioned that Churchill had promised to train the Polish

and Czechoslovak semi-trained pilots, 'a promise which we shall, sooner or later, have to implement'.

7. Maguire, C.E., *Anglo-American Policy Towards the Free French* (Macmillan 1995), pp. 1–17.
8. Collier, R., *The Years of Attrition, 1940–1941* (Allison & Busby 1995), pp. 106–8.
9. Maguire, p. 17.
10. Maguire, p. 6.
11. AIR 8/371: Medhurst to Sinclair and others, 20.7.40.
12. FO 371/24339: Air Ministry circular, 24.7.40.
13. FO 371/24366: Home Office to all police authorities, 20.7.40.
14. FO 371/24366: Report from Intelligence Section, Coastal Command to DAAC, 7.8.40. The covering letter to the report suggests that it may have originated with a Mary Trevelyan of the Student Movement House following research conducted in mid-July.
15. C8512/1419/62: Minute to file by Ward. Ward's remarks concerned the 'violent prejudice' shown by the writer to the Czechoslovak contingent, but the report was treated as a whole by the various departments of the Foreign Office, therefore most of the observations would have been regarded thus. Roberts also noted that many such reports had filtered through from various sources.
16. FO 371/24368 (AFO(40)66), 2.11.40. It was estimated that a further 200 Norwegian air personnel would arrive from Canada in early 1941 after undergoing their basic training.
17. See COS reports 1–7, CAB 66/10. Above 'good' on the ranking scale of morale was 'very good', 'high', 'very high' and 'excellent'.
18. CAB 66/10; COS Reports 8–10; AIR 2/5212: Minutes, DAAC meeting, 12.9.40; Medhurst to CAS, 18.9.40.
19. AIR 2/5595: Collier to Sholto–Douglas, 20.11.40.
20. AIR 2/5595: Boyle to ACAS(I), 26.6.41.
21. AIR 2/5595: Minutes, Anglo-French Conference, 27.6.41; also DAFL minutes, 5.7.41.
22. AIR 2/5595: Correspondence, 13.10.41 to 10.11.41.
23. AIR 2/5595: Valin to Sinclair, and reply, 14.11.41.
24. AIR 2/5595: Correspondence, 14.11.41 to 22.1.42.
25. AIR 2/5595: Report by Skepper to DAFL, 15.4.42.
26. FO 371/32207: Anglo-French agreement correspondence and minutes, 3.4.42 to 1.5.42.
27. AIR 2/5595: Correspondence, 4.8.42 to 21.12.42.
28. Porch, D., *The French Secret Services* (Macmillan 1996), p. 205.

29. AIR 2/5931: DAFL Report, 29.4.43; Memorandum from Macmillan, 12.4.43.
30. AIR 2/5931: Correspondence, May–June 1943. This file contains extensive details of the re-equipment policy relating to the French squadrons in North Africa.
31. AIR 2/8238: DAFL reports, allied forces; FO 371/41870, minute to file, 7.1.44.
32. FO 371/50747: Mack to Orme Sargent, 6.2.45; Air Ministry to Foreign Secretary, 22.2.45; Eden to Churchill, 26.2.45; Eden to Reconstruction Department, 3.3.45.
33. FO 371/50748: COS(45)111(0), 15.2.45.
34. FO 371/50749: Duff Cooper to Ward, 19.3.45; Halifax to Foreign Office, 21.3.45.
35. FO 371/50749: Foreign Office correspondence, 20/21.3.45.
36. FO 371/50749: Foreign Office and Air Ministry correspondence, 18.4.45 to 27.4.45.

CHAPTER FIVE

The Norwegians

The arrival of the Polish, Czechoslovak and French air crews received plenty of public attention. *The Times* and the *Daily Mirror*, for example, both ran a series of short articles highlighting the splendid nature of many individual escapes, and spoke in glowing terms of the immediate and effective contribution each contingent would make to the war effort. This was propaganda, designed to impress the political leaderships as much as the average Briton. These three countries all had special places in the hierarchy of allied forces: the Poles because they were the people in whose defence Britain had supposedly gone to war in the first place; the Czechoslovaks because people of all political persuasions recognised that something distasteful and decidedly un-British had been done to them in 1938; and the French because they were our stout and faithful allies. The press and the BBC, by emphasising the unshakeable *esprits de corps* and the relentless courage of each group, helped to reassure and inspire the British people, who were still wrestling with the twin horrors of the awesome prospect of imminent invasion and mass infiltration by enemy agents.

Less fanfare greeted the military evacuees from Norway, Belgium and Holland. This was not because they were in any way inferior, but simply because they came in smaller groups and did not command as much political attention as the other three. Even so, this did not mean that serious questions were not asked about their morale and commitment. In each case, pre-war political relations played a major part in the British assessment of the new allies, and the behaviour of their countrymen and national leaders during the short but devastating western war also deeply conditioned the attitudes with which they were initially received.

The first to arrive were the Norwegians. The fate of their
nation, which had contributed so much to the eventual downfall
of Neville Chamberlain, meant that they were in need of refuge
much earlier than any of the other national groups. The battle
for Norway had begun in April 1940, though the Norwegians
themselves had not thought it likely that they would have been
dragged into the war at all. In effect, the Germans and the
allies conducted part of their war on Norwegian territory, and
eventually the country had been overrun while bringing this
sideshow to a conclusion. The Norwegian forces fought hard
and valiantly, scoring some notable victories over the German
invaders, but neither they nor the allies could prevail. Vidkun
Quisling, with Hitler's tacit support, assumed control of Norway
on 8 April while the official Norwegian government was still
technically in existence, but by 9 June all effective resistance was
at an end. Two days earlier, King Haakon VII had set sail for
England on HMS *Devonshire* with most of his ministers and the
remnants of the Norwegian armed forces, which had, with great
credit, fought to the last moment.[1]

Churchill had already nailed his colours to the Norwegian
mast. After all, he had taken the premiership in the midst of
the crisis, and on 23 May had promised the War Cabinet that
the King and his entourage would be given refuge in Britain if
the campaign ended in defeat.[2] What had begun as an attempt
by Chamberlain to stamp his name on the war had finished with
Churchill accepting some of the responsibility for its failure,
therefore the Norwegians expected, with good reason, every
political and military consideration by the British government.
This they were not given, at least not entirely, but still the Anglo–
Norwegian liaison during the latter's time in exile remains
probably the smoothest of all such relationships during the war.

From the outset, the major problem facing the Norwegian
government was similar to that of the Free French: how to
establish and retain credibility as a sovereign administration in
the face of hostile propaganda issued from the home territory.
Indeed, the Norwegian Foreign Minister, Halvdan Koht,
warned his countrymen against getting too close to a formal
alliance with Britain, for any binding commitments made by
his government could possibly have rebounded disastrously
had Britain lost the war and a negotiated settlement with the
Germans been forced upon them. This was practical politics,
for the outlook in the late spring of 1940 was truly ghastly as far
as the allies were concerned. One factor was in the Norwegians'
favour, however. King Haakon had demonstrated that he had

acted at all times in the best interests of his country, and Norway being a placid, democratic monarchy, he became a natural rallying point for the resistance. By contrast, de Gaulle had to overcome the tendency of many of his countrymen to reject him as an alternative leader, hence he was fighting two political battles at once, whereas the Norwegians were fighting only one. Yet this caution was not one-sided traffic, for in early April a meeting of the Allied Military Committee decided that Norway had 'retreated into a form of jealous neutrality', and though it is not clear exactly of whom the Norwegians were supposed to be jealous, the report concluded that they were more likely to be hostile to the allies if forced to make a choice. Thus, on both sides of this new alliance, there was room for reflection and perhaps even distrust.[3]

Norway also had another useful asset in her merchant fleet. Despite substantial losses in the battle of April–June, no less than 1,876 merchant vessels of all sizes reached allied ports. Apart from rendering a significant contribution to the Atlantic supply chain, the income generated by this fleet also enabled the Norwegian government to finance its allied war effort without assistance from Britain, and this had a small but direct impact on the air policies which emerged. Nevertheless, the Norwegians still felt excluded from the high table during their time in Britain. As Olav Riste has shown, the Norwegians were presented with a novel experience when it came to negotiating allied agreements, for their long-standing principles of neutrality were inevitably compromised by the new situation. Even though the British kept effective control of the merchant fleet, and persistently refused to grant access to matters of strategic policy, the Norwegians stoically accepted their position and pledged full co-operation for the duration of the war.[4]

The composition of the Norwegian air forces at the outbreak of war was reflected in their eventual deployment during their time in Britain. Both their Army and Navy had their own air forces, but modernisation had been put on hold for some time before the outbreak of war. François Kersaudy noted that the military had ordered a batch of Caproni aircraft from Italy, 'not because they were the best, but simply because they could be paid for in dried cod'.[5] The British were also aware of the limitations, and the abilities, of the Norwegian air services. In a report supplied to the Chief of the Air Staff in February 1940, Norwegian pilots and ground crew were described as disciplined and well-trained, but the equipment was 'largely obsolescent and in some cases unsafe.' In fact, the reserve officers' association

had petitioned the parliamentary military committee in the
spring of 1939 and bluntly informed it that the aircraft of the
Naval Air Arm were 'wholly unserviceable'.[6]

At the time of the German assault on Norway, a long overdue
order for new aircraft from America was still in crates awaiting
delivery. On 11 May Porri (then still with the Directorate of
Intelligence) wrote to various administrators noting that nine
officers and five other ranks of the Royal Norwegian Naval Air
Service (RNNAS) had arrived in the country and were seeking
immediate training. He had been informed by the Norwegian
Legation in London that there were plans to evacuate a
further twenty to thirty pilots from Norway to form a unit in
Britain supplied with British aircraft and maintained by British
mechanics, which could then be posted back to Norway for
active operations. In his view, however, this was an unlikely
event; therefore he suggested that the detachment should be
split between the Royal Navy base at Calshot and the Army depot
at Aston Down. This would allow the men 'to absorb a certain
amount of atmosphere, technique and language which would
facilitate any further arrangements made'.[7] He received a reply
two days later which amended the proposal in favour of sending
the men to Coastal Command for initial assessment.

The Chief of the Air Staff in Norway was Col Thomas Gulliksen.
He informed Porri that the men had engineered their escape
from Fornebo aerodrome on 9 April, proceeded to Lillehammer,
where they destroyed some other aircraft to prevent their capture,
and then boarded SS *Sjogutten* to arrive at Lerwick in Scotland. In
Gulliksen's opinion, the men were all fully trained and capable
of flying Gladiators, but the Air Ministry replied that insufficient
aircraft of this type existed to form a separate flight, though it was
content to begin training on British planes. It was also noted by
Porri that Gulliksen was already manoeuvring himself to be the
senior officer in a reconstituted Norwegian air force in Britain.[8]

Things then moved quickly for the Norwegians. On 17 May,
the Air Ministry hosted an inter-departmental conference to
discuss the position of the air force personnel then in England.
The C-in-C of the Royal Norwegian Army Air Service (RNAAS),
Capt Bjarne Øen, informed the delegates that 10 Army and 6
Navy pilots, plus 4 or 5 skilled mechanics, were then in England
awaiting orders. He added that the maximum number likely to
arrive from Norway would be 100, though a possibility existed
that more might arrive from America. As for aircraft, 5 Curtiss
Hawk P36s were in crates at Kirkwall, but another 36 were due
from America plus a further 36 Northrop float-planes. All in all,

suggested Øen, this was more than enough to form a solid core of a Norwegian air force in Britain.[9]

But this proved to be only the first hurdle, not the end of the race. Porri and Wg Cdr Garraway (attached to the Directorate of Plans) rejected the idea on the premise that maintaining Curtiss aircraft in Britain would be impossible due to lack of spares and the unpredictability of the supply routes from America. Porri suggested sending the men for training in Canada, thereby solving the spares problem and making use of the incoming aircraft from America. Garraway added that it would be of little use to create a new squadron in Britain which used different planes from the RAF, and since they had no aircraft to spare at that moment, he suggested drafting the men into the RAFVR for training in RAF squadrons; once competent, they would then be posted back to Norway for service. This would go some way towards solving the language problem, and it might therefore be possible to consider the formation of a Norwegian squadron once the situation in Norway had been resolved. Øen accepted this proposal, with the added caveat that RAFVR enlistment should not prejudice the formation of a truly independent unit composed entirely of Norwegian personnel, should the opportunity arise. The meeting then heard that the Norwegian government was prepared to pay all expenses connected with the training scheme, and in a later minute of 18 May, all relevant departments were brought up to date. Most of the personnel spoke English 'reasonably well', and it was accepted in principle that a full Norwegian squadron would be formed as and when the men became available, but in the mean time every effort would be made to get their aircraft out of America and into service. The scheme was commended to the Foreign Office, which swiftly replied on 27 May, raising no points of objection.[10]

The minutes of the May meeting give rise to a small controversy. According to Gen Wilhelm Mohr, the proposal to send the men to Canada for training was a suggestion made by the Norwegians themselves, but the documents clearly indicate that it was Porri and not Øen who tabled the scheme. Indeed, Mohr goes as far as to state that the British were 'reluctant' to go along with the idea, citing the urgency of using trained pilots in the Battle of Britain as his evidence, but we can see here that the RAF was making its decisions on a realistic basis, and despite the enthusiasm of the allied pilots to go into action in their own national squadron, insurmountable problems of supply and maintenance meant that their ambition would have to be postponed. Mohr's error was to rely on documents dated

June and July 1940 – a different case altogether so far as the air war was concerned – but these papers merely confirmed the arrangements made at the earlier time. Sholto Douglas stated in a short note to the DAAC in July 1940 that he had not been a supporter of the training scheme when it had first been suggested, 'but I did not pursue the matter [because] on security and political grounds it was highly desirable to let the Norwegians go'. Unfortunately, his reasons are not recorded, but it is likely that his views were those which gave rise to Mohr's interpretation of reluctant acquiescence.[11]

By early July, the Norwegian ministry of defence had reorganised itself in London. The army wing contained thirty-five fully trained pilots, and the Air Force had thirteen pilots in various stages of training, and a handful of other ranks. The land forces and the navy were much better off. As well as a submarine, a couple of MTBs and various patrol vessels, the destroyer *Sleipner* lay alongside at Portsmouth, while at Rosyth the destroyer *Draug* was waiting for orders. Also in Scotland, at Dumfries, about forty officers and a thousand other ranks had regrouped at a camp vacated by the British Army. Compared to some other allied exiles, therefore, the Norwegians had arrived with the nucleus of a credible force.

The proposal to train Norwegian crews in Canada was swiftly executed. By mid-August 1940, Medhurst was informing the Air Council that all the selected personnel had left British territory. Uppermost in the minds of his superiors, however, was the importance of maintaining healthy relations with the Canadian government, and Medhurst was told that the situation would require 'careful handling', and that the Canadians 'should not be requested to take on any additional commitments'. This was a euphemistic way of saying that they should not be expected to foot the bill, but there would never be any worries for the British on that score. The income generated by their extensive merchant fleet promised a steady flow of resources for the Norwegian war effort, and besides paying for their training in Canada, they bought their own planes as well.

Training continued at a furious pace in 'Little Norway' near Toronto. Recruits continued to stream in from the Continent, and by September 1940 the Norwegian Legation informed the Air Ministry that it could list 70 trained pilots, 100 partly trained, and 100 more awaiting basic instruction. To this it could add radio operators, navigators and about eighty mechanics, but even all of this expertise could not fulfil the basic establishments of the three independent squadrons it had asked the RAF to form when the time was right. Yet again, the aspirations of an allied force broke down because of the shortage of ground crew, but unlike some other exiled groups the Norwegians were pragmatic enough to accept this, and scaled down their proposals accordingly.

In fact, by the summer of 1941, all the indications were that the Anglo–Norwegian relationship promised to be a stable, mutually beneficial alliance considerably lacking in the tensions which had marred air arrangements with other exiled groups. This might have been because of the blunt yet important fact that they could pay their own way; or because of clear political objectives of either side which had no strings attached fore or aft, or because of the Norwegians' attitude to the alliance itself, whereby they recognised the seniority of the British but felt in no way inferior themselves. These were all powerful factors, and though it is scarcely possible to pinpoint one as being definitive, it remains true that the files contain very little which is critical of the Norwegian air forces during their time in Britain. Even the Canadians informed the Air Ministry in January 1941 that their Scandinavian guests had acquitted themselves with honour and impeccable behaviour. In short, this was an alliance which needed the barest minimum of political or military maintenance – a gift for the British, and a relief for the Norwegians.

The full agreement with the Norwegians was not signed until 28 May 1941. The delay was caused partly by the Canadian training scheme, but mainly by some skilful Norwegian manipulation of the jurisdiction clauses which signposted the route to independent status. Øen had made his case plain from the very start – 'identifiable' units would be created from the available personnel at the earliest opportunity, and this as far as the RAF interpreted the term, meant independence. Yet whereas much spleen had been vented in other cases where independence had been demanded, this was not the case with Norway. The preamble to the agreement promised the 're-establishment of the freedom and independence of Norway through its complete liberation from German domination', and the implications deep within this statement meant that Norway's pre-war territorial integrity would be preserved and restored, something wholeheartedly avoided with the Polish and Czechoslovak contingents. The key to the whole relationship lies in the fact that Norway brought no complicated political agenda to Britain – at least in so far as postwar British interests were concerned – therefore independence, and all that the status implied, was not something to be feared. The RAF went so far as to permit the application of Norwegian air force law to the point where a man could *choose* the military code under which he wish to be tried – an unheard of option in the other exiled groups.[12]

One of the other clauses in the agreement amalgamated the two air arms into one Royal Norwegian Air Force (RNAF), placed under the command of Capt Hjalmar Riiser-Larsen, with Øen as his chief of staff. In Canada, overall responsibility was held by Capt Ole Reistad, and it was he who filtered the steady number of volunteers from Canada and America. In contrast to the Poles and the Czechoslovaks, Norway enjoyed a better recruiting campaign in North America, and though the numbers were never high for any of the allied forces, the numbers of expatriate Norwegians coming forward were at least consistent and enabled training at 'Little Norway' to function smoothly without interruptions for want of new fliers. Almost certainly the reason for this was political. The Poles and the Czechs met with stubborn resistance from former nationals who had gladly left their homelands to seek a better life in America, therefore it was all the more difficult to persuade them to fight and perhaps die for a country which they had freely chosen to leave, often with bitter memories. By contrast, the Norwegians in North America rallied to the flag because they held no lasting grudges against the home country, Norway having been spared the seismic shifts in the political and economic terrain which had afflicted so much of Eastern and Central Europe in the twentieth century. So successful was the campaign to attract North American volunteers – and to this must be added the constant stream of escapees from occupied Norway itself and through neutral Sweden – that the Norwegians announced in January 1942 that they would be able to form fully national squadrons when the RAF was ready to do so. This was music to the ears of the DAFL, a pleasant change from the running battles fought with the French and the Czechoslovaks.

In all, the Norwegians had four main squadrons during the war, with a fifth (334) coming into service after VE Day. The first to be created was 330 on 25 April 1941, under the control of Coastal Command, for at long last the freighter *Fjordheim* had made the journey across the Atlantic with eighteen Northrop N-3PB float-planes, which were then assembled in Reykjavik. Designed and operated primarily as an anti-submarine squadron, 330 was manned by naval personnel throughout its period of service, first off Iceland and then over the North Atlantic. The Northrops were jettisoned in June 1942 in favour of the Catalina III, then these were also replaced in February 1943 by Sunderlands. Thus, 330's range was pushed further

as the war progressed, and although it could be argued that
the squadron had a successful if largely tedious war, the long
Atlantic patrols took their toll. By 1945, the squadron had lost
sixteen aircraft and sixty-three men, most of them in flying
accidents caused by adverse weather conditions. But a loss is
a loss, and when the squadron passed back into Norwegian
hands in November 1945, it did so with full honours gratefully
bestowed by the RAF.

Another maritime unit was formed in May 1943 at Leuchars.
Divided into two flights – one equipped with Mk II Mosquitoes,
the other with Catalinas – 333 Squadron joined 330 in shipping
reconnaissance duties along the Norwegian coast, and convoy
protection in the Atlantic. In contrast to 330, however, 333
enjoyed slightly more excitement in its coastal operations, often
being used for close engagements with shipping, and transporting
agents and saboteurs to and from occupied Norway. Early losses
were high, mainly due to a lack of training on the Mosquito,
and for a short while the Air Ministry suspended the operational
status of 333 until the problem had been rectified. Wilhelm Mohr
attributes this to 'Norwegian impatience and over-confidence,
and British trust', but this still serves to demonstrate how easy the
relationship was between the two allies.[13]

Inevitably, though, most of the public's attention fell upon
the two Norwegian fighter squadrons, 331 and 332. The first was
formed on 21 July 1941 at Catterick, when the personnel had
finished training in Canada. Mounted on Mk I Hurricanes, 331
became operational on 21 September and then moved north
for a long sojourn in Scotland, returning to the south seven
months later where it remained until the Normandy invasion.
The second squadron was formed on 16 January 1942, also at
Catterick, on Spitfires. There was to be no Scottish expedition
for 332, however, and together with 331, it saw most of its action
in the south. The COS reports speak highly of both units,
never describing the morale as anything less than 'excellent'
or 'exceedingly high', though as time went by the morale in
330 began to fall as the long winter weather and seemingly
perpetual darkness depressed them all, especially the ground
crew. Numerous sorties were cancelled due to engine failure,
and requests for transfer to the fighter squadrons were frequent
yet seldom upheld. Furthermore, the Germans had managed
to block most of the escape routes from Norway by mid-1943,
so much of the hitherto constant flow of recruits had begun to
dwindle, and most of those who got through went to the fighter
squadrons, which suffered greater losses.[14]

The two fighter squadrons came of age in OPERATION JUBILEE, the flawed raid on the French coastal town of Dieppe in August 1942. The surviving operations records books (ORBs) clearly reveal the extent to which the allied squadrons committed themselves to the raid, and the entries for the two Norwegian units in particular give us a fascinating and sometimes moving glimpse into the day's events. What follows is an edited extract from the ORB of 331 for 19 August 1942:

> It was fine and clear at sunrise. Everyone was up at 0400 hours for the second day in succession. Today will be hard work for us all, and its importance was stressed yesterday at the briefing. We know that 332 Squadron has felt the lack of sleep too. We had an early breakfast and arrived at dispersal excited and in good spirits, but soon most were sleeping in all sorts of queer positions all over the place.
>
> We took off at 0610 with 242 and 332 Squadrons and arrived over Dieppe at 0650. Almost at once we were attached by enemy aircraft from above and the squadron became split in the general melee. Second Lieutenant Greiner was attacked by two Fw190s and was hit in the starboard wing root which flung his plane into a spin and showered splinters all over the cockpit, some into his right leg. He managed to recover from the spin and climbed to 4,000 feet where he baled out.[15]

The second sortie was at 11.15 hours, and produced two 'kills' and four 'probables'. The squadron returned for refuelling and then took off again at 14.25, nearly diving in to attack half-a-dozen Typhoons which the Norwegians mistook for Fw190s. After more successes, the tired pilots returned to refuel and take off yet again on the fourth sortie of the day, this time covering the retreating forces. The records show that the total score for the day was 7 enemy aircraft destroyed, 2 probably destroyed and a further 8 damaged. In return, 331 had lost 2 aircraft, but both pilots had been rescued by the Royal Navy. The ORB perfectly captures the mood at the end of the operation:

> It has been a hell of a day with everyone working at top pressure – no time for meals, but there were masses of sandwiches and soft drinks and coffee – in fact, one seemed to be eating most of the day. The ground crew have had a hard day too, but they have done very well. Everyone enjoyed the day and got a great kick out of the fact that they were

taking part in something vital. 'Yes, let's have some more like this tomorrow', is the general opinion. After dinner, we heard that Berg and Greiner were both safe and unhurt. Everyone weeping and jumping for joy at the news.

The men of 332 squadron also had a busy day over Dieppe, scoring 3 destroyed, 1 probable and 4 damaged. Unlike their brother squadron, however, they lost two of their comrades on the first sortie, Sgt Plts Staubo and Bergsland. Staubo was left behind as they turned to leave Dieppe. Someone spotted him way below and behind the main formation, and although a warning was called to him on the radio, he took evasive action too late to avoid being jumped by three or four Fw190s. Sgt Plt Eriksen turned and dived to assist his countryman, but before he was in position the Germans had opened fire and Staubo's Spitfire burst into flames. Eriksen accounted for one of the enemy planes, but by then Staubo's machine had been lost from view. Bergsland was also caught alone after losing his place in the formation. He was warned on the radio, but was immediately attacked by four Fw190s. The records note that he did not change course even under fire, and very soon his Spitfire was seen to fall blazing into the sea.

Such tales do not convey even the tiniest fraction of the reality which these men experienced in action. They were brave men, perhaps reckless at times, but then they were also young. They were fighting for their homeland, not Britain, and that holds true for every other allied squadron which flew with the RAF during the Second World War. This may be contrasted with the views of one British officer who completed the day's ORB for 310 (Czechoslovak) Fighter Squadron on 31 August 1940. Plt Off J. Sterbaček was seen going down in the Thames having been surprised by German fighter in support of a bomber squadron. He was presumed dead. 'Thus,' said the report, 'he has the proud distinction of being the first Czech fighter pilot to give his life for England.'[16] Nothing could have been further from the truth. He gave his life for Czechoslovakia, that is all.

OPERATION JUBILEE was counted as a success by the RAF, for although the raid itself was generally considered to be a disaster on the day, the air support provided was universally acknowledged by land and sea commanders to have been of the highest quality. The average loss rate per squadron was calculated at 7 per cent, or two losses per unit, and this from a total of 2,403 sorties flown by sixty-one squadrons in all.[17] The European allied air crews had a strong presence in the raid, and stories similar to those related above may be found in the ORBs of the Free French, Dutch, Belgian, Czechoslovak and Polish squadrons that were involved. After Dieppe, the files contain hardly any criticisms at all except for those provoked by political considerations, and even these originated with the various governments, and not the military men under their command. It might therefore be advanced that the performance of the European exiles in the Dieppe raid, leaving aside all other interpretations of the event in the context of the wider war, finally confirmed in the minds of many senior British commanders the importance of the contribution made by them to the prosecution of the combined effort, and utterly dispelled once and for all any vestiges of the old notions of distrust or lack of belief in their will to fight.

Wilhelm Mohr records in his personal assessment of the Norwegian air forces that the RAF rated the fighter squadrons among the highest of those available in terms of efficiency, servicing, motivation and safety. They also featured regularly in the upper divisions of the monthly and quarterly calculations compiled by the Air Ministry which reflected operational successes against enemy aircraft and losses to the squadrons. These achievements, however, threatened to disturb the otherwise sound equilibrium of the Anglo–Norwegian alliance in the air. For so effective were the fighter squadrons, the RAF fought hard to keep them within the Tactical Air Force being assembled in preparation for OPERATION OVERLORD in 1944, and this conflicted with the Norwegian government's desires to use its forces as part of a separate battle group designed to assist in the liberation of the home territory. With strong protests, the terms of the 1941 agreement were waved under the collective nose of the Air Ministry. The text clearly stated that Norway's forces in exile would be used 'either for the defence of the United Kingdom or for the purposes of regaining Norway', and it was obvious to both parties that the intended attack on occupied Europe met neither criterion. As Mohr notes in his 1995 essay, no record of the discussions resolving the situation has yet come to light, but it is apparent that the RAF won the argument, because the squadrons stayed with the Tactical Air Force right throughout the campaign. Even so, the fact that the Norwegians *did* agree to the use of their squadrons in Normandy merely underlines the strength of the alliance at its core.[18]

When victory was in sight in early 1945, the Norwegian government – like all the other exiles – began to liaise with the appropriate British departments regarding reconstruction and rearmament. One of the earliest Norwegian requirements was a training school located in Britain for immediate postwar needs. The RAF acted swiftly, establishing such a unit at RAF Winkleigh, and all training provided would be under the terms of Mutual Aid. Then, in a return to the dispute over the separate utilisation of its forces, the Norwegian Military Mission formally requested the withdrawal of its squadrons from the Tactical Air Force and their transfer to Norway re-equipped with Mustangs. Its argument was sound enough. It pointed out that its units had been on first-line duty since 1942 and had fulfilled the Air Ministry's desires by contributing to the liberation of Europe; now the time had come for them to assist in the final liberation of Norway. The request also had a political edge to it, in that it hinted that the people of Norway would not understand why their own air force was not participating in the final defeat of the Germans who were operating a bitter scorched-earth policy in retreat. For these reasons, the Norwegians insisted that the squadrons should be transferred at once.

But as with the Czechoslovaks, who argued for the return of their units to help with the Slovak uprising in 1944, the Air Ministry remained entirely unmoved. In fact, in rejecting the proposal, it also used similar tactics to those employed against the Czechs. In both instances it focused on technical matters rather than the military or political dimensions, and in the Norwegian case the DCAS (AM Sir James Robb) considered the aerodromes in Norway to be unsuitable for Mustangs, and more importantly that supply and maintenance would be difficult, if not impossible, over such a distance. In a letter full of platitudes, he hoped that the Norwegian Military Mission would understand his position, and he closed by hoping that they would continue to assist with the final liberation of Europe.[19]

When Robb rejected the transfer request, Hitler had nine days to live. Eight days after that, the war in Europe was over. On 22 May, the Norwegians units left the Continent for home – and in that they were lucky. Churchill had ordered a 'stand firm' attitude in Europe because he feared a sudden push by Soviet forces further west, and though the poor Czechs had to wait until August before they could return, again because of complications with the Russians, the Prime Minister gave his personal permission for the Norwegians to take their leave and fly home in triumph. Four days before they left, Maj-Gen Riiser-Larsen wrote to the Air Council expressing his thanks for a 'memorable five years' and the great friendship which now existed between the two kingdoms. In closing, he promised the British government and people that 'whenever called upon,

be certain that the Royal Norwegian Air Force will be at your
side'. It was a fitting and sincere tribute from an officer knighted
by the British King, and it brought to an end to an alliance
in which the admiration and respect for each other was truly
mutual. It now seems clear that in the context of the whole exile
experience, here was the exception to the rule.[20]

'THE CINDERELLA FLIERS': DANES IN THE NORWEGIAN AIR FORCE

The attack on Denmark by German forces was timed to coincide
with the strike against Norway. On 9 April 1940, the Danes
were taken so totally by surprise as German tanks and marines
overwhelmed their country that only one fighter of the Danish
Air Force managed to get off the ground – and that was promptly
shot down. There was a short, hopelessly one-sided battle in
and around Copenhagen, and by mid-morning King Christian
X had ordered a full ceasefire and immediate capitulation.
In what must count as one of the fastest wars in history, a
constitutional monarchy of over four million people had been
conquered at a cost of thirteen war dead and twenty-three other
injuries – and all before lunch. Hitler called Denmark his first
'model protectorate', whereas Churchill preferred 'the sadistic
murderer's canary'.[21]

To the British Foreign Office, Denmark had given in far
too easily. All the wrong signals had been sent when, in May
1939, she had signed a non-aggression pact with the Nazis,
and this eagerness to co-operate with her hostile neighbour
seemed to be more than just pragmatism when it quickly
became apparent that the German occupation was benign in
the extreme. More than 25,000 Danes volunteered for lucrative
jobs in Germany, and another couple of hundred swiftly signed
up with the Waffen SS. The Danish government was permitted
considerable freedom in its administration of home affairs, and
by the end of 1940 serious speculation in London was drifting
towards the conclusion that Denmark would be formally and
willingly incorporated into the Third Reich – a fate which befell
Luxemburg in August 1942. Any notion of an alliance in exile
was therefore entirely out of the question as far as the British
were concerned.

But the ease with which Denmark gave in to Nazi pressure
was deceptive. It was first and foremost the only logical option,

because any spirited resistance would have been utterly crushed with a massive loss of life. Furthermore, it is hardly surprising that so many Danes chose to throw in their lot with what seemed to be an invincible force in 1940, and a great many saw themselves as being as Aryan or as Germanic as the most fanatical Nazi. Indeed, in June 1941, when Hitler launched the attack on the Soviet Union, Denmark responded by organising a national unit – the Frikorps – to fight alongside the German Army in the east, and by 1942 the SS had enough Danes in its ranks to form a regiment with three battalions. Eventually, these land forces were strong enough to be merged with the 11th SS Division, a sizeable portion of which, it should be noted, was composed of Norwegian volunteers.

However, this is not to argue or even imply that German occupation was uniformly welcomed by all of the Danes. True, many resigned themselves to the situation with heavy hearts, but more than a few made good their escape into neutral Sweden, and from there to Britain. The reception they received was cool but not hostile; in fact, as far as the British government was concerned, the less official contact between the two parties, the better. By August 1940, a number of exiles had gathered in and around London and had formed a National Committee of Free Danes, each one of them prepared to serve with any allied force in any capacity. This was no clandestine organisation, but the British drew back from giving it any formal recognition, and the policy line issued from Whitehall was that in the mean time it was 'highly undesirable that the committee's activities should receive any publicity'. A parliamentary question directed at 'Rab' Butler in the Commons received a similar brush off. When asked if His Majesty's Government intended to mobilise Danes in exile, Butler replied: 'The Government welcomes assistance from all quarters in the prosecution of the war.' When pressed about the National Committee, Butler merely said that he knew of its existence and the work it was doing.[22]

Later in August, the British Council wrote to Anthony Haigh at the Foreign Office and suggested the formation of a 'Danish House' similar to the establishments created or considered for the other exiled nationalities. The precedent was the existence of a long-standing 'Danish Club' in Britain, plus a branch of the Danish Church and the Anglo-Danish Society, all of which were organisations with impeccable reputations. Even so, the Council recognised that the essential problem lay in the fact that there was no Danish government in exile, therefore any official sanction would remain a thorny issue. In replying to the Council, Lawrence

Collier directed it towards certain trusted Danes known to the
Foreign Office, and invited it to proceed with extreme caution
and absolutely no publicity.

The question of putting a few Danes into uniform then arose.
An inter-departmental meeting at the Foreign Office on 19
August reviewed the situation and immediately strangled the idea
of a Danish Legion. The War Office argued that since there was
no official Danish authority in Britain, any Danes who wished to
fight should be enrolled in the British Army as private individuals.
The Air Ministry was also lukewarm, agreeing to accept only those
Danes 'with special qualifications' into the RAF. The Foreign
Office saw things differently. At Collier's prompting, Cdr Frank
Stagg of the Ministry of Shipping suggested taking some of the
younger Danes and thrusting them forward as propaganda icons,
enlisting maybe one man to each service and maximising the
publicity potential. 'This,' he said, 'would act as a great fillip
to morale and would serve generally to ginger up the Danish
Committee who are in the main a supine lot.'[23]

His ideas were taken seriously, and within a couple of months
a Danish Bureau had been created, composed of the interested
service departments and empowered to act on behalf of Danish
volunteers. Some senior Danes had been awarded honorary
seats, but at the earlier meetings not a single one was present.
The token Dane chosen for the RAF was one Olaf Poulsen, who
apparently had over 200 hours' flying experience and had owned
a private aircraft before the war. Of greater interest, however,
were the activities of the Danish Minister in London, Count
Eduard Reventlow, who had been waging a counter-propaganda
campaign. He had been most energetic in his mission to
encourage Danes in exile to reject the lure of a service career
with the allies and to opt for repatriation instead. By all accounts,
many had already done so. Lawrence Collier, in a textbook
example of diplomatic verbiage, wrote to the Count and informed
him that 'it might not be possible to extend the present courtesy
and privileges to him' if he were to persist in maintaining an
attitude unhelpful to His Majesty's Government. In point of fact,
Reventlow was within an ace of being shown the door, but the
plan was shelved because it was felt that such a move would have a
negative effect on Danish morale.

It was the issue of morale and the stimulation of resistance in
the occupied territory which finally brought all minds into focus.
The Foreign Office heard that the Danes had shown perhaps
more disillusionment with German rule than they had previously
been given credit for, therefore by the autumn of 1940 it was

felt that Denmark should feature more prominently in official speeches, especially in the type which promised a better world after the war. MI6 reports from agents within Denmark gave the impression that a visible sign of exile activity would pay dividends, so the Foreign Office approached the service departments to sound out their views on taking suitable Danes into the services. Each one concurred, and the Air Ministry let it be known that a small number of Danes had tagged along with the Norwegians heading for Canada.

A year later, in the summer of 1941, the first batch of trained men returned to England and began to form the Norwegian squadrons; with them were the few Danes who had been cleared by MI5. At the eleventh meeting of the Danish Bureau, the Air Ministry expressed the hope that enough Danes might be found to form a national squadron of their own. This idea was soon dashed through lack of numbers, but good news came in the form of a Danish Spitfire Fund which had been established by the Danish Council, then on a fundraising tour in America. Considerable sums had been pledged and much publicity generated as a result. On 10 April 1942, three Spitfires were proudly handed over to the RAF, but unfortunately all were lost in combat. The Danes also contributed to the 'Little Norway' training camp in Canada, providing two of the Fairchild PT-26 aircraft. In the end, the RAF negotiated with the Royal Norwegian Air Force, and an unwritten agreement was reached whereby Danish pilots would be filtered into those squadrons where vacancies existed. The numbers were never high, perhaps twenty or so by 1941, but where successes were scored through the efforts of Danes in the cockpit, maximum publicity would be drawn from the event.[24] In such a manner would the Danish cause be kept alight, and the British could relax in the knowledge that another 'ally' had been gained with no commitments from London whatsoever.[25]

In the end, it proved to be a shrewd investment. Although no new Danish air crew were trained after 1940, their presence in the RAF was sufficient to maintain tentative links with Denmark which bore fruit in 1945. In March of that year, the Danish military mission confirmed its interest in securing RAF assistance with rebuilding its national air force once the liberation was complete. The plans were lavish indeed, with up to 500 fighters, light bombers and torpedo bombers being brought into service over a seven-year period. The Air Ministry rubbed its hands with delight and instantly promised extensive training facilities in Britain along with the first batch of equipment to be delivered as soon as it became available.

The war experience also shaped the future Danish Air Force from the moment reconstruction began in 1945. Whereas before the war the air power had been divided into navy and army wings, a new unified command under Lt Col Kaj Birksted resolved to rebuild the force on the RAF model. Birksted had won the DSO and DFC, later commanding a Spitfire wing in his own right. He kept open his channels of communication with the Air Ministry, and before the end of 1945 many of the men who had seen action with the RAF were on their way back to England for retraining or to serve as instructors to a new generation of Danish pilots. But Britain's hopes of funnelling in aircraft by the ship-load were disappointed. The Air Ministry supplied several trainers from surplus stock, and a number of Supermarine Sea Otters to the Danish Navy, but the promised expansion on a massive scale never happened, mainly due to Denmark's postwar economic priorities. Even so, a valuable and friendly ally had been gained by the RAF for scarcely any effort; and although the Danes had a relatively small presence in Britain during the Second World War, they won many admirers for their attitude and commitment to the common cause.

NOTES

1. See Kersaudy, François, *Norway 1940* (Collins 1990) for an excellent and thorough study of the Norwegian campaign as seen from all sides of the conflict.
2. CAB 65/13: War Cabinet minutes, 23.5.40.
3. CAB 85/16: 'The Major Strategy of the War', 11.4.40. This is an invaluable document for students of early allied strategy and the British assessments of the neutral countries.
4. Salmon, P. (ed.), *Britain and Norway in the Second World War* (HMSO 1995), Olav Riste: 'Relations between the Norwegian government in exile and the British government', pp. 41–9.
5. Kersaudy, p. 11.
6. AIR 10/3938: Efficiency Report A, February 1940. Most of the observations in the report were themselves obsolescent by the time they were compiled, the details having originated with the intelligence officers aboard HMS *Courageous* which visited Norway during the summer of 1938.
7. AIR 2/5122: Porri to all relevant departments, 11.5.40.
8. AIR 2/5122: Porri, minute to file 10.5.40.
9. AIR 2/5122: Air Ministry conference, 17.5.40.
10. AIR 2/4213: DCAS Meeting on utilisation of allied air force personnel, 27.5.40.

11. Salmon, P. (ed.), 'Mohr: Wilhelm' The contribution of the Norwegian air forces', p. 85. See also AIR 2/5152; Sholto Douglas to DAAC, 7.7.40.

12. AIR 2/4806: Documents on Norwegian Air Force Personnel (Jurisdiction). Also FO 371/24368, minute to file by J.G. Ward, 12.10.40.

13. Mohr, p. 93.

14. AIR 2/8238: DAFL quarterly reports, October 1942–October 1943.

15. AIR 27/1724: Combat Reports, 331 Squadron; 19.8.42. See also AIR 50/129 and AIR 50/130 for the combat reports of individual pilots.

16. AIR/27/1680 (ORB) 31.8.40.

17. AIR 8/883: COS Report on OPERATION JUBILEE; see also AIR 37/199.

18. Mohr, pp. 90–2.

19. WO 202/876: Correspondence, 27.3.45 to 21.4.45.

20. Dr Christopher Mann of King's College London has written extensively on the subject of the Norwegian forces in the Second World War, and his work is an invaluable resource for all students of Norwegian history and foreign relations.

21. Reilly, R. *The Sixth Floor* (Leslie Frewin 1969), p. 16.

22. FO 371/24790: Minute to file and PQ, 9.8.40.

23. FO 371/24790: Minutes, inter-departmental meeting, 19.8.40. Frank Stagg had travelled extensively in Norway and Denmark before the war, and he produced several works on Scandinavian issues in the 1950s.

24. Some authorities place the total number of Danish pilots in allied service at sixty-six, though if these had all flown with the RAF, then pressure to form a Danish squadron would have been intense. Much more likely is that this number includes Danish-born pilots who flew with the Americans.

25. FO 371/29302: Danish affairs, correspondence, August 1941.

CHAPTER SIX

The Belgians and the Dutch

The air contingents from Belgium and Holland were two of the smaller groups to see service in Britain, and they were distinct from the others previously examined, in that their governments began their time in exile with substantial colonial holdings still in their possession. True, the French also had imperial territories, but because of the partition of France into the occupied northern area and the puppet administration in Vichy, de Gaulle was sometimes forced to seek colonial loyalty to his cause at the point of a gun. This is not to say, however, that either Belgium or Holland enjoyed a trouble-free time in exile. In the Belgian Congo there were some 48,000 white Europeans and approximately 200 indigenous tribes, some friendly, some not so. The Belgians would have preferred to conscript a large army of liberation from the Congo, but this would have exposed the rest of the population to a potentially disastrous situation, therefore the government's fears for the safety of those settlers led them to rely only upon volunteers.

The Dutch position was more complex still. Out in Indonesia, the Netherlands East Indies (NEI) comprised some seventy million souls kept in check by a mere 80,000 Dutch colonists. Like the Belgians, they could in theory have drafted a vast force from the NEI, but they probably would not have had a colony to go back to at the war's end. Worse still, the territories lay in the direct path of the Japanese. The Dutch had taken a stand against the Japanese invasion of French Indo-China by refusing to transport oil and other goods via the NEI to Japan, and since the holdings promised fabulous wealth for any power which could secure them, Tokyo made elaborate invasion plans long before the 1941 attack on Pearl Harbor. The military defences that existed were thinly spread and in some cases obsolete, such as Gen van Oyen's air force, and it was believed by many and known by some that any spirited attack by the Japanese would have been impossible to repel. Both governments therefore had plenty of problems with which to contend when they arrived in Britain during 1940. From the British point of view, however, colonies were good. Colonies meant first and foremost that they might not have to pay for the military upkeep of the reconstituted armed forces, and they also meant that having such external preoccupations might keep the governments themselves relatively stable.

But each administration's reputation preceded it into exile. The Belgians had been totally overwhelmed by the German Sixth Army in May 1940 as part of Hitler's attack in the west. Some 6,500 Belgian soldiers, many of them reservists, were killed in the onslaught, and about 15,000 civilians also died. Faced with a defeat on this scale, King Leopold surrendered his country and her defences to the invader on 28 May. What darkened the skies as far as the British authorities were concerned were the rampant accusations of treachery which accompanied the collapse of the Belgian war effort. The French were even more convinced that a substantial Fifth Column had been active inside Belgium. As one historian phrased it, the circumstances under which Belgium succumbed 'led to a marked decline in appreciation of all things Belgian.'[1] Furthermore, the French were adamant that Belgian refugees, and even some of the military made themselves scarce on French soil, such was the fear of a stab in the back. As a result, Britain was virtually forced to admit large numbers of civilians both before and after the defeat of France in June 1940.

As for the Dutch, they clung to their neutral status as if it were a talisman warding off evil spirits. Dutch intelligence warned time and again that the Germans, if only for strategic reasons, were almost certain to invade should a war in the west ignite, but the government preferred to hope that such predictions were wrong. To that extent, the Dutch forces had not even mobilised when the Germans attacked on 10 May. The reservists were hastily contacted, but only the small regular army was able to do battle, though it managed to scramble together an impressive show of resistance. But the real damage to the Dutch cause had all been in the planning, or lack of it, and after six days the government ordered a general surrender. By that time the army and navy had sailed for Britain, and Queen Wilhemina had arrived to take up her royal exile. The small Dutch Air Force had also managed to get some of its personnel onto the boats.

Yet even though the government had been forced into exile, it still preferred to adopt a largely neutral stance, at least for the first few months. Holland had endeavoured to maintain good relations with Britain since the mid-sixteenth century. It was a relationship which was mutually beneficial, for Holland recognised and promoted Britain's interests in the Western European balance of power, and Britain in return promised to uphold Dutch neutrality. That cosy arrangement no longer applied after 1940. As Janet Eisen has demonstrated, the Dutch government 'gradually accepted the doctrine of mutual obligation and co-operation'.[2] In other words, it would *have* to throw in its lot with Britain – economically, militarily and politically – because there were no other options available to it.

The early contacts with both governments were therefore on the cool side, but at a military level things were a little better. In theory at least, both nations had a good stock of air expertise which could be effectively utilised in the service of the RAF. The Belgian pre-war order of battle comprised 198 first-line aircraft spread across a range of uses, with army co-operation work, fighters and reconnaissance bombers formed into a regiment each. The Dutch had a smaller force and a different organisation. The emphasis here was on army co-operation, and the second of the two Dutch air regiments was formed entirely for that purpose, the aircraft being the Fokker C.5 and the Koolhoven F.K.51. One group of the first air regiment was reserved for fighters, and the British estimated in 1939 that the Dutch were operating thirty-six Fokker D21s and six Fokker G1s. In all, Holland was defended by approximately 146 first-line aircraft with little in reserve, but no one seriously doubted the professionalism or the abilities of the men in either air force.[3]

The initial assessment of the incoming aviators after the fall of France was in the same vein, and there was none of the furrowing of brows which had greeted the news that the Poles and the Czechs were heading across the Channel in large numbers. Even before France had asked for an armistice, the Air Ministry was busy discussing plans for the formation of national units, and it is clear from the records that the Dutch and the Norwegians were to be granted squadrons as soon as the personnel became available – a status initially denied the Poles, despite their considerable numbers. The Directorate of Intelligence estimated that the number of suitable Belgians who had made their escape might not be sufficient to man a full squadron, but they had no objection to the rapid formation of flights which could then be attached to British squadrons. This must be set against the decision taken at the same time to reject Czechoslovak crews, and Archibald Boyle was the guiding hand behind all of it. There can be no doubt that Slavs of whatever nationality were not to Boyle's liking, but the West Europeans were an altogether different matter.[4]

By late May 1940, the Belgians had 180 pilots and ground crew in Britain. They insisted that this was enough to form two squadrons, but it was apparent that the British were not going to entertain the idea because a large injection of RAF technical personnel would have been required to make the units operational. The Belgian government had requested thirty Hurricanes and twenty Blenheims, the argument being that they could re-train pilots quickly enough to fly them in action. Boyle said no, but then offered to take the best pilots available for individual service. 'The Belgians were disinclined to accept this,' he minuted, and it was clear from their attitude that they expected the reconstitution of the Belgian Air Force in its entirety. This was always going to be out of the question – they had far fewer men than the Czechoslovaks who had already been pushed into the RAFVR – but on this occasion the British could reasonably use their argument that insufficient numbers made the formation of national squadrons unrealistic. As a result, individual Belgian airmen soon found their way into British fighter squadrons with the blessing of Hugh Dowding, AOC Fighter Command, who needed them badly as the air war with Germany developed.[5]

On the political front, it was Churchill again who was driving the policies forwards. By early June 1940, the Belgian government was still on French soil, and proposals to form national units of any kind were still subject to French sensitivities. As with the Czechoslovaks, the British decided to play safe and direct any conscripts or volunteers over to the Continent for enlistment. A parliamentary question in the Commons requested confirmation that the Belgians were determined to continue conscripting men in spite of King Leopold's surrender, and the answer received was an emphatic yes. But this did *not* mean that Britain would turn away airmen who were considered to have the skills necessary to join British units if vacancies existed, and in response to some urgent prodding by Churchill, the Air Ministry elicited the approval of the Belgian authorities in Paris. The reaction was largely negative. Col Wouters, the Assistant Air Attaché, let it be known that if any transfers to the RAF organisation were to take place, they had to be conducted in the spirit of a future intention to form national squadrons when the circumstances permitted. This the British were reluctant to promise, so as the battle of France drew to a close, those airmen who had been selected for service in Britain got on with their re-training in the knowledge that they might well do their combat flying in France. In the event, most of them returned only to seek evacuation a few days later.

However, yet again the British were faced with a resolute ally, and we have seen before that standing firm usually produced a determination to resist in equal measure. The Belgians were making reasonable demands, but in no way would the RAF allow the establishment of any precedents in regard to allied service in its ranks. Besides, it was clear by July 1940 that yet another government was moving into exile with divisions in its ranks. The Foreign Office heard that several hundred Belgians – mainly Walloons – had applied for service with the Free French, their leaders declaring that they were 'disgusted with King Leopold and the Belgian government'. Some souls in Whitehall thought the idea a good one, not least because it removed a potential responsibility from British shoulders onto those of de Gaulle, but in the end it was vetoed at a higher level.[6]

Nevertheless, such divisions merely warned the British that the Belgians would need careful handling if they were to become a bona fide ally in exile. The British experience of Belgian refugees had not been a happy one in general, and it was important to regenerate public confidence in their abilities and commitment to the common cause. As the dust settled on the French beaches after the evacuations in June, it became clear that only a handful of Belgian pilots had managed to get out successfully. The Chiefs of Staff report noted that some twenty or thirty trained men had reached British soil, and about another twenty were believed to be on their way. This was plenty to form a squadron with air crew only, but scarcely any ground crew had managed to get away, therefore Wouters was told firmly that all men would be commissioned or enlisted into the RAFVR. By mid-August, the numbers had risen to ninety-four, of which twenty-eight were already in service with British squadrons or passing through OTUs. But as with the Czechoslovaks, the contingent was top-heavy with officers or professional fliers, both civilian and military, and pleased though the British were that another sixty or so pilots were said to be en route from North Africa, there still remained the problem that no Belgian squadrons could be formed without the necessary ground crew.[7]

This was a situation which embittered the early relationship with the Belgian military authorities, and as preparations got under way to create the usual agreement with them, the Foreign Office was aware that its guests were a little touchy regarding their new status. It was pointed out in an exchange of notes that Belgium had sought and preserved a strict neutrality both before and after the German attack on Poland, therefore demands that she be treated as a full ally now that her strategy had been exposed as worthless were, to put it mildly, a bit rich. In the eyes of the British, RAFVR membership was a fair compensation, and one which guaranteed active service against the enemy. Anything else would not be on offer, no matter how hard the Belgians pushed. Roger Makins at the Foreign Office decided to soothe the tattered nerves by showing the Belgians a copy of the standard agreement being touted around the offices of the other governments then setting up shop in Britain, but 'to invest the occasion with slightly more significance', he thought Alexander Cadogan should be the prime communicator, the logic being that by dealing with the Permanent Under Secretary to the Foreign Office, the Belgians might not feel so put out by the otherwise frosty attitude.

The text of the main agreement differed little from those arranged with the other allied powers in exile. There was no promise to liberate Belgium in the preamble, merely a recognition of 'the common interest in maintaining the armed forces of Belgium'. This was enhanced by a statement which carefully skirted the term 'liberation'. All of Belgium's forces in exile would 'be employed either for the defence of the United Kingdom, or for the purpose of regaining Belgium, or for other tasks to this end'. This provision contained a multitude of possibilities, and it gave rise to some inter-governmental squabbles later on, most of the emphasis falling on the last clause. In theory, this meant that Belgian forces could have been deployed in any theatre of the war if it could be argued that their activity was helping to win the war as a whole, and therefore by extension, free Belgium from occupation. Furthermore, and unlike other agreements, this one contained no Air Appendix, the Air Ministry having decided at a very early stage that all Belgian aviators would be drafted directly into the RAFVR.[8] Thus the British were keeping their hands free of yet another entanglement with an allied power, for in the Belgian case its forces were either directly absorbed into those of the hosts, or remained flexible enough to be deployed anywhere on a technicality. This gave the British the power to prevent the Belgian government from insisting that its forces only took part in operations directly connected with defending Britain or the battle for Belgium – a useful loophole should the Belgians decide that their forces be kept in reserve for such a purpose.

The new agreement was a long time in coming, and the Belgian government spent the first six months of 1941 arguing about jurisdiction. Where no specific Air Appendix existed, the airmen were automatically subject to Royal Air Force law; but in the Belgian Army (approximately 800 strong) their own military codes applied. The Belgian government wanted a re-draft which noted the 'temporary arrangement' in regard to the pilots and ground crew, a clause specifying that British law would only apply to RAFVR personnel 'so long as they continue to serve in that force'. The British were well aware that this created the potential for a later argument based on demands for independent status or at least national squadrons, but in order to see the thing through to a reasonable conclusion, the Foreign Office relented with some reluctance. It was a smart move by the Belgians. By means of the long delay they tested Whitehall's patience, and without an explicit call for independence they managed to push open the door a little with a carefully worded amendment.[9] Yet even this draft failed to satisfy all the parties, and it would not be until 4 June 1942 when the final version was signed, and by that time the Belgians had succeeded in gaining a clause explicitly promising 'liberation from German occupation' *and* a provision which allowed for inter-governmental discussions on the use of their forces.

The Belgians had a long wait before they acquired their first squadron within the RAFVR arrangement. This was not due to the delays surrounding the agreement, but because of the lack of trained air crew and ground staff. Their numbers in Britain increased only gradually, and they were almost entirely dependent on escapees from Europe rather than volunteers from elsewhere. It was not until 12 November 1941 that 350 Fighter Squadron was formed, and even then it took a further six months before the unit was declared fully operational. Once active, however, it delivered a fine record of service. It saw action at Dieppe, and accompanied the advancing allies into France after OVERLORD, finally moving onto its home soil in December 1944.

But before the formation of 350, most Belgian airmen fought their war from within British squadrons, the South African Air Force, and even the occasional French unit, this latter option being open to them for reasons of language and the short but effective joint training scheme initiated in 1940. The Chiefs of

Staff reports regularly paid tribute to the skill and courage of the Belgians, and the tally, even by August 1940, stood at ten enemy aircraft confirmed destroyed and one unconfirmed: an impressive haul from a contingent which only had thirty pilots in the air. But still it took a long time to gather and train enough men for a squadron of their own. By August 1941, they felt strong enough to press for a national unit, having amassed a total of 22 men in British fighter squadrons (with 11 of those in 609), a further 38 in fighter OTUs, and another 8 in training schools. When the proposal was put before Sholto Douglas (then AOC Fighter Command), Dore at the DAFL noted that the chances of getting enough ground crew to form a fully integral unit were slight, though he accepted that a slow trickle of about six pilots per month should be enough to cover losses in the air. Dore accepted that the situation was a little touchy, especially given the amount of time and trouble taken with the French to ensure that they manned their own units, but he added: 'I feel that some weight should be given to political considerations and national prestige', and if British ground crew could be found, then the squadron should be formed.[10]

Yet even though their numbers were limited, the Belgians continued to put in a fine performance. By March 1943, they had a total of only 353 men in service, but had accounted for sixty-seven enemy aircraft. The Chiefs of Staff reported the morale in 350 Squadron to be 'very high' to 'excellent' in all of their reports down to the end of the war. Furthermore, the Belgians had received an added boost on 10 November 1942, when a second fighter squadron, 349, was formed in Nigeria from men who had volunteered for service in the Belgian Congo. At first they flew Tomahawks and spent much of their air time in ferrying duties, but the reputation of 350 prompted the Air Ministry to bring 349 to Britain in the summer of 1943, when it re-formed on Spitfires, becoming operational on 5 June 1943. In fact, by that time the Belgians were in the happy position of having surplus pilots, and entire crews were posted to British units to form Belgian flights. Most of the men in 349 came from the Force Publique, a training scheme in the Congo which provided pilots for both the RAF and the South African Air Force. Apart from around 200 pilots in various stages of training, there was a welcome fillip to the low ground crew numbers with another eighty-five mechanics going through trade testing in Africa. In all, the Air Ministry was becoming decidedly content with its Belgian allies by the end of 1943, and a DAFL minute noted that morale 'was very high throughout', and the attitude 'exemplary'.[11]

The strength of the relationship should not, however, lead one to suppose that the RAF was unaware of the political problems which plagued most of the exiles during their time in Britain. As with the Czechoslovaks, who pursued their own disastrous attempt at gaining independence in 1943, the Belgian government also made a lunge at the same prize at the same time. At the end of June, the DAFL informed the Air Ministry that there were three types of Belgian personnel then in service: those in the Belgian section of the RAFVR; those of the Belgian Military Aviation section attached to the government, all of whom wore Belgian uniform and were subject to their national military laws, and those of the Force Publique in the Congo. Most of the latter group had escaped through Spain and had trained in South African air schools, later to see action with the South African Air Force. This organisation was too fragmented, argued the DAFL: 'The total personnel of these three sections combined is only about 1,200 but owing to petty intrigue, personal jealousies and the lack of a co-ordinating head, the problems attached to them and the administrative work entailed is out of all proportion to their size.'[12]

To solve the problem, the DAFL recommended that *all* of the Belgian air sections be brought into the RAFVR, in line with the Czechoslovak precedent. In return for sacrificing that slice of independence, they would be granted an inspectorate and a national depot. Wouters, the Air Attaché, was said to be in favour of the scheme, and he seemed to think that most of his airmen would feel likewise. Resistance came from the Minister of National Defence, Pierlot, who preferred to push for independent status in tandem with the Czechoslovaks. It might have been coincidence, but in the very week when the DAFL issued its devastating critique of the Czechoslovak proposals, Pierlot was reported to have been 'coming round to our way of thinking'. As for the man most likely to become Inspector-General, the DAFL supported Wouters, but in so doing they rejected others who would be unacceptable at any price. Again, as with Janoušek in the Czechoslovak Air Force, the British selected rather than accepted the men who would lead the national sections of the RAFVR.

Further resistance came from the Congo. A request had been made for ambulance and coastal aircraft which had subsequently been rejected by the Air Ministry as unnecessary, but that did not stop at least one senior commander from refusing to transfer any men to Britain. According to the DAFL, he was trying to gather more power to himself 'irrespective of the greater and more important needs of the Belgian Air Force as a whole.' In retaliation, the Air Ministry threatened to withdraw training provisions from the Force Publique, and put pressure on the Belgian government to insist that the whole Congo contingent, around 250 men, be posted to Britain for enlistment in the RAFVR. Pierlot at first agreed, then changed his mind, apparently suspecting that there was an ulterior motive behind the plan to gather all the men in Britain. In all probability, there was. Standard Air Ministry procedure when dealing with the smaller allies was to minimise the risk of intrigue and division in the air forces as a result of similar tensions in the national governments, and their method of stabilising the situation usually meant throwing a British blanket in the shape of the RAFVR over the whole force.

In the event, this particular round ended in a draw, at least in the short term. With Pierlot still proving obstructive, the British baited the hook with a promise of six Oxford air ambulances for service in the Congo if all the surplus personnel were then sent to Britain. Pierlot accepted the aircraft with thanks, and in the mid-summer of 1943 they duly made their way to Africa. The DAFL waited patiently for the Belgians to fulfil their side of the agreement, but after a couple of sharp prompts, Pierlot wrote to Portal in mid-August and declared that the Belgian government of the Congo had decided to keep as many men as necessary to service *all* the aircraft then in the territory, plus the six Oxfords. Unfortunately, this left only 102 out of the 250 men available for service in Britain, and even they had been informed that RAFVR service was not compulsory, so they might well end up in the land army after all. The British had been outflanked, and it is a pity that the DAFL's response is no longer in the London files, though we might guess that it was not a pleasant read.[13]

But the DAFL would not be thwarted. It applied more pressure on the Belgian government, mainly through Wouters, who was growing tired of being the middle man. Then the Belgians launched another gambit. They let it be known in November that the remaining men in Africa would soon be on a ship bound for England. Then it was suggested that in return for a new protocol to the existing agreement – a termination date when Belgium had been liberated – everything would be done to persuade the Congo authorities to send the remaining men to Britain. Nonplussed, the DAFL sought guidance from a higher power, the Allied Forces Committee (AFC). No other allied agreements had termination dates. The arrangement had always been that each nation would continue to serve until the war was won, no matter which was liberated first. It was not so much a question of what the Belgians would actually do when their country was free – there had been no hint of a sudden severance of the alliance – but the bare fact that they had the gall to request the option in the first place, even if by implication. The Air Ministry advised the AFC that the whole thing was to do with internal Belgian politics and should be ignored – advice the AFC handsomely appreciated. Wouters, it seems, had not been consulted on the matter, and again it would appear that his government treated him with as much suspicion and disdain over political matters as the Czechoslovak administration treated Janoušek. Yet again, this stands as another case of a government with its own axes to grind using its most visible fighting arm to further its own agenda.[14]

This time, the Belgians came unstuck. The AFC had no hesitation in rejecting the proposed protocol because it would have been a dangerous precedent to set at a time when plans for OVERLORD were well advanced. The Air Ministry held two trump cards. The first was the fact that Wouters had made clear his irritation at not being consulted on the matter, and the British thoroughly disliked it when inspectors were unhappy because that threatened the harmony of the relationship. Second, the men in the Congo were entirely unemployed apart from routine work, and there had been some pressure from them upon their own officers to let them be with their countrymen. In any case, the Air Ministry knew well that the Congo detachment was unsustainable, and its very existence outside the main war effort was embarrassing to the Belgians anyway. It was, however, being used as a chip in a game of political poker played by its government, and the net result was a general cooling of relations between all parties. From then until the end of the war in Europe, the British treated the Belgian politicians with just a touch more contempt.

As always, the inevitable compromise was struck. A new protocol to the agreement was signed on 30 March 1944, but although it did not substantially alter the relationship, it did allow for the establishment of an Inspectorate-General and a fully-fledged Belgian section of the RAFVR, formalising the de facto arrangement which had existed since the previous autumn. The British also agreed as far as possible to group all Belgian personnel into national squadrons, but that was their policy anyway. However, the Protocol did not give them independence, which was what they actually wanted, though they were permitted to wear Belgian uniforms with national ranks when not on duty. These were small concessions, but they kept the peace.[15]

When victory was in sight early in 1945, the British offered to maintain and expand the Belgian Air Force once Germany had been defeated. Again, this was in line with the provisions of COS 120 and the policies directed towards the other allied governments. But again, as with the French, the Americans objected. It was Washington's policy to resist all attempts by the British to steal the march on matters of postwar rearmament, and apart from the Mutual Aid agreements, no military supplies not destined for the common war effort were to be sent to any allied force. The British sidestepped this by following expansion plans which could easily have been claimed as legitimate provisions: the supply of aircraft for training purposes, the formation of a pilot school, and the enrolment of a few men on specialist and instructor courses, all of which were supposed to maintain the supply of men for the western front, even though everyone knew the war would be over long before they were ready for action.[16]

Both 349 and 350 Squadrons finished their war with the occupation forces stationed at Fassberg. In Britain, meetings were held to discuss the final disbandment of the Belgian Section of the RAFVR and the termination of all agreements. As with the previous years, many thoughts were turned towards the likely rearmament policies, and more to the point, whether those policies would be acceptable to the Americans. Mutual Aid had provided the cover for the training and a large proportion of initial re-equipment, but a fillip was given to British hopes when the Belgians made it clear that they would reorganise their air force along RAF lines, implying that they would expect to receive new British machines when reconstruction began. The Americans could not intervene in this transaction. It was easy to veto British proposals to hold sales drives in Europe, but impossible for them to ban customers from choosing their own wares.

The official date for the restoration of a newly independent Belgian Air Force was set for 1 September 1946, with demobilisation and transfer of stores to be phased over a period of six weeks. On 15 October, the final day, Tedder wrote to the Belgian Chief of the Air Staff, Gp Capt Leboutte, and filled the page with thanks and hearty sentiments. The Belgian pilots and ground crew had fought a hard war and won much respect, not to mention three DSOs and over forty DFCs and DFMs. In addition, they had destroyed 138 enemy aircraft by VE Day; and by 1943, five RAF squadrons were commanded by Belgian Air Force officers. On 24 October, a lavish cocktail party in Brussels marked the end of a long alliance, and one which was only occasionally troublesome.[17]

In the years that followed, the Belgian Air Force drew heavily on RAF experience and equipment. Training continued at RAF Bottisham and Snailwell, and it was not until November 1948 that the first Belgian pilots trained on their home soil were ready for service. Much to the delight of the Air Ministry, the skies were thick with British aircraft heading for Belgium, primarily Tiger Moths, Spitfires and Mosquitoes. The British also assisted with the development of a transport wing which flew Ansons, Dakotas and Oxfords among others. In March 1948, Belgium, Holland, Luxemburg, France and Britain signed the Treaty of Brussels, a slightly backward-looking agreement which was directed against a resurgent Germany, but one which nevertheless symbolised European desires to move towards real stability on the continent. The alliance had ended with more smiles than tears, and that in itself was a victory when one considers the fate of the East Europeans.

Turning now to the Dutch, their experiences broadly mirrored those of the Belgians. However, previous experience tended to determine their war roles perhaps more than any other allied group. At the beginning of the war, Dutch air power had been divided into two arms: the Royal Netherlands Naval Air Service and the Royal Netherlands Army Air Service. Neither of these two had been particularly well maintained during the interwar years, but as a result of the political machinations which accompanied the arrival of the pilots in Britain, it was the naval wing which gained the first advantages and tended to dominate for the rest of the conflict.

This was demonstrated in the formation of 320 and 321 Squadrons at Pembroke Dock on 1 June 1940 – the fastest assimilation into the RAF's order of battle of any exiled force during the war. The Dutch had the advantage in that they brought most of their own aircraft with them, for when their home bases were in danger of being overrun they simply evacuated the entire unit to Britain. Thus, for several months until September 1940 when a shortage of spares forced them to re-equip with Ansons, 320 flew its own Fokker T-VIIIW float-planes on anti-submarine patrols – an interesting irony in itself. On the other side of the bay, 321 was formed on Ansons and flew similar patrols until 18 January 1941, when it merged with 320, at which time the combined unit operated Hudsons as well. In March 1941, the squadron moved to Scotland for a long year of North Sea patrols, scoring the occasional success against enemy shipping.

Although this neatly took care of the naval wing of the Dutch air forces, the men from the Army Air Service were not so easily employed. As the German assault in the west gathered pace, the French informed the Air Ministry that around 150 Dutch Army Air Service personnel had escaped from a flying school and reached Caen. Writing to Sholto Douglas, Cyril Porri noted that the French were 'very anxious' to get the men to England. Sholto Douglas contacted AM Sir Richard Peirse, the VCAS, who gave his assent to the immediate transfer of the group to Britain. Within two weeks, they had disembarked at Porthcawl. Other men had scrambled onto the boats as they left French shores, and a total of 191 were interviewed by the security services at Haverfordwest in Wales. Of these, eighty-seven were pilots, and at once politics entered the scene when the Dutch government announced that the men were to stay in Britain instead of the destination required by the Army, the Dutch East Indies.[18]

Their numbers continued to grow as the men were assembled for trade-testing and attestation. Towards the end of June, a further fifty had made their way to Britain and registered for service. Such a sudden influx, combined with all the other allies, was causing headaches at the Air Ministry because of the limited training opportunities which existed as the Battle of Britain began. The British were pushing through their own recruits at breakneck speed, but it was swiftly decided that the best of the Dutch would be hurried through into operations if they could fill establishment posts and had sufficient spoken English. The Dutch authorities had no objection to this idea, but they insisted that all of their personnel be brought together into national units when the opportunity arose. But this still left nearly ninety men idle, and the RAF argued that a British trainee would be displaced for each Dutch pilot, no matter how experienced he might be, who was fed into the training programme.

Then someone came up with a new idea. If the entire contingent was shipped en bloc to the training schools in Newfoundland, the problem would be solved. Sholto Douglas gave his enthusiastic approval, but there then followed an interesting mix-up in attitudes and actions. Dealing directly with the Dutch Liaison Officer, Capt Berdenis van Berlekom, the Air Ministry proposed to promote the plan over the heads of the Dutch government, which, in the mean time, rejected the idea. In a letter of 5 July from the Dutch Military Mission, the government informed the Air Ministry that 'after careful consideration', the Newfoundland plan had been deemed unsuitable and all personnel should instead be sent to the East Indies to reinforce the air force units there. Indeed, arrangements were in hand to begin the transfer immediately.

This was something of an embarrassment to Boyle who had despatched Berlekom to Hednesford on 6 July to test the waters on the Newfoundland plan, and to offer them the only alternative of going out to the East Indies as a full contingent or as a last resort, enrolment in the Dutch Army. The men were paraded and asked to make their choices, though to ease things along they were not given the full list of options, but asked only one question: 'Do you want to go to the East Indies?' Of the 24 officers present, 14 refused the offer outright, 7 agreed to go 'under the strongest protest', and the remaining 3 accepted. Of the 114 men other ranks, all but three refused to go. The minutes state that 'all the men there were most depressed and almost broken-hearted' at the thought of going to the East Indies. They were told that their own Minister of Defence had turned down the Newfoundland offer. In a longer note (made available to Berkelom), the feelings of the men were even more tragically recorded:

> They referred in bitter terms to the fact that the French, Poles and Czechs are going to be allowed to fight in the air against Germany, but that they, the Dutch, are apparently not going to be allowed to do so, and they consider this to be a reflection on their honour.

The report also claimed that many would have stayed in Holland with their families had they known that this shambles would have come to pass, and by this account they accused their Ministry of Defence of 'lacking courage and imagination'. The report closed with a recommendation that the Dutch government be informed of these views, and that 'it would be an act of criminal folly not to make use of this enthusiasm'.

Obviously, this gave the British a strong hand to play in its game with the Dutch government, and Boyle prepared a typical finesse to clinch the matter. He proposed writing directly to the Dutch Minister of War and asking whether his government was still prepared to fight alongside the British, and if the answer was yes, then the Army pilots should be trained in Newfoundland ready for service on the western front. If the answer was no, then the Dutch could do with them as they wished. Whether Boyle sent such a note is unclear, but he certainly engaged the help of Sinclair in communicating these ideas to the Dutch, though no doubt the Secretary of State for Air was a little more tactful in his representations.

Within a couple of days, the Dutch returned with a list of queries which, when amalgamated, cast many doubts upon the British ability to really secure the necessary materials if the Newfoundland plan went ahead. Could they, for example, guarantee that accommodation, food supplies and suitable aircraft would all be on hand if the army contingent were sent at once? Van Berkelom, batting for the British, assured his superiors that their hosts were quite capable of such a venture, that they had already demonstrated their commitment by rapidly setting up the two seaplane squadrons with Coastal Command, and that it was in everybody's interest to see the group return from Newfoundland as experienced pilots and ready to wage war in the common cause.

On 10 July, Medhurst chaired a meeting with various representatives of the departments affected by the problem. Mr R.B. Ewbank of the Dominions Office rang a negative note when he reported that the Canadian government 'did not view the plan with favour', and that the Newfoundland government might object 'to having in their midst a people of a Germanic race of whom only about 10% had a knowledge of English'. Medhurst retorted that the Norwegians had made similar approaches to the Canadians who had happily accepted them. The meeting then heard that most of the men were content to go to Newfoundland, but were being thwarted by the wishes of the Dutch Army. As for Ewbank's point, the political sensitivities might be overcome if the Dutch could be persuaded to involve the local community in the project, either as workers in the camp or even as trainees in their own right. The cost of the exercise was liable to be borne by the Dutch government, 'who have substantial reserves of gold in the United States', and the meeting decided in closing that every effort would be made to push the plan through. An added sweetener might be that the presence of a Dutch force on the North American continent could act as a banner for recruitment in America.

But no one on the British side seemed to pay much heed to the realities of training in Newfoundland – something the Dutch took the trouble to find out for themselves. For a start, the British would have needed to build several huts and hangars at the Hatties Camp, and because of the conditions in winter, the snow on the runways would need to be packed hard with rollers to enable aircraft to land and take off using wheels instead of skis. No operational flying at all could take place for four to six weeks in the depths of winter, and the spring thaw would also make conditions extremely hazardous. Extra water and sanitary services would also need to be supplied because the camp was already in use by a 900-strong battalion of the Canadian Army, and all utilities were stretched to capacity. For a race of people used to the relatively mild climate of Europe, or the cloying humidity of the Far East, such a sojourn would have been grim indeed, every bit as chilling to the Dutch heart as that which the poor Tahitians experienced when they were posted to the Free French unit in Scotland.

This was a battle which the British ultimately lost. It is not clear whether it was the result of sustained pressure from the Dutch Army, or the tendency of the Dutch government to still keep at least a little distant from foreign entanglements, or even the more logical desire to protect their imperial holdings in the Far East, but the end result was rejection for the Newfoundland scheme and an announcement that all untrained men would be sent to the East Indies while the more experienced pilots would go to the Coastal Command squadrons. A brief telegram sent to Hatties Camp on 2 August confirmed the decision, but it also seems unlikely that the Canadians would have given their blessing anyway. The Dutch, unlike the Norwegians, had still been tainted with a strong whiff of the Fifth Column after the collapse in the summer, and although we know now that this was a gross and unfair misjudgement, we are not in the fraught days of 1940 when defeat or survival hung by a thread. To a certain extent the Dutch suffered from this widespread suspicion, as indeed did the Belgians. In the event, not many men actually embarked for the Dutch East Indies. Apart from the trained personnel sent to 320 and 321 Squadrons – given as twenty pilots and thirty-three mechanics – eight instructors were retained, while fifty-eight other ranks either went to the Dutch Army or made the long trip to the east.

Looking at the figures, one feels compelled to call this tussle an honourable draw. The Dutch government recognised that Britain needed all the pilots she could lay hands on, and many Dutch pilots went straight into RAF squadrons if they had a sufficient command of English. Indeed, one such group flying with 167 (Gold Coast) Squadron eventually made up the core of the third Dutch unit in 1943. But we must also accept that Holland had imperial possessions which needed defending, and although her government had sought sanctuary in Britain after the French defeat, a vast and extremely vulnerable territory with tens of thousands of weakly defended citizens lay at the mercy of the Japanese. Therefore, we should not be surprised that the Dutch Army dug in its heels and demanded that at least *some* reinforcements be sent to the beleaguered colony. Equally, the British might well have had reasonable concerns about the commitment to the war effort demonstrated by small but powerful sections of the East Indies' community. In September 1940, the Foreign Office heard from the Consul-General in Batavia (now Jakarta) that many high-ranking members of the government 'are not particularly disposed towards the United Kingdom or the allied cause'. However, this was largely considered to be the result of the Gestapo placing 431 leading Dutch personalities into concentration camps as a reprisal for alleged ill-treatment of German internees in the Dutch East Indies. The Foreign Office noted the comments, but dismissed the tales as having originated from 'unreliable sources'.[19]

Balanced against this dark propaganda was the irrefutable evidence that the Dutch colonists had deep pockets. In October 1940, the *Sunday Times* reported that the people of the East Indies had raised £334,000 in a 'Spitfire Campaign' and a further £323,377 for bombers, enough to buy forty fighters and eighteen Hudsons, collectively known as the Wilhemina Fund. But the money was being delayed in Batavia, in the face of strong public protest, by elements within the government who believed the money should be spent in Java. The Foreign Office regarded the issue as a test of the government's will to resist supporting the Western allies. Besides, they were already aware of the fund-raising and a parallel recruitment drive as early as July, and an interesting comment on the matter reveals that the Air Ministry was not in favour of receiving Dutch pilots from the East Indies because of the 'Quisling danger', though why escapees from Europe were not so regarded is at present unknown.[20] However, this attitude *might* explain the reluctance of the Air Ministry to let the Dutch governments send men to the Far East, but when all is said and done, they were not there for very long.

The day after the Japanese attack on the American fleet at Pearl Harbor, the Netherlands declared war on Japan. Between then, December 1941 and 1 March 1942, the day when Japanese forces first landed on Java, the plucky but hopelessly outclassed Dutch forces suffered defeat after defeat. Ten days later, the entire territory had been lost to Tokyo, and in another mass evacuation what remained of the Dutch forces made their way to Britain, a few of them for the second time. During their absence, their countrymen had continued to fight the war in the west much to the satisfaction of the RAF. Perhaps more importantly, the Dutch government had succeeded in keeping a reasonable political distance between the two allies. The two Coastal Command squadrons stood as independent units of the Royal Netherlands Naval Air Services, a condition granted by the Air Ministry largely because of the golden purse with which the Dutch financed themselves, but also because they could supply nearly all of the ground crew for the two squadrons.[21]

By the time the eighty or so men arrived in Britain after the Japanese conquest of Indonesia, the Dutch government had been picking away at the drafts of the usual military agreement for more than two years, a major sticking point being the application of Dutch military law in the two Coastal Command squadrons. Despite the best efforts of the British to convince them that it would be easier 'for reasons of practical convenience' to apply RAF law, the Dutch held out for this supreme symbol of independence. Neither did the Dutch request a 'liberation clause' to be inserted into the agreement's preamble. Even this would have bound them in some degree to an alliance which we cannot interpret as anything other than a reluctant one, not for reasons of distrust or compulsion, but because it so perfectly mirrored traditional Dutch foreign policy since the seventeenth century. From the very start, and to the very end, they were determined to keep their hands free, and what makes them so different from all the other allies (with the possible exception of the Norwegians) is that they succeeded.[22]

The new influx from Java were interviewed and trade-tested before being sent to 320 Squadron, now even more self-sufficient after its merger with 321 in January 1941. But in August 1942, 321 Squadron was reborn in the Far East. Dutch crews had managed to salvage a number of Catalinas and fly them from Java to Ceylon, and another detachment marooned in Australia joined them at China Bay, which became the unit's base until the end of the war. In Britain, the Dutch Army pilots at last realised their dream in June 1943, when 322 Fighter Squadron was formed at Woodvale. Drawing upon the experienced core of pilots who had seen much service with RAF units, 322 was initially mounted on variants of the Spitfire V and flew convoy patrols and sweeps over the Irish Sea and the English Channel. Here, however, the Dutch success in gaining independence petered out, for one of the conditions attached to the squadron's formation was that it should be within the RAFVR. This was not a retaliatory strike by the British; rather, to have granted the unit independent status when its physical presence was so small would have been a tempting challenge to other exiled governments who sought similar status for their own larger air forces.

By 1943, the Dutch had a total of 614 officers and men in units attached to the British home forces, but by this time recruitment had become spasmodic. All who could have escaped – or who wanted to escape – had largely been accounted for, and only the occasional soul brave enough to risk his life managed to report for duty. Even so, unlike the Czechoslovaks, the Dutch had no qualms about maintaining their highly active air forces by drawing from their army contingent, recognising that apart from their propaganda value, the air crews were becoming highly experienced, combat-toughened individuals who would have much to contribute to a postwar reconstruction policy. Karel Janoušek in the Czechoslovak camp had exactly the same vision, but Edvard Beneš was a man who wanted everything and came out with half-measures.

Much of the work of 322 Squadron was taken up in 'Diver' patrols, or the shooting down of V1 flying bombs launched from the continent as part of Hitler's last stand. Towards the end of 1943, a Combined Dutch Navy and Army Committee was formed to co-ordinate the expansion of a unified air force principally for service in the war against Japan after the final defeat of Germany. After the launch of OVERLORD, morale in 320 Squadron began to dip over concerns of the fate of Holland as the Germans fell back before the allied advance, but the Chiefs of Staff accepted that little could be done to employ the naval crews in any meaningful operations while the land engagement was of such vital importance. As for 322, its success in destroying 110 flying bombs earned it a mention in the allied forces report for the third quarter of 1944, but at least the recruitment problem was eased with the early liberation of southern Holland, and a mission from Britain was sent to campaign for volunteers to top up the air force establishments.

This in itself was a successful operation, and numbers surged. The Air Ministry was presented with a plan which envisaged fifty-four men a month for air crew training, and a further 200 a month for the maintenance teams. The long-term view was that all three Dutch squadrons would eventually depart for the Far East to liberate the East Indies from the Japanese occupation. To act as a central authority for this reorganisation, a recruiting centre was opened in Eindhoven with the full blessing of the Americans who saw much to be gained by having an experienced ally in the war against Hirohito. But it was not to be. For apart from 321 Squadron, already in Ceylon, the two British-based units finished their war on European soil with the occupation forces. One reason was that Holland proved remarkably difficult to liberate in its entirety. Five years of occupation had given rise to a formidable police state and a pro-Nazi force of about 50,000 men, many with the SS. The Dutch government admitted in 1949 that it had imprisoned nearly 150,000 collaborators, though a great many others simply disappeared, their fate decided by the Resistance.

After the war, the Dutch government pursued much the same rearmament policy with the British as did the Belgians. The Air Ministry happily supplied spares and maintenance materials for the Spitfires flown by 322 up until 1951. Training also continued in Britain for a few years after the war, for the air force as well as the army, and the re-equipment agreement reached in May 1946 enriched the British coffers by £1.8 million. As for the Dutch government, they had learned well that small nations need big friends if they are to survive, and in the postwar environment they lent themselves more readily to co-operation in the wider interests of European security, and from the unsteady alliance of 1940, a stronger, more communicative friendship emerged from the common battle so bravely fought and deservedly won.

NOTES

1. Buck, M., *'Feeding a Pauper Army': War Refugees and Welfare in Britain, 1939–1942* (Berghahn Books 2000). Extract from pre-publication paper.
2. Eisen, J., *Anglo-Dutch Relations and European Unity, 1940–1948* (Hull University, 1980), p. 1.
3. AIR 40/2031: Orders of Battle, 1939. In a subsequent report prepared for the Chiefs of Staff, the airmen of both nations were considered to be of the highest quality in Europe.
4. AIR 2/7196: DCAS Conference (Conclusions), 25.5.40. Sholto Douglas later minuted that Polish pilots should be used in British fighter squadrons if they were satisfactorily trained.
5. AIR 2/4213: Minute to file by Boyle; DCAS Conference minutes, 27.5.40.
6. FO 371/24366: Correspondence, 5.6.40 to 23.7.40.
7. CAB 66/10: COS Reports 1–3, 22.7.40 to 12.8.40.
8. FO 371/24368: Drafts, Anglo–Belgian Military Agreement and comments, 13.8.40 to 7.10.40.
9. FO 371/24369; Correspondence, 15.11.40 to 30.11.40. See also FO 371/26448, minute to file by J.G. Ward, 13.6.41. Ward noted that the details had been 'exhaustively discussed', and regarded the entire debate as 'extremely tiresome'.
10. AIR 2/5595: Dore to Sholto Douglas, 22.8.41. This letter was written in the middle of the heated debate over the maintenance of 340 (Free French) Squadron by French naval

personnel. Most of the Belgian air recruits were being drawn from the army.

11. AIR 2/8238: DAFL Quarterly Reports, 10.10.42 to 16.4.43.
12. AIR 8/778: DAFL to CAS, 30.6.43.
13. AIR 8/778: Correspondence, 1.7.43 to 17.8.43.
14. FO 371/42298: Correspondence, January 1944.
15. FO 371/42299: Correspondence and minutes, 11.3.44 to 14.4.44.
16. FO 371/50748: Reconstruction correspondence, 9.2.45 to 15.2.45.
17. AIR 20/7270: Correspondence, 8.10.46 to 26.10.46.
18. AIR 2/5152: 'Disposal in England of Dutch Army Air Force Personnel and Aircraft'; general correspondence, June–July 1940. Subsequent references are drawn from this file until otherwise noted.
19. FO 371/24717: Walsh to R.G. Howe (Far Eastern Dept), 16.9.40.
20. FO 371/24717: Correspondence, 9.7.40 to 27.10.40.
21. FO 371/24366: Medhurst to Coleridge, 14.8.40; Air Council minutes, 12.7.40.
22. FO 371/32207: Anglo-Dutch Agreement, May 1942; see also CAB 85/20 (AFO(41)12), 17.2.41. The no 'liberation clause' was a final compromise to a dispute which had started in August 1940. The Dutch had originally wanted RAF command to cease the moment they crossed into Dutch territory, but we have seen earlier how the Air Ministry refused to sanction such a clause when the Belgians advanced a similar demand.

CHAPTER SEVEN

Conclusion

Perhaps one of the most misunderstood lines in the written history of warfare originated with Carl von Clausewitz in his 1832 treatise, *On War*. For what is actually a rather a large book with many fascinating musings and arguments, it seems that only one thought has gone forward to keep Clausewitz near the top of the quotation league table: his famous phrase, 'war is merely the continuation of policy by other means'. But as Christopher Bassford has argued, the German word *Politik* can mean 'policy' or 'politics', and these are two different things. The first is a rational programme of action designed to produce a desired result, whereas the second is an abstract concept central to human existence, a force which determines the shape of the lives of everyone on the planet. According to Bassford's interpretation, therefore, Clausewitz required us to understand that war can represent two things at once: a policy in itself whereby the political objectives are pursued by force, and a complete breakdown of all normal political dialogue, leading to the march of armies to resolve the issues. In Bassford's words, 'war is what happens when political conflict reaches an emotional level that leads to organised violence'.[1]

This penetrating reading of the old Prussian's philosophy neatly underpins the idea that the Second World War was not so much a war between nations in the style of the first great conflict of 1914–18, when the great empires collided in a struggle for European supremacy, but rather it was a war between the three most prominent political ideologies of the era, ideologies which had attained a level of development whereby the conflict between them reached critical mass. Fascism had been around in various forms for at least a century; communism was relatively new, but in the Russian revolutions it had acquired real power. The oldest of all, the democracies, had been badly shaken by the near-collapse of their economic system in the Depression, and had yet to fully recover psychologically from the previous world war.

Three systems, three different political aims. Thus, between the years 1939 and 1945, the war of arms between these three claimed over fifty million lives. We know now that the communists and the democracies prevailed after six years of bloody struggle – if only to begin immediately a new war of ideology which lasted a further forty-five years. It could even be argued that the war of ideas is only now finally over; that the liberal democracies have at last achieved victory, and that the world will forever be governed by stock markets and unknown men in suits, not tin-pot dictators with ludicrous uniforms and a taste for genocide. But that is a matter for future historians to ponder upon. In the autumn of 1939, the ideological elements of the conflict were not invisible to the leaders of the hour, but perhaps they were not so clearly understood either.

The explanation of the war in the minds of many people was still cast in the terms of 1918: a German nation which had not learned its lesson and been allowed to slip the chains forged at Versailles. People spoke of 'empire' and 'colonies' and the exportation of *Kultur* as much in 1939 as they had in 1914, but in fact these were nineteenth-century concepts which had been dealt a mortal blow by the First World War, though they proved to be a long time dying. For it was not *Kultur* which was being exported by Germany this time, it was national socialism. The German nation became the carrier of the Idea, as an organic cell is host to a virus. Those who thought German national aspirations could be satisfied by tinkering with the Treaty of Versailles entirely missed the point, and each concession made to Hitler convinced him not of Germany's right to a seat at the table of the Great Powers, but of the intrinsic strength of his perverse system of social order. He and his gangsters were naught but bullies in the continental playground, throwing their weight around in greater measure until at last their harassed victims summoned the courage to make a collective stand. Only then did Hitler realise that his power was not irresistible.

The appeasers took most of the blame, of course, not that they wholly deserved it. There was very little that could have practically been done to stop Hitler between 1933 and 1939, given the weaknesses of the British and French military, the lack of public support for war, and the simple but honest fear of another western front like the one where so many millions had died in vain. When Churchill took the premiership in 1940, it was not because he was the best man for the job, he was the *only* man for the job, for there was no one else to be called upon who had his combination of credibility and experience. A government led by Lord Halifax, the only other serious contender, would have probably sued for peace after Dunkirk. But although Churchill was far from secure until at least the early part of 1941, he nevertheless had one great asset which propelled him into office and kept him there until victory in Europe had been secured: his deep understanding of the philosophy of the Right and the grim fascination it inspired in the minds of the weak. Churchill understood Hitler far better than Chamberlain did. He recognised earlier than most that Hitler was a man driven, not by love of country or even love of himself, but by love of power for its own sake. He also knew that he was not dealing with a single nation, but with a disease which had infected half of Europe. Inside every one of the six nations which sought exile in Britain during 1940 were significant fascist parties or other organisations sympathetic to rightist ideology. Aside from the military pressures after Dunkirk, Churchill knew that he must keep Britain free from the contamination of the fascist idea, and it mattered not to him that a man might be from Austria or Czechoslovakia, Poland or even Germany, only that he did not carry with him that insidious virus which would, as he put it, wreck Christian civilisation if the infection were to become incurable.

In the War Cabinets of June 1940 we see him putting this philosophy into practice. He alone was prepared to throw open the doors of Britain to any man who was prepared to carry on with the fight against Nazism, and while others around him urged caution – and wisely so – he swept aside their concerns and demanded that the soldiers of the six nations be granted refuge, and that their airmen be given the chance to continue the struggle immediately. He justified this policy by claiming that it would give the British war effort that 'broad international character which will add greatly to our strength and prestige', which in practice meant a defiant salute to America.[2] Fascists and communists were excluded as a matter of course, but the British media made hay with many glorious (and sometimes fantastic) tales of allied heroism and escapology, and the Foreign Office made sure that American journalists got the best scoops. To Churchill, the collapse of the European democracies meant that their spirits could be kept alive not so much in Britain, but in America, where millions of European emigrants had made their homes. As symbols of freedom, fortitude and courage, they were worth their weight in gold – or so it seemed at the time. We know now that recruitment for the allied forces in America was not especially successful, but at least their presence in Britain kept the war alive in the minds of the expatriate communities in America.

But having encouraged Britain to welcome them with much bonhomie and flag-waving, Churchill lost interest in the European exiles after America joined the war in December 1941. He seldom mentioned them in his broadcasts after that date, whereas before that they had a place in almost every major speech. One can easily take the view that to him they had fulfilled their function by enabling the British war effort to be the prototype of his 'Grand Alliance', a small community of many flags whose very existence demonstrated that the unspeakable evil could be resisted. In the eighteen months between Dunkirk and Pearl Harbor, Churchill could thus be relied upon to act decisively in matters concerning the exiles; but with the entry of the Americans and the Russians, the responsibility fell entirely upon the service departments and the Foreign Office to maintain the allied relationships, and we have seen how varied and sometimes volatile those relationships could be.

The security services, acting in concert with the national governments, weeded out the suspect, the fanatical and the merely discontent from each group upon arrival. Avowed communists were swiftly shunted off to internment, as were political figures known to have paid too much attention to the principles of fascism. Those men who were critical of their political leaders received sympathetic treatment from the British, hence the decision to allow them to serve in British forces rather than suffer intimidation and victimisation in their own. Anti-Semitism among the exiles was commonplace, but the British did very little to discourage it, preferring instead to leave this highly sensitive issue to the governments concerned. Besides, being anti-Semitic did not mean that a man was pro-Nazi, and it was this that mattered most. Curiously, very few genuine spies were discovered during the filtering process, and it seems that the Germans missed their chance to place efficient agents within the contingents as they escaped from France. Perhaps it had all happened too quickly even for the Abwehr to take further advantage of victory in the field.

Once in Britain, the great priority was to organise and employ all the service personnel as rapidly as possible, primarily in order to maintain morale, but also in preparation for the expected German invasion later in the summer. For its part, the War Office encountered few difficulties with the allied land forces. From the very outset, each one stood as an independent, self-contained contingent which would take its place in the line when the time came for action. The Poles had a huge army in their own right – nearly a quarter of a million men, most of whom saw fierce combat in Italy – but the rest had much smaller forces, little more than brigades in most cases. Each allied government supplied men from its land forces for specialist training and covert operations with the Special Operations Executive, but still the majority of soldiers based in Britain had a long wait for action until the opening of the Second Front in 1944. As for the Royal Navy, it too enjoyed the benefits of having self-regulated, highly efficient naval forces and merchant fleets at its command, and although further research is needed in this area, it would seem that the Admiralty absorbed its new allies with little difficulty or disruption to the Navy's organisation or general routine.

However, for the Air Ministry, none of these advantages applied. Its war was very much a hot one, being fought by the day, by the hour, even by the minute, therefore Churchill's directive that all suitable allied air personnel should be thrown back into the fight presented a far greater peril to the Royal Air Force than any of the other services. The slightest error of judgement could have had disastrous consequences, and this is partly why so much suspicion and distrust is apparent in the history of the early allied air relationships. Another reason is that the Air Ministry had to make decisions quickly, and these decisions were often based on assumptions which in themselves were frequently rooted in naked prejudice. It is easy to condemn them from this distance, but it is no exaggeration to state that, at the time, the very existence of the British Empire was at stake. If the French said the Poles were not up to much, then such a view must have some substance, therefore it was better not to trust them. If the Foreign Office said that the Czechoslovaks were riddled with internecine political squabbling, then might that not affect the efficiency or the commitment of the air crews and pilots? Again, it was better to be safe than sorry.

That this 'safety first' principle was dominant in the RAF during the chaos of 1940 can be demonstrated by Hugh Dowding's attitude when he was informed that Fighter Command had at its disposal a number of Polish and Czechoslovak pilots as well as a smaller number of men from the other allied powers. At the emergency meeting convened on 14 July to discuss the integration of the new personnel, Dowding expressed strong reservations about, as he termed it, 'the infiltration of foreign pilots into British squadrons'. He claimed that pilot morale was the greatest asset he possessed, and unless he could be assured of the fighting spirit of the exiles, he would rather do without their services altogether. He made these statements in a week when he had an establishment deficit of 115 pilots and would lose a further seventy in action, but it soon became clear that he was using the term 'foreign pilots' diplomatically, for he had no qualms about was using the French and Belgian pilots immediately. As for the Slavs, however, he argued that he would 'roll up' British squadrons before taking any more of them into existing British units. It has been argued that this attitude demonstrated his commitment to the formation of integral Czechoslovak and Polish squadrons, but he insisted that such units be sent to 'thicken the line in the west' – that`is, the southern Atlantic approaches, well away from the heart of the action in the south-east.[3] In short, Dowding was one of the influential band of men who at first drew back from the prospect of East Europeans fighting in the front line, and it is highly likely that sheer desperation – not allied solidarity – drove him to employ the Czechs and Poles in the Battle of Britain.

Why Dowding and others chose to direct most of their criticisms towards the Slav pilots is still a difficult question to answer conclusively, especially since very few British officers had witnessed them in action and the only firm reports came from the French, heavily biased as these were. In all probability, the reasons lay in the pre-war attitudes towards Poland and Czechoslovakia explored in earlier chapters: that they above all others were most likely to be tainted with either fascism, communism or both. When the truncated state of Czechoslovakia was occupied by German forces in March 1939, the reaction of the Czechs appalled senior figures in the Foreign Office. There had been no real resistance from the armed forces, the national organisations, the communists or the general population to establishment of the Protectorate. By May 1939, the rightist National Assembly in Prague had more than two million members, or 98 per cent of all adults qualified to join.[4] By the outbreak of war in September, there were 80,000 Czech contract workers in Germany – all volunteers – and in the Protectorate itself there was a manpower shortage as industrial production in service of the Germans got into full swing.

This was hardly the kind of vision to inspire the West into trusting a Czech or a Slovak as an automatic ally, and it goes a long way towards explaining the suspicious attitudes of 1940 in civilian and military circles. That the War Cabinet was aware of this is demonstrated by the memoranda supplied by Robert Bruce Lockhart, in which he drew the government's attention to the possible collapse of pro-allied support without steps to improve morale. In the case of the Poles, they had sought accommodation with Hitler's Germany almost from the start, and their bullish diplomatic attitude coupled with their extensive anti-Semitism did nothing to endear them to the liberal powers. However, whereas the Poles could shrug off suspicion relatively quickly once the German atrocities in Poland became commonly known, the attitude of the Czechoslovak population as a whole did not reflect the qualities expected of a committed ally, at least until the appointment of Heydrich as Reich Protector; hence the doubts, hence the ambivalence.

This is not to suggest that the Slavs were perceived as the only obstacles to a successful integration of the allied forces. The French were fighting a war among themselves as well as against the Germans, and it is possible to study the documents and come away against the conclusion that the British would have preferred it if no Frenchman had set foot on British soil for the remainder of the war. The Air Ministry in particular was delighted to receive instructions to post most of them out to North Africa; and although victory there meant that they would return in great numbers for reorganisation, that was at a much later stage when the earlier political bitterness had considerably subsided. We can see through the history of 340 Squadron exactly what some of those problems were, and even though the Air Ministry does not emerge from this study with a great deal of credit to its name, still we must feel some sympathy for the British officers on the ground as they found themselves waist-deep in a vicious struggle for power and influence inside the French forces.

As for the Belgians, the Dutch and the Norwegians, these contingents were either too small to present many problems to the RAF or accepted their lot with a good deal more grace than others. It is possible to make sweeping judgements on the essentially smooth nature of these three relationships simply by acknowledging how few documentary traces they left behind in the London archives. The British trusted the Norwegians to run their own affairs with scarcely any interference at all, and once the Dutch had recovered from the shock of defeat and occupation, they too kept themselves to themselves. Even so, it is important to recall that they also had relatively stable political administrations above them, and once the Belgians had reached an acceptable compromise, they too settled down into a fairly contented alliance. This can not be said of the Czechoslovaks. Their political milieu was volatile in the extreme, even after apparent stability had been reached with the full recognition of the Beneš government in 1941. Beneš himself persisted in seeking to restore his own career and prestige at the expense of his forces in exile, especially the air force, and if the Foreign Office men were troubled by these affairs, they inevitably corrupted, or at least distorted, the perceptions of the Air Ministry.

When all is said and done, the *real* alliance was with the Poles. They had huge reserves of manpower and an unquestionable commitment to the defeat of Germany, although it took the British a while to believe this. Once demonstrated, however, the relationship was a sound one. All the problems were at the start or at the end, and it could be argued with some justification that the British compensated for their earlier scepticism by supporting the Poles when the communist tragedy struck them in 1945. Much credit must go to the Air Ministry here. It rallied behind the Polish Air Force in its hour of need, and we need only compare its attitude to the Poles with the rather shabby treatment of the Czechoslovaks to see how British postwar policy was by no means uniform. What mattered in the Czechoslovak case, as far as the British were concerned, was securing a military foothold in Central Europe, and no document dealing with the Poles in 1945 contains the kind of language used by Portal when he spoke of being 'rid of the commitment' to the Czechoslovak Air Force. It was a brutal and unwarranted comment, but also indicative of the kind of grudging tolerance with which many senior British officers had regarded the Czechoslovak Air Force from the start. This was grossly unfair, and in all probability the irritation was not caused by the men in uniform, but by the constant interference from above.

So the history of each allied air force had a beginning, a middle and an end. This seems logical enough, but in most cases 'the middle' was simply the business of war. Only the Czechs ran into difficulties, when Beneš attempted to gain independence again through 1942 and 1943. However, for the others, the resistance encountered in 1940 soon dissipated once they had proved their worth. With each contingent there were political and military problems to be resolved at the beginning, but even the French had put aside most of their grumblings against the British to fully close ranks with them by 1944. At the beginning, every nation, including the British, felt aggrieved and discomfited by the sorry situation in which they found themselves, but to the credit of everyone these emotions were pushed aside in favour of the overwhelming desire to survive.

Yet the ends were not so similar. With the Poles, it ended in sadness and permanent exile. With the French, it ended in brief glory and then swiftly became an interminable struggle to ward off American meddling with their affairs, and to rebuild again the brittle alliance with Britain. With the Belgians, Dutch and Norwegians it ended relatively quietly, each of them prepared to re-evaluate their pre-war positions and seek security within a wider European alliance and model their reconstituted air forces on the experiences they had gained within the RAF. But with the Czechoslovaks, it ended in disgrace. The constant dithering over whether or not the Russians would approve of the squadrons' return home merely left the Czechs dangerously exposed to further Russian influence. It seems likely that a similar debacle would have arisen over the Polish return had it not been for the faster establishment of a communist regime in Warsaw than in Prague. Beneš and his men managed to hang on to a form of independence until 1948, when they too succumbed to the will of Stalin, and then we find many of the old heroes from the war imprisoned or sent down the mines as 'enemies of the people'. If anything, the Czechoslovaks came out worst of all, for although the Poles were condemned to life in a foreign land, at least they had a chance to rebuild their lives in a democracy. For the Czechs, they had three short years of hope before their freedom was smashed by Moscow.

In the final analysis, the Anglo-allied air relationships were powerful structures. To be sure, the British do not emerge from the difficulties of 1939 and 1940 looking too good, their reputation for even-handed tolerance having been scuffed and torn by the tussles with the Poles, the Czechs and the French. But it is hard to condemn them entirely. The Air Ministry was trying to do its best in most cases, and although it was certainly guilty of neglect when it came to language instruction and welfare, it was in the unique position of having to check with the Foreign Office before any new initiatives could be advanced. Quite often, the Foreign Office vetoed or amended strictly military proposals which might have had political implications either at the time or in the postwar environment, and perhaps we might feel some sympathy for the Air Ministry at having to work under such a system. Once Halifax had been replaced as foreign secretary by Anthony Eden, he to some extent filled the vacuum of interest at the top, and he played an active role in exile affairs, especially in the Polish and French cases, where he instinctively foresaw postwar difficulties.

But the real credit goes to the officers and men of the six nations. In the face of humiliating defeat, they had picked themselves up and fought on, often against fearful odds, and too often in the excruciating knowledge of what was happening at home. Such pressures never applied to British pilots, for they knew that apart from the bombing, home was safe. The Poles and the Czechs were regularly taunted by German radio when family names were read out followed by accusations of treason, sabotage, or notice of deportation. Such cruelty never dented their determination to fight on. Many drank to kill the pain, a few – very few – lost control altogether. They can be little doubt that they had it worse than the rest, for although the Germans at times ruled with a heavy hand in the other countries, the levels of oppression were nowhere near as constant or as severe as they were in Poland and Czechoslovakia, particularly the latter after the assassination of Heydrich in 1942.

However, one need only read the memoirs of those men who flew in the uniform of the RAF but fought for the freedom of their homeland to understand what the experience meant to them. To this author's knowledge, there is no dedicated veterans' organisation for *all* the air personnel who fought in exile during the Second World War, though the Royal Air Force Association acts as a clearing house for correspondence and locating old comrades, and of course national societies exist in each of the countries. But the collective experience was unique in the history of modern warfare, and perhaps it is time to encourage the exchange of those rich memories as the generation which defeated Hitler moves into old age. As Shakespeare had Henry V say on the field of Agincourt: 'Old men forget; yet all shall be forgot, but he'll remember with advantages what feats he did this day.' Most certainly, every man was proud to wear RAF blue, win RAF medals, and play a small but none the less vital part in the banishment of Nazism from the Continent. But at the same time, he participated in the liberation of his homeland, even if indirectly – and that, to all of them, was where the *real* satisfaction lay.

NOTES

1. See Christopher Bassford's review of *On War* in *Defense Analysis* (Brassey's, June 1996). At the time of writing, the entire English text of *On War* is available on the Internet at the following site: <http://www.bibliomania. com/ NonFiction/Clausewitz/War/index.html>.
2. AIR/8/370: Prime Minister to Chiefs of Staff via General Ismay, 12.7.40.

3.   See AIR/8/370: Conference Minutes 14.7.40; AIR/2/5196: Sholto Douglas to Peirse, 15.7.40; Wood, D. and H.D. Dempster, *The Narrow Margin* (Arrow Books 1969) Appendices 11 and 13, and Zamoyski, A., *The Forgotten Few* (John Murray 1985), pp. 75–6. Zamoyski adduces Dowding's 'infiltration' remark as a reason for the rapid establishment of independent Polish squadrons, leading to the formal Agreement of 5 August establishing the Polish Air Force on British soil. Although Zamoyski includes Dowding's succeeding remark that 'apart from the language difficulty he [Dowding] is uncertain to the effect this will have on the morale of his squadrons', he dovetails this with his own observation that 'the creditable conduct and above-average results of these pilots [and] their growing popularity with their British colleagues and commanders', leading to the inference that British morale would be sapped by having to fly with better men. In this, he somewhat misses the point that Dowding was pressing for national units for negative, not positive, reasons.

4.   Mamatey, S. & Luža, R. (eds), *A History of the Czechoslovak Republic, 1914–1948* (Princeton UP 1973), Rhode, Gotthold, 'The Protectorate of Bohemia and Moravia', pp. 302–6. The National Assembly (Národní Souručenství) was a collective movement headed by a National Committee (Národní Výbor) consisting of fifty members appointed by Emil Hácha, and was composed of representatives of all the major parties, with the exception of the communists. Membership was restricted to adult males. Its first proclamation denounced Freemasons and Jews. Rhode quotes figures for unemployment as dropping from 93,000 in March 1939 to 57,000 in May and less than 17,000 in June.

Allied Air Strengths, 1940–44

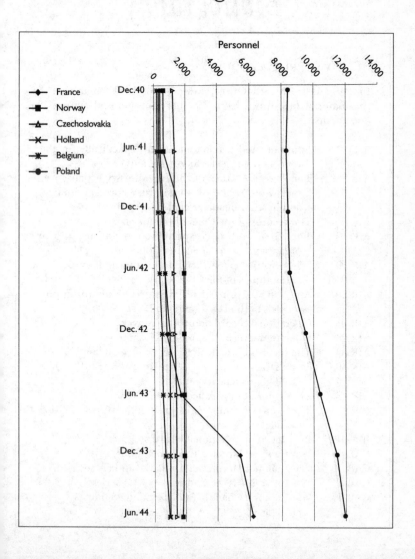

Bibliography

ARCHIVAL PRIMARY SOURCES

In the Public Record Office, Kew, London, the majority of the material was drawn from the following general classes of documents:

ADM 1	Admiralty and Secretariat papers, specifically for the report on OPERATIONS AERIAL and CYCLE
AIR 2	The registered files of the Air Ministry which cover the whole range of Air Ministry correspondence, administration and related subjects
AIR 8	The records of the Chief of the Air Staff
AIR 16	The files and correspondence relating to the organisation, etc. of Fighter Command
AIR 19	Private office papers, including the memorandums and minutes of the Chief of the Air Staff
AIR 20	Air Ministry unregistered papers, including the records of the DAAC and the DAFL
AIR 27	Operational record books – squadrons
AIR 28	Operational record books – RAF stations
AIR 33	The records of the RAF Inspectorate-General
AIR 40	The Directorate of Intelligence and other intelligence-related papers
AIR 46	Air Missions to the Allied Forces
BW 2	The papers and correspondence of the British Council
BW 108	British Council: National Hearths
CAB 65	War Cabinet: Minutes and Conclusions
CAB 66	War Cabinet: Mermorandums (WP and CP series)
CAB 67	War Cabinet: Memorandums (WP(G) series)
CAB 79	War Cabinet: Chiefs of Staff Commitee minutes

CAB 85   War Cabinet: Anglo-French Committees and the
          minutes and papers of the Allied Forces (Official)
          Sub-Committee
CAB 111   Files and correspondence of the Allied Supplies
          Executive
CAB 120   Minister of Defence: Secretariat Files
CAB 121   Cabinet Office: Special Secret Information Centre,
          files and papers
FO 371   Foreign Office: Correspondence, political
WO 32   War Office: Allied contingents

Printed Primary Sources (Memoirs and Correspondence, etc)

British Parliamentary Debates, 5th Series (Hansard)

Bruce Lockhart, R.H., *Comes The Reckoning* (Putnam 1947)

Čapka, J., *Red Sky At Night* (Anthony Blond 1958)

Colville, J., *The Fringes of Power: Downing Street Diaries 1939–1955* (Hodder & Stoughton 1985)

Dilks, D. (ed.), *The Diaries of Sir Alexander Cadogan, 1938–1945* (Cassells 1971)

Donnet, M., *Flight To Freedom* (Ian Allan 1991)

Eden, A., (The Rt Hon. Earl of Avon), *The Eden Memoirs, Volume 1: The Reckoning* (Cassells 1965)

Goddard, V., *Skies to Dunkirk* (William Kimber 1982)

Kennan, G.F., *From Prague After Munich* (Princeton University Press 1968)

Liškutín, M.A., *Challenge in the Air* (William Kimber 1988)

Moravec, F., *Master of Spies* (The Bodley Head 1975)

Taborsky, E., *President Beneš Between East and West* (Hoover Press 1981)

Van Der Kop, H., *The Flying Dutchman* (Patrick Stephens 1985)

White, L.M., (ed.), *On All Fronts: Czechoslovaks in WW2, Volume 1* (East European Monographs, Boulder 1991)

——, *On All Fronts: Czechoslovaks in WW2, Volume 2* (East European Monographs, Boulder 1995)

Young, K., (ed.), *The Diaries of Sir Robert Bruce Lockhart 1915–1938* (Macmillan 1973)

——, *The Diaries of Sir Robert Bruce Lockhart 1939–1965* (Macmillan 1980)

Published Secondary Sources

Andrew, C., *Secret Service* (Heinemann 1985)

Bell, P.M.H., *John Bull and The Bear* (Edward Arnold 1990)

Beneš, E., *Democracy Today and Tomorrow* (Macmillan 1939)

Benešova, M., *et al.*, *Terezín 1940–1945* (Terezín Memorial Publications 1996)

Bradley J.F.N., *Czechoslovakia: A Short History* (Edinburgh University Press 1971)

Brivati, B. & Jones, H. (eds), *What Difference Did The War Make?* (Leicester University Press 1993)

Bury, J.P.T., *France, 1814–1940* (Methuen 1985)

Calder, A., *The Myth of the Blitz* (Pimlico 1995)

——, *The People's War* (Jonathan Cape 1986)

Chapman, G., *Why France Collapsed* (Cassells 1968)

Charmley, J., *Chamberlain and the Lost Peace* (Hodder & Stoughton 1989)

Collier, R., *The Years of Attrition, 1940–1941* (Allison & Busby 1995)

Cynk, J.B., *History of The Polish Air Force* (Osprey 1972)

Dagan, A. (ed.), *The Jews of Czechoslovakia, Volume III* (The Jewish Publication Society of America, New York 1984)

Darlington, R., *Nighthawk* (William Kimber 1985)

Derry, T.K., *A Short History of Norway* (Allen & Unwin 1957)

Donaldson, F., *The British Council: The First Fifty Years* (Jonathan Cape 1984)

Dunn, S. & Fraser, T.G. (eds), *Europe and Ethnicity* (Routledge 1996)

Engel, D., *In the Shadow of Auschwitz: The Polish Government-in-Exile and the Jews, 1939–1942* (University of North Carolina 1987)

Flint, P., *Dowding and Headquarters, Fighter Command* (Airlife 1996)

Foot, M.R.D., *S.O.E. – The Special Operations Executive, 1940–1946* (BBC 1984)

Franks, N., *R.A.F. Fighter Command, 1936–1968* (Patrick Stephens 1992)

Garlinski, J., *Poland in the Second World War* (Macmillan 1985)

Garrett, R., *Sky High* (Weidenfeld & Nicolson 1991)

Gaujour, R., *The French Air Force, 1940–1944* (French Air Forces Press 1944)

Gilbert, M., *Second World War* (Fontana 1990)

——, *Winston S. Churchill, Volume 6: 1939–1941* (Heinemann 1983)

Gillman, P. & Gilman, L., *'Collar The Lot!'* (Quartet 1980)

Glees, A., *Exile Politics During the Second World War* (Oxford 1982)
——, *The Secrets of the Service* (Cape 1987)
Hennessey, P., *Never Again* (Jonathan Cape 1992)
Hirschfeld, G. (ed.), *Exile in Great Britain* (Berg 1984)
Holmes, C., *John Bull's Island* (Macmillan 1988)
Horne, A., *To Lose A Battle* (Macmillan 1969)
Irving, D., *Churchill's War* (Veritas 1987)
Kersaudy, F., *Norway 1940* (Collins 1990)
Kitchen, M., *British Policy Towards the Soviet Union During the Second World War* (Macmillan 1986)
Lafitte, F., *The Internment of Aliens* (Libris 1988)
Lamb, R., *Churchill as War Leader – Right or Wrong?* (Bloomsbury 1993)
Lukeš, I., *Czechoslovakia Between Stalin and Hitler* (Oxford University Press 1996)
MacDonald, C., *The Killing of SS Obergruppenführer Reinhard Heydrich* (Macmillan 1989)
Maguire, C.E., *Anglo-American Policy Towards the Free French* (Macmillan 1995)
Mamatey, S. & Luza, R. (eds), *A History of the Czechoslovak Republic 1918–1948* (Princeton University Press 1973)
Mastný, V., *The Czechs Under Nazi Rule* (Colombia University Press 1971)
Mountfield, D., *The Partisans* (Hamlyn 1979)
Pajer, M., *Ve Stínu Slávy* [In the Shadows of Glory] (Svět Křídel, Prague 1992)
Porch, D., *The French Secret Services* (Macmillan 1996)
Prazmowská, A., *Britain and Poland 1939–1943: The Betrayed Ally* (Cambridge University Press 1995)
Rajlich, J. & Sehnal, J., *Slovenští Letci* [Slovak Airmen] (Label, Prague 1991)
——, *Stíhači Nad Kanálem* [Fighters Over the Channel] (Naše Vojsko, Prague 1992)
Ray, J., *The Battle of Britain: New Perspectives* (Arms & Armour 1994)
Reilly, R., *The Sixth Floor* (Leslie Frewin 1969)
Rhodes James, R., *Anthony Eden* (Weidenfeld & Nicolson 1986)
Salmon, P. (ed.), *Britain and Norway in the Second World War* (HMSO 1995)
Taylor, A.J.P., *English History 1914–1945* (Oxford University Press 1988)
——, *From the Boer War to the Cold War* (Hamish Hamilton 1995)
Taylor, P.M. (ed.), *Britain and the Cinema in the Second World War* (Macmillan 1988)

Wells, M.K., *Courage and Air Warfare* (Frank Cass 1995)

West, N., *MI5* (The Bodley Head 1981)

——, *MI6* (Weidenfeld & Nicolson 1983)

Wheeler-Bennett, J.W., *Munich* (Macmillan 1963)

Zamoyski, A., *The Forgotten Few* (John Murray 1995)

Zeman, Z., *The Life of Edvard Beneš 1884–1948* (Oxford University Press 1997)

——, *The Masaryks* (Weidenfeld & Nicolson 1976)

REFERENCE WORKS

Armitage, M., *The Royal Air Force* (Arms & Armour 1993)

Ashworth, C., *Action Stations, Volume 9* (Patrick Stephens 1985)

——, *R.A.F. Coastal Command 1936–1969* (Patrick Stephens 1992)

Delve, K., *A Source Book of the Royal Air Force* (Airlife 1994)

Everitt, C. & Middlebrook, M., *The Bomber Command War Diaries 1939–45* (Midland Publishing 1995)

Falconer, J., *R.A.F. Fighter Airfields of World War Two* (Ian Allan 1993)

Foreman, J., *1941 – The Turning Point* (Air Research Publications 1993)

Halley, J.J., *The Squadrons of the Royal Air Force* (Air Britain 1980)

Jefford, C.G., *R.A.F. Squadrons* (Airlife 1988)

Wood, D. & Dempster, D., *The Narrow Margin* (Arrow 1969)

DISSERTATIONS AND THESES

Blaylock, W., 'Britain's Attempts to Maximise U.S. Participation in the Second World War, 1939–41' (PhD, University of London 1980)

Brown, A., 'The Czechoslovak Air Force in Britain, 1940–1945' (PhD, University of Southampton 1998)

Buck, M., *'Feeding a Pauper Army': War Refugees and Welfare in Britain, 1939–1942* (Berghahn Books 2000)

Callcott, W.R., 'British Attitudes to the Czechoslovak State, 1914–1938' (PhD, University of Newcastle-upon-Tyne 1986)

Eastment, D.J., 'The Policies and Position of the British Council from the Outbreak of War to 1950' (PhD, University of Leeds 1982)

Eisen, J., 'Anglo–Dutch Relations and European Unity, 1940–1948' (Hull University, 1980)

Kernberg, T., 'The Polish Community in Scotland' (PhD, University of Glasgow 1990)

Krosby, V.M., 'Host to Exiles: The Foreign Office and the Norwegian Government in London, 1940–45' (PhD, London School of Economics 1979)

Stenton, M.M., 'British Propaganda and Political Warfare, 1940–1944' (PhD, Cambridge University 1979)

Index

Air Ministry (UK)
  and Allied air agreements, 70–1,
    182–3, 203, 231 n.
  and Foreign Office, 41–2
  and Polish repatriation, 86–94
Allied forces
  Air Ministry policy, 23–8, 66–9,
    110–11, 202–3, 236–7
  anti-Semitism in, 17, 32 n., 73,
    167, 235
  as national units, 14–15,
  conscription of, 16–17
  discipline in, 72–73
  education of, 19–20
  jurisdiction in, 15–18, 32 n.,
    67–8, 114–117, 197–8, 227
  morale in, 21–8, 35, 73, 75–7,
    165–66, 176–77, 189,
  public perception of, 71–3,
    76–7, 82–5, 100–1, 191
Allied Forces Act (1940), 14, 16–18
Allied Forces (Official) Sub-
  Committee, 110
Anders, General Wladyslaw, 78,
  82–4, 89–93

Beaumont, Gp Capt Frank, 60, 62,
  130, 141, 179
Belgian Air Force, 210–22, 237–9,
  in the Belgian Congo, 217–19
Belgium
  pre-war position of, 210–11
Beneš, Edvard, Chapter 3 passim,
  229, 238–9
Bevin, Ernest, 86–93
Birksted, Lt Col Kaj, 208
Boyle, Archibald
  and Belgians, 213

  and Czechoslovaks, 60, 213
  and Dutch, 224–5
  and Free French, 168–9
  and the JIC, 103–4
  and Poles, 41–2, 44–6
British Council, 18–23, 32 n.,
  205–6
British Government,
  and alliances, 48–9
  as coalition, 32
Bruce Lockhart, Robert, 108, 111,
  152–3 n., 155 n., 237
  and William Strang, 152–3 n.,

Cavendish-Bentinck, Victor, 82–4,
  89
Chamberlain, Neville
  and Polish guarantee, 37, 47–8,
    184
Churchill, Winston Spencer
  and Belgians, 213–14
  and COS (120) 28–30
  and Czechoslovaks, 121–2, 144
  and de Gaulle, 83–4, 162
  and Denmark, 204
  and exiles, 101–3
  and French collapse, 36, 159–61
  and Norway, 192
  as Prime Minister, 234
COS (120) 28–30, 184, 187, 221
Czechoslovak Air Force, Chapter
  3 passim
  and Slovak Uprising, 135–41
  and the Soviet Union, 135–51
  dissent in, 112–17, 154
  in Britain, 61–65, 212–3,
  in France, 36–7, 53–9, 110
  independence of, 117, 126–35

post-war re-equipment of,
142–51, 156 *n*.
recruitment of, 117–27
repatriation of, 140–9
Czechoslovak Land Forces, 110–11,
117–27
Czechoslovakia
liberation of, 78, 140–1
occupation of, 236–7, 242 *n*.
Provisional Government, 104–5,
108, 163
refugees in UK, 104–5
UK relations with, 104–9

DAAC, *see* DAFL
DAFL, 61, 71, 115, 116, 127, 129,
130, 133, 138, 141–2, 148, 174–
83, 198, 217–19
Danish airmen in exile, 204–8
Davidson, Alexander, 39, 52, 69–70
De Gaulle, General Charles,
159–85, 214
Denmark
and the British Foreign Office,
204–6
war in, 204–5
Dickson, AVM Sir William (ACAS),
91, 141–7
Dill, General Sir John (CIGS),
101–3
Dowding, ACM Sir Hugh, 213,
230–7
Dutch Air Force, 222–30
See also Royal Netherlands Air
Force
See also Netherlands

Eden, Anthony, 53, 59, 101–4,
124–7, 139–40, 184, 186, 240
Evill, Sir Douglas, 39, 43, 92

France
agreements with UK, 177–8
collapse in 1940, 160–2
post-war rearmament of, 183–8
pre-war relations with UK, 100–
1, 159–60
Free French Air Force, Chapter 4
passim, 236–40
and Belgians, 169, 213–14
Free French Navy, 165–180
French Government
and Belgians, 213

and Czechoslovaks, 109–10
and Poles, 35–43, 48
and the Soviet Union, 185–6

Giraud, General Henri, 180–2
Grigg, Sir Edward, 16–18
Gulliksen, Col Thomas, 194

Halifax, Lord, 101–3, 107–8, 234,
240
Hollinghurst, Gp Capt Leslie
(DDO), 66

Ingr, General Sergěj, 116–20,
124–37, 154–6 *n*.
Izycki, Gen Mateusz, 85, 90–4

Janoušek, AVM Sir Karel, Chapter
3 *passim*, 218, 220, 229
Joint Intelligence Committee (JIC),
41, 103–4, 151–2

Kalkus, Gen W.J., 69–70
Kalla, Lt Col Josef, 69–62, 115
Kubita, Lt Col Alois, 62

Masaryk, Jan, 132, 134–5, 138–9
Medhurst, ACM Sir Charles, 60–1,
63–6, 87, 97 *n*., 161, 164–6,
169–70, 182, 196, 225
Mitkiewicz-Zoltek, Col Leon, 50
Mohr, General Wilhelm, 195–6,
199, 202
Muselier, Admiral, 169–74, 179
Mutual Aid Protocols, 28–30, 80,
203, 221

Netherlands
East Indian colony, 210, 223–9
pre-war position of, 210–11
Newall, Sir Cyril (CAS), 45, 63, 164
Nichols, Philip, 126, 131–4, 137,
139–40, 144–50
Nižborsky, General Antonin,
112–14
Norway
occupation of (1940), 191–2
pre-war attitude of, 192
See also Royal Norwegian Air
Force

Øen, Capt Bjarne (RNAAS), 194
Operation AERIAL, 57

Operation JUBILEE, 200–1
Operation MENACE, 164, 168
Operation OVERLORD, 182–3,
  202, 216, 220, 229

Poland
  Military Mission (1945), 83–4
  pre-war attitudes, 47–8, 94–5
  post-war debts, 80
  post-war environment, 74–5
  post-war government, 80–1,
    88–9
  Provisional Govt of National
    Unity, 78
  Warsaw Uprising, 75–6
Polish Air Force, Chapter 2 *passim*,
  236–241
  recruitment of, 121
Polish Land Forces, 61, 77–81,
  91–4, 235–6
Polish Resettlement Corps, 91–4
Porri, Wg Cdr Cyril
  and Czechoslovaks, 59–60,
    110–11
  and Dutch, 223
  and Free French, 166
  and Norwegians, 194–5
  and Poles, 52–3

Rathbone, Eleanor, 16–17
Reventlow, Count Eduard, 206
Riiser-Larsen, Capt Hjalmar, 198,
  203
Rola-Zymierski, Marshal, 84–6
Royal Air Force Volunteer Reserve,
  40, 51–2, 64–5, 68–70, 109–111,
  115–16, 129, 148, 150, 165, 167,
  179, 195, 213–221, 228
Royal Netherlands Air Force,
  222–236, 237–8
  pre-war composition of, 212, 222
  training of in Newfoundland,
    224–6

Royal Norwegian Air Force,
  Chapter 5 *passim*, 238–40
  pre-war composition of, 193–4
  recruitment of, 198
  training in Canada, 195–7

Sholto Douglas, AM Sir William,
  95–7 *n.*
  and Belgians, 217
  and Czechoslovaks, 60–2
  and Dutch, 223–4
  and Free French, 170–4, 179–80
  and Poles, 52–3, 84–5
Sinclair, Sir Archibald, 60, 117–20,
  124, 133, 138–9, 164, 173, 224
Sikorski, General Wladyslaw, 39,
  41–5, 58, 67–8, 71, 104
South African Air Force, 216–18
Special Operations Executive
  (SOE), 136–7, 156 *n.*
Stagg, Cdr Frank, 206
Strang, William, 110–11, 153 *n.*,
  166

United States of America
  and post-war plans, 14
  and post-war rearmament,
    184–8
  and strategic affairs, 66–7

Van Berkelom, Capt Berdenis,
  224–225
Von Clausewitz, Carl, 232
Vuillemin, General, 161

War Office, 14–15
  and Poles, 50–1
West, Air Cdre Ferdinand, 148
Wouters, Colonel, 169, 213–14,
  218–20

Zajac, General, 38–9, 65